250
Essential
Chinese
Characters

250
Essential
Chinese
Characters

Volume 1
Revised Edition

Philip Yungkin Lee
Revised by **Darell Tibbles**

TUTTLE PUBLISHING
Tokyo • Rutland, Vermont • Singapore

Published by Tuttle Publishing, an imprint of Periplus Editions (HK) Ltd., with editorial offices at 364 Innovation Drive, North Clarendon, Vermont 05759 U.S.A. and at 61 Tai Seng Avenue #02-12, Singapore 534167.

Library of Congress Cataloging-in-Publication Data in Progress

ISBN 978-0-8048-4035-4

Distributed by

North America, Latin America & Europe
Tuttle Publishing
364 Innovation Drive
North Clarendon, VT 05759-9436 U.S.A.
Tel: 1 (802) 773-8930
Fax: 1 (802) 773-6993
info@tuttlepublishing.com
www.tuttlepublishing.com

Asia Pacific
Berkeley Books Pte. Ltd.
61 Tai Seng Avenue #02-12
Singapore 534167
Tel: (65) 6280-1330
Fax: (65) 6280-6290
inquiries@periplus.com.sg
www.periplus.com

First edition
14 13 12 11 10 09   10 9 8 7 6 5 4 3 2 1

Printed in Singapore

Contents

Introduction

Beginning Chinese language learners frequently wonder as to the number of Chinese characters necessary for basic written fluency. Effectively answering that question is neither simple nor straightforward. Simple conversations and interactions can be covered with a few hundred known characters. Advanced and specialized conversations would, on the other hand, require specialized vocabulary.

This first volume of *250 Essential Chinese Characters for Everyday Use* demonstrates the essential characters necessary to cover basic conversations and language situations. Complete information is given for each character including the meaning, pronunciation, and written components.

The 250 characters have been selected and arranged based on a range of criteria. First, many characters should be instantly familiar in meaning for any language learner. These characters are foundational structures necessary to communicate in almost any language setting. Second, characters have been chosen for usefulness in a variety of word and language settings. A frequent indicator of usefulness and variety was the range of two character compound vocabulary words that utilize the character. Knowing these characters can increase vocabulary acquisition as the patterns of use and meaning are built. Finally, characters have been selected that show great frequency and meaning in spoken language.

Each **character** is presented in an independent entry that provides both the simplified (*jiantizi*) and traditional (*fantizi*) form for the character. Each character's stroke order, the recognized order for character composition, is given for the simplified character form. *Pinyin* romanization is also provided. The meaning and radical for each character is given, along with the radical index number found in standard dictionary indexes. A variety of examples are given that demonstrate effective use of the character. These examples feature use of the two character compound vocabulary and multiple character phrases that often appear in modern written and spoken Chinese.

The character entries are arranged into 23 lessons of 10 to 12 characters per lesson. A longer review appears every fourth or fifth lesson, after each new 50 characters as appropriate. A short selection of exercises at the end of each lesson provides different opportunities to practice the vocabulary of the lesson.

The **Review Activities** for each lesson provide 3 related components for character mastery. Generally, the first section of the exercises focus on *pinyin* or character recall. The second section asks for effective grammatical utilization of the previous vocabulary. The final section is a broader exercise to develop communicative proficiency. Exercises in this section require short paragraphs or responses that depend on understanding the lesson. These offer each learner the opportunity to grow and strengthen individual proficiency.

Each **Section Review** is composed of 4 sections, with each section growing in linguistic complexity. The first exercise is a larger vocabulary and character recognition for the combined lesson vocabulary. Next, the second exercise will challenge for grammatical understanding and accuracy. The bulk of the section review is a longer open format exercise to allow individual proficiency growth. The topic of discussion for the section will depend on the characters from the previous lessons. Taken together, these first 3 exercises in the section review can provide effective opportunity to review and practice for advanced proficiency examination such as the College Board AP examination or an American Council on the Teaching of Foreign Languages Oral Proficiency Interview (OPI). The final exercise in each section review is a series of questions offered to prompt greater depth in the previous section. If possible, these questions can be asked and answered orally, preparing the learner for oral interview interactions and assessments.

A key for exercises is provided for those exercises formatted for single answers. Those exercises that ask for open answers will not be included in the answer key. Also, in language, there are many effective strategies to express similar concepts. Therefore, please understand the key is in many cases an illustration of possible effective responses.

The activities and exercises provided are intended to allow each learner to grow at their level and individual pace. For a new language student the character entries will provide much to consider and many new examples of language use. Lesson exercises will often challenge and exceed the domain of one particular lesson. For a language student reviewing previously known characters, many entries will confirm examples and constructions well practiced. Lesson exercises will review and strengthen existing skills.

For each learner the process of mastering Chinese character writing is also a development of individual learning and recall strategies. With the stroke order given for each character and many different examples of vocabulary use, each learner is invited to utilize the most effective learning strategy for him or her. Best practices in character memory include mindfulness and repetition. When practicing character formation, be aware of each stroke, stroke order, and composition. Character recall is further strengthened by much repetition including the physical act of character writing. Learners further strengthen character recall by repetition, especially writing individual characters and words multiple times.

This new edition's contents have been revised to match the development of Chinese language instruction. The character order has been restructured to help learners connect characters based on function. This has necessitated slight variations in lesson length, with some lessons of 10 characters, and some lessons of up to 12 characters. As a result, the expressive possibilities of the vocabulary have been increased for each lesson. Additionally, the exercises have been completely revised to reflect the growing focus on proficiency assessment throughout the field. Each lesson and section review features exercises designed to challenge and grow expressive proficiency. Finally, greater attention is paid to incorporating spoken language throughout the exercises. While the volume focuses on character vocabulary growth, examples throughout the exercises invite learners to engage in spoken review and development.

The 250 characters contained in this volume when taken together compose a strong foundation for basic language proficiency. Whether you are new to the subject or coming back for review, each of these characters provides a wealth of expressive opportunity.

Learners' Guide

Chinese Characters

For many learners of Chinese language, one of the most engaging and fulfilling challenges is mastering the Chinese character writing system. From the first character learned, understanding and utilizing a refined system with a long history is very compelling. In this book you'll be introduced to 250 characters, with a demonstration of the writing system for each.

Every character has a basic form recognized for reading and visual accuracy. The basic form is the result of a precise stroke order that allows for clear and accurate character formation. Through accurate stroke order, the composition of each character is achieved. Every character is the formation of several components. As important as the shape of the overall character is the relationship between these different components. These relationships are seen in the composition of the character. Finally, characters contain many repeated components, and across the 250 characters in this volume many components will repeat. These commonly used character components help create predictable patterns for composition, stroke order, and pronunciation.

Most characters contain a significant component: the character radical. In the Chinese character writing system, the vast majority of characters are considered to be "radical-phonetic" characters. By identifying the radical component you often reveal a key insight into the character meaning and use. Additionally, the remaining character component, the "phonetic," is a clue to pronunciation. The identification of character radicals is critical to utilizing a character index by radical, which is common in Chinese dictionaries.

These 250 characters establish the foundation for identifying patterns in the Chinese character writing system. There are patterns in character stroke order, composition, and overall form. There are also patterns in meaning, pronunciation, and use identified in part by character components. Yet there are also those characters that defy easy compartmentalization. Often these are fundamental characters and constructions for expressive language.

The Basic Strokes

Chinese characters are written in various strokes. Although we can identify over 30 different strokes, only 8 are basic ones and all the others are their variants. Certain arrangements of strokes form components, or the building blocks for characters.

The strokes that make up a component of a character and by extension the whole character are given names. Here are the 8 basic strokes:

[—] The *héng* or "horizontal" stroke is written from left to right.

[|] The *shù* or "vertical" stroke is written from top to bottom.

[ﾉ] The *piě* or "downward-left" stroke is written from top-right to bottom-left.

[＼] The *nà* or "downward-right" stroke is written from top-left to bottom-right.

[ヽ] The *diǎn* or "dot" stroke is written from top to bottom-right, finishing firmly. It can also be finished to bottom-left, depending on how the dot is written.

[ㄱ] The *zhé* or "turning" stroke can begin with a horizontal stroke with a downward turn, or it can be a vertical stroke with a horizontal turn to the right.

[⅃] The *gōu* or "hook" stroke is written by a quick flick of the pen or Chinese brush. There are five types of *gōu* "hook" strokes. They are:

    [⟶] the *hénggōu* or "horizontal hook,"

    [⅃] the *shùgōu* or "vertical hook,"

    [⌊] the *wān'gōu* or "bending hook,"

    [＼] the *xiégōu* or "slanting hook,"

    [⌣] the *pínggōu* or 'level hook."

[╱] The *tí* or "upward stroke to the right" is written from bottom-left to top-right.

Stroke Order

The long history of Chinese character writing has developed a strong aid to character memory and recognition: stroke order. Each character has a recognized stroke order that is the preferred method of character formation. Learning and repeating this stroke order for every written character is recommended as an aid for memory, recognition, and writing clarity.

Stroke orders are the product of a long continuous history of the writing system. Each stroke order offers benefits to character production. First, the recognized stroke order is the most accurate method for character composition. With each stroke in proper order, a character is clear, readable, and accurate. Second, the recognized stroke order is the most efficient method for character construction. The progression of strokes between character components have developed to move effectively through each component and to the next character to be written. Third, the recognized stroke order, when practiced, is the most repeatable method to write the character. Mastering a stroke order allows, much like a singer mastering a song, the character to be produced without having to cognitively recall each component. Instead of having to learn all of the constituent components, a character is learned as a process.

The recognized stroke orders have developed for right-handed character writing. This is shown in the stroke progression and stroke formation. For left-handed writers the stroke orders may appear inefficient or counter-intuitive. There is no easy remedy for this aspect of character writing; the benefits for consistent stroke orders are still valid for left-handed writers and should be considered.

The following examples illustrate patterns in character stroke orders. These general rules can help you understand specific stroke orders.

1. From top to bottom:

三		一	二	三	
学		丷	丷	丷	学
是		曰	旦	早	是

2. From left to right:

你		亻	亻	亻	你
好		女	奵	好	
她		女	如	妑	她

3. The horizontal before the vertical:

十		一	十		
七		一	七		
天		二	千	天	

4. The horizontal before the down stroke to the left:

大		一	大	大	
有		一	大	右	有
在		一	大	才	在

5. The down stroke to the left before that to the right:

人		丿	人	
八		丿	八	
文		亠	宁	文

6. The enclosing strokes first, then the enclosed and finally the sealing stroke:

四		丨	冂	冂	四
国		冂	国	国	国
回		冂	冋	回	回

7. The middle stroke before those on both sides:

小		亅	小	小	
你		亻	仁	你	你
水		亅	扌	水	水

8. Inside stroke before side stroke:

这		亠	亠	文	这
过		寸	寸	讨	过
道		丷	丷	首	道

Simplified Characters versus Traditional Characters

Many of the 250 characters in this volume have both simplified and traditional character forms. If only one character form is given for a character then the simplified and traditional forms are identical. Becoming acquainted with both forms is useful for many reasons. First, the simplified form is related to the traditional form of the character. The techniques for simplification are outlined below, with many of the simplifications being a confirmation of the evolution of character writing through the history of Chinese characters. Second, both forms are used in current Chinese language communities. Different communities generally prefer the use of one character form or the other; however both forms can be seen and used within one community. Advanced Chinese language use necessitates at least basic familiarity with both character forms.

Simplified characters have existed long before the government of the People's Republic of China sanctioned their use in 1986. For example, the characters **cóng** 从 (from), **wàn** 万 (ten thousand), and **bǐ** 笔 (writing brush) existed side by side with the traditional forms 從, 萬, and 筆 in classical Chinese. The official sanction only means the elevation of the simplified forms.

Several techniques were employed to create simplified characters. One was to replace the original component of a character with a component of fewer strokes but having the same sound as the given character. For example, the simplified character for "recognize" is **rèn** 认. The component 人 is pronounced **rén** which is also the pronunciation for **rěn** 忍 in the traditional form 認 (despite different tones).

Another technique was to take one section of a traditional character and use it as the simplified character. Compare the traditional form for "family" **qīn** 親 and the simplified form 亲 that uses only the left component. Other examples in this volume of such simplification include **ér** 兒 (son), **yī** 醫 (doctor), and **xí** 習 (practice) with respective simplified forms of 儿, 医, and 习.

Some characters are simplified on the basis of having adopted cursive forms and in the process eliminating some strokes. For example the radical **yán** 言 (speech) is simplified to 讠 by the adoption of its cursive form. Other radicals in this volume simplified on the same basis include 门 (door) and 车 (vehicle). Simplification involving radicals is responsible for many simplified forms being created as it is often the case that only the radical is simplified; **shuō** 说, **yǔ** 语, and **wèn** 问 are examples. Other cursive forms are adopted as the simplified form such as **ài** 爱 for 愛 and **lè/yuè** 乐 for 樂.

Some cursive forms use an arbitrary stroke order created for the sake of writing a character quickly. These are used to replace some complicated phonetic components. One common example is **yòu** 又 written in only two strokes. It is used in the characters **huān** 欢, **hàn** 汉, and **duì** 对 replacing 歡, 漢, and 對 respectively.

The Pinyin System of Romanization

The system used in this book to write Chinese with Roman letters is the *Hanyu Pinyin* system which is the standard in the People's Republic of China and is now used almost everywhere else in the world. The imitated pronunciation should be read as if it were English, bearing in mind the following main points:

Consonants

b, d, f, g, h, k, l, m, n, p, s, t, w, y as in English

c	like English **ts** in i**ts**
j	like English **j** in **j**eer
q	like English **ch** in **ch**eer, with a strong puff of air
r	like English **ur** in leis**ur**e, with the tongue rolled back
x	like English **see** (whole word)
z	like English **ds** in ki**ds**
ch	like English **ch** in **ch**urch, with the tongue rolled back and a strong puff of air
sh	like English **sh** in **sh**e, with the tongue rolled back
zh	like English **j**, with the tongue rolled back

Vowels

a	like English **ar** in f**ar**
e	like English **ur** in f**ur**
i	like English **ee** in f**ee**
o	like English **or** in f**or**
u	like English **ue** in s**ue**
ü	like French **u**

Tones

A tone is a variation in pitch by which a syllable can be pronounced. In Chinese, a variation of pitch or tone changes the meaning of the word. There are four tones each marked by a diacritic. In addition there is a neutral tone which does not carry any tone marks. Below is a tone chart which describes tones using the 5-degree notation. It divides the range of pitches from lowest (1) to highest (5). Note that the neutral tone is not shown on the chart as it is affected by the tone that precedes it.

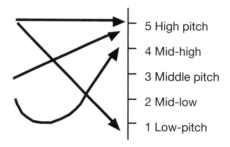

The first tone is a high-level tone represented by a level tone mark (–).

The second tone is a high-rising tone represented by a rising tone mark (′).

The third tone is a low-dipping tone represented by a dish-like tone mark (˅).

The fourth tone is a high-falling tone represented by a falling tone mark (ˋ).

In addition to the above tones, there is a neutral tone which is pronounced light and soft in comparison to other tones. A neutral tone is not marked by any tone mark. A syllable is said to take on a neutral tone when it forms part of a word or is placed in various parts of a sentence.

How to Use the Alphabetical Index

The words and phrases collected in the Chinese-English Glossary (approximately 1,200 items) are arranged alphabetically according to the *Hanyu Pinyin* system of romanization. In this system each syllable (represented by a character) is a unit. The first character in a word or phrase is the head character. Each word or phrase is ordered in the first instance according to the phonetic value of this character. In a succession of entries having the same head character, alphabetical order is then determined by the phonetic value of the second character. This arrangement has the advantage of enhancing meaning by grouping together words which share a common character root, even though it is done at the expense of a straight alphabetical ordering.

The ordering of characters is affected by two other considerations. Firstly, in the case of characters represented by the same Roman letters, alphabetization is determined by the tone of each character (represented in *Hanyu Pinyin* by diacritics), in the order first, second, third, fourth and neutral tone. Secondly, in the case of characters represented by the same Roman letters which also have the same tone, alphabetization follows the principle that simpler characters (those composed of fewer strokes) are listed before more complex characters (those composed of more strokes).

For example, the first 17 entries under Q have as their head character variations of the syllable **qi** (pronounced like *chee* in English). These entries are **qī** — first tone (5 instances of a 2-stroke character, 1 of a 7-stroke character, 2 of a 12-stroke character); **qí** — second tone (1 instance); **qǐ** — third tone (4 instances of the same character); **qì** — fourth tone (5 instances of a 4-stroke character). The neutral tone **qi**, written without any tone mark, is absent in this collection.

In the case of a character taking more than one tone, e.g. **bu** 不 which can take on **bú**, **bù** or **bu**, the words or phrases sharing the head character are also arranged in the descending order of the tones.

How to Use the Radical Index

The radical index is based on the 189 radicals used by *The Chinese-English Dictionary 1995*, published by the Foreign Language Teaching and Research Press in Beijing. When you look up a character, first determine which part of the character constitutes the radical and then count the remaining number of strokes to locate the character under that radical. Where a character is made up of two components which can function as radicals, it is sometimes classified under both radicals. For example, the character **měi** 美 "beautiful," is classified under both components which are treated as radicals: **yáng** 羊 "sheep" and **dà** 大 "big" in the same way as found in the *Chinese-English Dictionary 1995*.

Explanatory Notes for Character Pages

Below is an annotated character page, showing the range of information offered:

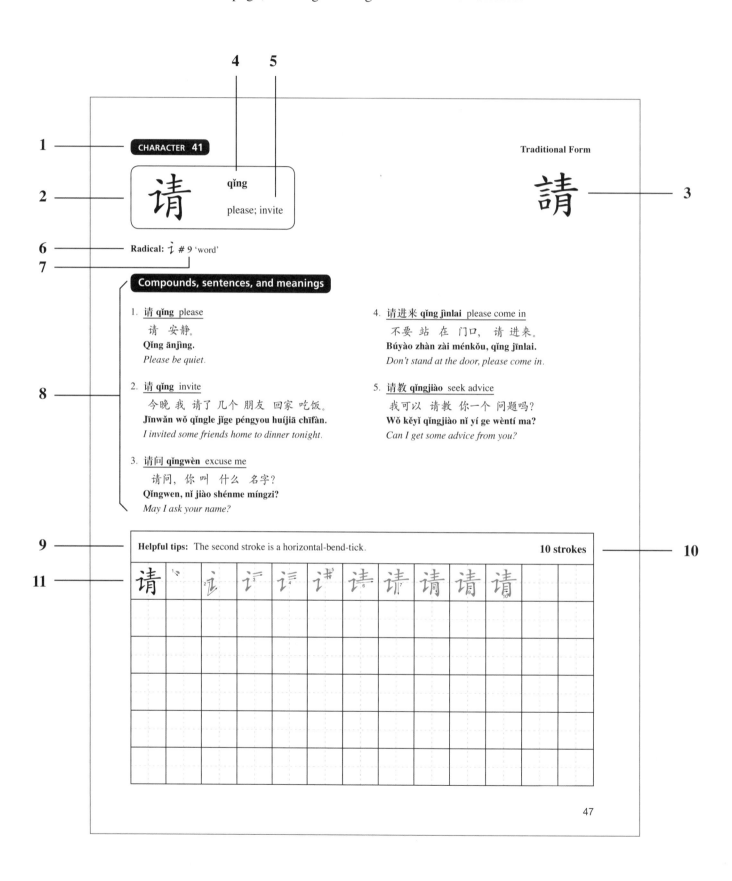

4 **5**

1 CHARACTER 41

Traditional Form

2 请 qǐng

please; invite

请 **3**

6 Radical: 讠 # 9 'word'

7

Compounds, sentences, and meanings

8

1. 请 **qǐng** please
   请 安静。
   Qǐng ānjìng.
   Please be quiet.

2. 请 **qǐng** invite
   今晚 我 请了 几个 朋友 回家 吃饭。
   Jīnwǎn wǒ qǐngle jǐge péngyou huíjiā chīfàn.
   I invited some friends home to dinner tonight.

3. 请问 **qǐngwèn** excuse me
   请问, 你 叫 什么 名字?
   Qǐngwen, nǐ jiào shénme míngzi?
   May I ask your name?

4. 请进来 **qǐng jìnlai** please come in
   不要 站 在 门口, 请 进来。
   Búyào zhàn zài ménkǒu, qǐng jīnlai.
   Don't stand at the door, please come in.

5. 请教 **qǐngjiào** seek advice
   我 可以 请教 你 一个 问题 吗?
   Wǒ kěyǐ qǐngjiào nǐ yí ge wèntí ma?
   Can I get some advice from you?

9 **Helpful tips:** The second stroke is a horizontal-bend-tick. **10 strokes** **10**

11 请 讠 讠 讠 请 请 请 请 请

KEY:

1. character number as sequenced in volume
2. character
3. traditional form of character (when appropriate)
4. *pinyin* Romanization and tone
5. character definition
6. character radical
7. radical index number (based on *The Chinese-English Dictionary 1995*)
8. character vocabulary examples with sentences, pronunciation, and meaning
9. points to note when writing character
10. number of strokes of the character
11. character stroke order

一 **yī / yí / yì**

one

Radical: 一 # 2 "horizontal stroke"

Note: When 一 is used in a stream of numbers, it is usually pronounced **yāo**.

Example: 九一一 (September 11) is pronounced **Jiǔyāoyāo**.

Compounds, sentences, and meanings

1. 一 **yī** one

   一 二 三
   yī èr sān
   one two three

2. 一个 **yí ge** one (general objects, usually roundish)

   请 给 我 一个 面包。
   Qǐng gěi wǒ yí ge miànbāo.
   Please give me a bread roll.

3. 一本（书）**yì běn (shū)** one (book)

   我 买了 一 本 书。
   Wǒ mǎile yì běn shū.
   I bought a book.

4. 一次 **yí cì** once

   我 来过 北京 一次。
   Wǒ láiguo Běijīng yí cì.
   I've been to Beijing once.

5. 第一 **dìyī** first

   这 是 第一次。
   Zhè shì dìyī cì.
   This is the first time.

Helpful tips: Begin boldly and end firmly.

1 stroke

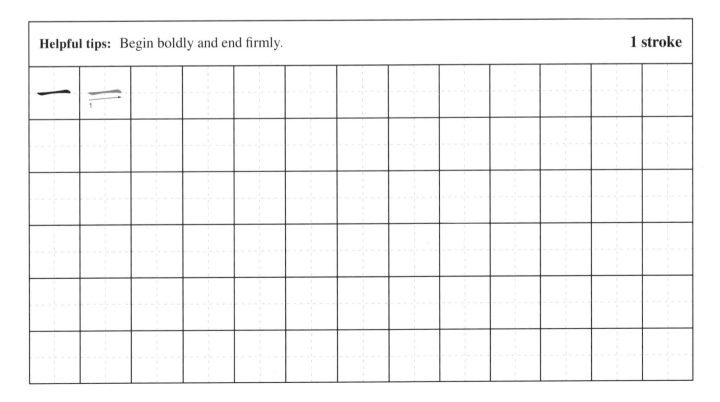

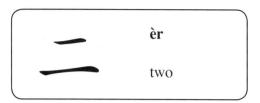

二 èr

two

Radical: 二 # 10 "two"

Compounds, sentences, and meanings

1. 二 **èr** two

   一加一 等于 二。

   Yī jiā yī děngyú èr.

   One plus one equals two.

2. 二哥 **èrgē** second older brother

   我 二哥是 中学 老师。

   Wǒ èrgē shì zhōngxué lǎoshī.

   My second oldest brother is a high school teacher.

3. 二月 **Èryuè** February

   北京 二月 还很 冷。

   Běijīng Èryuè hái hěn lěng.

   Beijing is still quite cold in February.

4. 二等 **èrděng** second class

   我 买了 二等 舱 的票。

   Wǒ mǎile èrděng cāng de piào.

   I've bought a second class cabin ticket.

5. 独一无二 **dúyī-wú'èr** unique

   她的 想法 独一无二。

   Tāde xiǎngfǎ dúyī-wú'èr.

   Her way of thinking is unique.

Helpful tips: The bottom stroke is longer.												2 strokes
二	二	二										

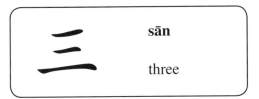

sān

three

Radical: 一 # 2 "horizontal stroke"

Compounds, sentences, and meanings

4. 三 **sān** three

一不离二，二不离三。

Yī bù lí èr, èr bù lí sān.

Things don't happen once; they come in twos and threes.

2. 三角形 **sānjiǎoxíng** triangle

这 是 个 三角形。

Zhè shì ge sānjiǎoxíng.

This is a triangle.

3. 三个月 **sān ge yuè** three months

我 来了 中国 三个月。

Wǒ láile Zhōngguó sān ge yuè.

I've been in China for three months.

4. 星期三 **Xīngqīsān** Wednesday

今天 是 星期三。

Jīntiān shì Xīngqīsān.

Today is Wednesday.

5. 三心二意 **sānxīn-èryì** undecisive

就 这样 吧，别再 三心二意了。

Jiù zhèyàng ba, bié zài sānxīn-èryì le.

That settles it, don't be indecisive. (literally, three hearts, two minds)

Helpful tips: The strokes are equally spaced; the middle stroke is the shortest.												**3 strokes**
三	一	二	三									

四 sì

four

Radical: # 51 "4-sided frame"

Compounds, sentences, and meanings

1. 四 **sì** four

   二二得四。

   Èr èr dé sì.

   Two times two equals four.

2. 四方 **sìfāng** square

   我 家 有 一个 四方 的 盒子。

   Wǒ jiā yǒu yí ge sìfāng de hézi.

   I have a square box at home.

3. 四季 **sìjì** four seasons

   这里的 气候四季如春。

   Zhèlǐ de qìhòu sìjì-rúchūn.

   The climate here is like spring in all seasons.

4. 四川 **Sìchuān** Sichuan (province; literally, four rivers, referring to the four tributaries of the Yangzi which flow through the province)

   四川菜 很 好吃。

   Sìchuāncài hěn hǎochī.

   Sichuan food is delicious.

5. 四通八达 **sìtōng-bādá** in all directions

   美国 的 公路 四通八达。

   Měiguó de gōnglù sìtōng-bādá.

   Highways of the United States go in all directions.

Helpful tips: The inner strokes do not touch the frame.													**5 strokes**
四	丨	冂	四	四	四								

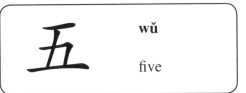

wǔ

five

Radical: 一 # 2 "horizontal stroke" or 二 # 10 "two"

Compounds, sentences, and meanings

1. 五 **wǔ** five
   五路 公共 汽车
   Wǔlù gōnggòng qìchē
   No. 5 bus

2. 五月 **Wǔyuè** May
   五月 一号 是 劳动节。
   Wǔyuè-yīhào shì Láodòngjié.
   The first of May is Labor Day.

3. 五个月 **wǔ ge yuè** five months
   他的汽车 买了 五个 月。
   Tāde qìchē mǎile wǔ ge yuè.
   He bought his car five months ago.

4. 五体投地 **wǔ tǐ tóu dì** prostrate oneself before someone (literally, the five extremities of the body)
   他 为人 正直，让 我 佩服得五体
   Tā wéirén zhèngzhí, ràng wǒ pèifúde wǔ tǐ
   投 地。
   tóu dì.
   I admire his uprightness greatly.

5. 五颜六色 **wǔyán-liùsè** multi-colored
   五颜 六色的 云霞 真 美丽。
   Wǔyán-liùsè de yúnxiá zhēn měilì.
   The multi-colored clouds are really pretty.

Helpful tips:	There is equal spacing between the 3 horizontal strokes. The bottom stroke is longer than the ones above.	**4 strokes**

五 二 丆 石 五

CHARACTER 6

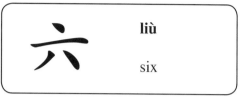

liù

six

Radical: 亠 # 6 "the top of 六"

Compounds, sentences, and meanings

1. 六 **liù** six

   二 三 得六。

   Èr sān dé liù.

   Two times three equals six.

2. 六月 **Liù yuè** June

   六月 十 二号 是 我的 生日。

   Liùyuè-shí'èrhào shì wǒde shēngrì.

   The 12th of June is my birthday.

3. 星期六 **Xīngqīliù** Saturday

   星期六 我 不 上班。

   Xīngqīliù wǒ bú shàngbān.

   I don't go to work on Saturday.

4. 六一 **Liùyī** June 1st

   六一 是 国际 儿童节。

   Liùyī shì Guójì értóngjié.

   June 1st is International Children's Day.

5. 三头六臂 **sāntóu-liùbì** superhuman (literally, three heads and six arms)

   你 别怕, 他 没有 三头 六臂。

   Nǐ bié pà, tā méiyǒu sāntóu-liùbì.

   Don't be scared, he's not superhuman.

Helpful tips: End the last stroke firmly.											4 strokes
六	丷	亠	亣	六							

6

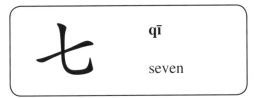

七   qī

seven

Radical: 一 # 2 "horizontal stroke"

Compounds, sentences, and meanings

1. 七 **qī** seven

   七七得四十九。

   Qī qī dé sì shí jiǔ.

   Seven times seven equals forty-nine.

2. 七天 **qī tiān** seven days

   一个 星期 有 七天。

   Yí ge xīngqī yǒu qī tiān.

   There are seven days in a week.

3. 七月 **Qīyuè** July

   北京 七月 很 热。

   Běijīng Qīyuè hěn rè.

   Beijing is very hot in July.

4. 七七八八 **qīqībābā** miscellaneous

   这里七七八八的 事情 很多。

   Zhèlǐ qīqībābā de shìqing hěnduō.

   There are plenty of odd jobs to do here.

5. 七上八落 **qīshàng-bāluò** be agitated
   (literally, like 15 buckets, 7 going up and 8
   going down)

   我的 心头 如同 十五 个 吊桶

   Wǒde xīntóu rútóng shíwǔ ge diàotǒng,

   七上 八落，静不下来。

   qīshàng-bāluò, jìngbuxiàlai.

   My heart was racing erratically.

Helpful tips: The second stroke ends with a hook.   **2 strokes**

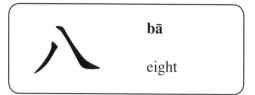

八 **bā**

eight

Radical: 八 #17 "eight"

Compounds, sentences, and meanings

1. 八 **bā** eight

   我 家 离 市区 八 公里。

   Wǒ jiā lí shìqū bā gōnglǐ.

   My house is 8 km from the city.

2. 八成 **bāchéng** 80 percent

   事情 有了 八成 了。

   Shìqing yǒule bāchéng le.

   It's as good as settled (80% complete).

3. 八折 **bāzhé** 20% discount

   八折 优惠 顾客。

   Bāzhé yōuhuì gùkè.

   20% discount.

4. 胡说八道 **húshuō-bādào** to speak nonsense

   别 胡说 八道。

   Bié húshuō-bādào.

   Don't talk nonsense.

5. 乱七八糟 **luànqībāzāo** in great disorder

   他的 屋子 乱七八糟 的。

   Tāde wūzi luànqībāzāo de.

   His room is in a mess.

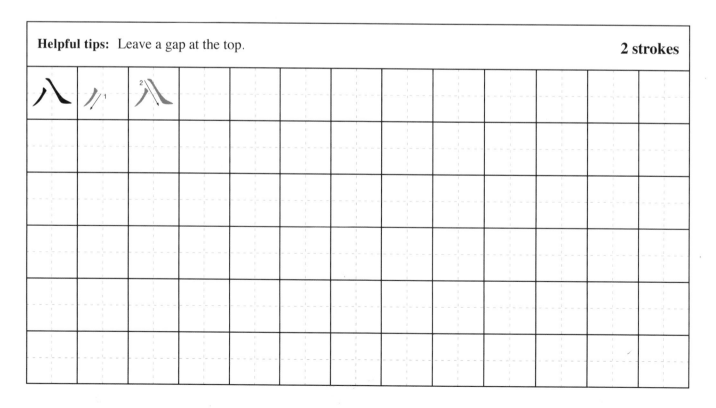

Helpful tips: Leave a gap at the top.   **2 strokes**

九　**jiǔ**

nine

Radical: ノ　# 4 "downward-left stroke"

Compounds, sentences, and meanings

1. 九 **jiǔ** nine

   三 三 得 九。
   Sān sān dé jiǔ.
   Three times three equals nine.

2. 九九表 **jiǔjiǔbiǎo** multiplication table

   你的 九九表 背熟 了吗?
   Nǐde jiǔjiǔbiǎo bèishú le ma?
   Did you learn the multiplication table?

3. 九级风 **jiǔjífēng** force 9 wind

   今天 吹 九级风。
   Jīntiān chuī jiǔjífēng.
   A strong gale is blowing today.

4. 九宫格儿 **jiǔgōnggér** 9-grid paper

   九宫格儿 是 用 来 写 汉字 的。
   Jiǔgōnggér shì yòng lái xiě Hànzì de.
   A 9-grid squared paper is used for writing characters.

5. 九一一 **Jiǔyāoyāo** September 11

   美国人 难忘 九一一。
   Měiguórén nánwàng Jiǔyāoyāo.
   Americans will never forget what happened on September 11.

Helpful tips: The second stroke ends with a hook.											2 strokes
九	ノ	九									

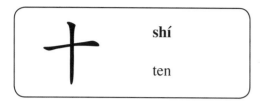

Radical: 十 # 11 "ten"

Compounds, sentences, and meanings

1. 十 **shí** ten

   我 妹妹 今年 十 岁。

   Wǒ mèimei jīnnián shí suì.

   My younger sister is ten years old.

2. 十分 **shífēn** fully

   你 康复了, 我 十分 高兴。

   Nǐ kāngfúle, wǒ shífēn gāoxìng.

   I'm very pleased that you've recovered.

3. 十足 **shízú** 100 percent

   这 个 小伙子 干劲 十足。

   Zhè ge xiǎohuǒzi gànjìng shízú.

   This young man is full of energy.

4. 十字路口 **shízì lùkǒu** intersection

   前面 有 个 十字路口。

   Qiánmiàn yǒu ge shízì lùkǒu.

   There's an intersection farther ahead.

5. 十全十美 **shíquán-shíměi** be perfect in every way (literally, complete and beautiful)

   人生 很 难 会 有 十全 十美 的。

   Rénshēng hěn nán huì yǒu shíquán-shíměi de.

   It's very hard to find perfection in life.

Helpful tips: The lower part of the vertical stroke is longer.　　　　**2 strokes**

十	十	十								

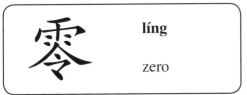

零 líng

zero

Radical: 雨 # 172 "rain"

Compounds, sentences, and meanings

1. 零 **líng** zero

   现在 六点 零 八分。

   Xiànzài liùdiǎn-líng-bāfēn.

   The time now is 6:08.

2. 零下 **língxià** below zero

   今天 气温 是 摄氏 零下 五度。

   Jīntiān qìwēn shì shèshì língxià wǔ dù.

   Today's temperature is 5°C below zero.

3. 零钱 **língqián** small change

   我要 换 点 零钱。

   Wǒ yào huàn diǎn língqián.

   I want to get some small change.

4. 零碎 **língsuì** piecemeal

   我 还 有 点儿 零碎 事情 没有 办完。

   Wǒ hái yǒu diǎnr língsuì shìqing méiyǒu bànwán.

   I still have some loose ends to tie up.

5. 零用钱 **língyòngqián** pocket money

   你一个 月 给孩子 多少 零用钱？

   Nǐ yí ge yuè gěi háizi duōshao língyòngqián?

   How much pocket money do you give your child a month?

Helpful tips: Finish the last stroke firmly.											**13 strokes**
零	一	厂	帀	雨	雨	雫	雫	雫	霚	零	零	零
零											

CHARACTER 12

百	**bǎi**
	hundred

Radical: 一 # 2 "horizontal stroke" or 白 #147 "white"

Compounds, sentences, and meanings

1. 百 **bǎi** hundred

   我 认识 两百 个 汉字。
   Wǒ rènshi liǎngbǎi ge Hànzì.
   I know 200 characters.

2. 百分之百 **bǎifēnzhībǎi** absolutely (literally, 100%)

   这 是 百分之百 的 谎话!
   Zhè shì bǎifēnzhībǎi de huǎnghuà!
   That's an absolute lie!

3. 百货 **bǎihuò** general merchandise

   这 是 一家 高档 的 百货 公司。
   Zhè shì yì jiā gāodǎng de bǎihuò gōngsī.
   This is an upmarket department store.

4. 百万 **bǎiwàn** million (literally, a hundred ten thousands)

   她 想 嫁给 百万 富翁。
   Tā xiǎng jià gěi bǎiwàn fùwēng.
   She wants to marry a millionaire.

5. 百分点 **bǎifēndiǎn** 1 percentage point

   银行 利息 增加了 半 个 百分点。
   Yínháng lìxī zēngjiāle bàn ge bǎifēndiǎn.
   Bank interest has increased by half a percentage point.

Helpful tips: The top horizontal stroke is longer.   **6 strokes**

百	一	丆	丆	百	百	百					

Lesson 1: Review Activities

A. Pronunciation and *Pinyin* Practice

Please write next to each of the following numbers the character for each number. Then write the *pinyin* for each. Finally, practice reciting aloud the numbers in Mandarin Chinese.

1 (_____) _____   2 (_____) _____   3 (_____) _____

4 (_____) _____   5 (_____) _____   6 (_____) _____

7 (_____) _____   8 (_____) _____   9 (_____) _____

10 (_____) _____

11 (_____) _____   12 (_____) _____   13 (_____) _____

14 (_____) _____   15 (_____) _____   16 (_____) _____

17 (_____) _____   18 (_____) _____   19 (_____) _____

20 (_____) _____

10 (_____) _____   20 (_____) _____   30 (_____) _____

40 (_____) _____   50 (_____) _____   60 (_____) _____

70 (_____) _____   80 (_____) _____   90 (_____) _____

100 (_____) _____

B. Number Identification

Complete each of the following sections.

I. Please write the number for the following characters:

五 _____   十七 _____   二十三 _____

四十一 _____   八十六 _____   九十九 _____

一百 _____   五百五十 _____   七百二十五 _____

九百零一 _____

II. Please write the characters for the following numbers:

16 _____   38 _____   400 _____

205 _____   370 _____

III. Please select and write five numbers and their respective characters:

Number   **Character**

_____   _____

_____   _____

_____   _____

_____   _____

_____   _____

C. Chinese Language Sudoku

Please complete the following grid in Chinese characters. The grid is comprised of columns and rows that contain each number from 1–9. Each small box within the grid also contains each number from 1–9.

			七			九		
八			一	九	六			
		三	五		八			
五	六					二		九
	四				五			七
九		八	二				六	四
		六		一	七			
二			六	三			五	
三	八				二			一

wǒ

I, me

Radical: 戈 # 85 "spear"

Compounds, sentences, and meanings

1. 我 wǒ I, me

我 喜欢 学 汉字。

Wǒ xǐhuan xué Hànzì.

I like learning Chinese characters.

2. 我们 wǒmen we, us

我们 互相 帮助, 好 不好?

Wǒmen hùxiāng bāngzhù, hǎo buhǎo?

Let's help each other, shall we?

3. 我们的 wǒmende our, ours

我们的 将来 是 美好 的。

Wǒmende jiānglái shì měihǎo de.

Our future is bright.

4. 自我 zìwǒ self

我 建议 大家自我 介绍 一下儿。

Wǒ jiànyì dàjiā zìwǒ jièshào yíxiàr.

I suggest that we introduce ourselves.

Helpful tips: The fourth stroke comes up, the sixth stroke sweeps down.								**7 strokes**				
我	一	二	于	手	我	我	我					

你

nǐ

you

Radical: 亻 # 19 "upright person"

Compounds, sentences, and meanings

1. 你 **nǐ** you

   你 想 买 什么?

   Nǐ xiǎng mǎi shénme?

   What would you like to buy?

2. 你好 **nǐ hǎo** hello

   你好! 认识你, 我 很 高兴。

   Nǐ hǎo! Rènshi nǐ, wǒ hěn gāoxìng.

   Hi! I'm pleased to meet you.

3. 你们 **nǐmen** you (plural)

   我 给 你们 介绍, 这是…, 这是…。

   Wǒ gěi nǐmen jièshào, zhè shì ..., zhè shì....

   Let me introduce, this is ..., this is ... .

4. 你们好 **nǐmen hǎo** hello everyone

   你们 好!

   Nǐmen hǎo!

   Hi everyone!

5. 你们的 **nǐmende** your, yours

   你们的 东西 放好 了吗?

   Nǐmende dōngxi fànghǎo le ma?

   Have you put away your things?

Helpful tips: The fifth stroke is a vertical hook.											**7 strokes**
你	亻	亻	亻	你	你	你	你				

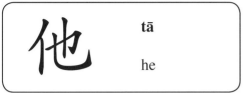

他　**tā**

he

Radical: 亻 # 19 "upright person"

Compounds, sentences, and meanings

1. 他 **tā** he

   他 是 我的 老朋友。
   Tā shì wǒde lǎopéngyou.
   He's an old friend of mine.

2. 他们 **tāmen** they

   他们 是 法国人，不是 美国人。
   Tāmen shì Fǎguórén, búshì Měiguórén.
   They're French, not American.

3. 其他 **qítā** other

   还有 什么 其他 事情 要 我们 做 吗?
   Háiyǒu shénme qítā shìqing yào wǒmen zuò ma?
   Is there anything else you want us to do?

4. 他人 **tārén** others

   别 吵, 这样 会 影响 他人。
   Bié chǎo, zhèyàng huì yǐngxiǎng tārén.
   Don't make so much noise as this will disturb people.

5. 他妈的 **tāmāde** damn it!

   他妈的, 你 怎么 走路 看 也 不看!
   Tāmāde, nǐ zěnme zǒulù kàn yě búkàn!
   Damn you, why don't you watch where you're going!

Helpful tips: The third stroke ends with a hook.　　　　**5 strokes**

他　丿　亻　仂　仳　他

她 **tā**

she

Radical: 女 # 65 "female"

Compounds, sentences, and meanings

1. 她 **tā** she

   她 说 汉语 说得 很 好。

   Tā shuō Hànyǔ shuōde hěn hǎo.

   She speaks Chinese very well.

2. 她的 **tāde** her, hers

   她的 汉语 说得 很 地道。

   Tāde Hànyǔ shuōde hěn dìdao.

   Her spoken Mandarin is very authentic.

3. 她们 **tāmen** they, them (female)

   你认得 她们 是 谁 吗?

   Nǐ rènde tāmen shì shéi/shuí ma?

   Do you know who these girls/women are?

4. 她们的 **tāmende** their, theirs (female)

   她们的 衣服 都 很 时髦。

   Tāmende yīfu dōu hěn shímáo.

   The clothes they are wearing are very fashionable.

Helpful tips: The fourth stroke ends with a hook.											

6 strokes

她	㇆¹	女²	女₃	奴₄	奻⁵	她₆					

们 **men**

[plural suffix]

們

Radical: 亻 #19 "upright person"

Compounds, sentences, and meanings

1. 你们 **nǐmen** you (plural)

请 你们 等 一下,我 马上 回来。

Qǐng nǐmen děng yíxià, wǒ mǎshàng huílai.

Please wait a moment, I'll be right back.

2. 咱们 **zánmen** we, us (referring to those spoken to)

咱们 商量 一下。

Zánmen shāngliang yíxià.

Let's talk it over.

3. 女士们 **nǚshìmen** ladies

女士们 先生们, 你们 好!

Nǚshìmen, xiānshengmen, nǐmen hǎo!

Ladies and gentlemen! Greetings!

4. 男士们 **nánshìmen** gentlemen

通常 是 男士们 邀请 女士们

Tōngcháng shì nánshìmen yāoqǐng nǚshìmen

跳舞。

tiàowǔ.

Generally it is the men who ask the ladies to dance.

5. 哥儿们 **gērmen** buddies

朋友 之间 分得太 清 就 不够

Péngyou zhījiān fēnde tài qīng jiù búgòu

哥儿们了。

gērmen le.

If friends become too calculating, then there's not much friendship between them.

Helpful tips: The last stroke ends with a hook.　　　　　**5 strokes**

们	丿	亻	亻	伀	们							

bù / bú

not

Radical: 一 # 2 "horizontal stroke"

Compounds, sentences, and meanings

1. 不 **bù** not

   昨天 他 说 今天 不 来了。
   Zuótiān tā shuō jīntiān bù lái le.
   He said yesterday that he won't be coming today.

2. 不错 **búcuò** quite good

   这 个 字 写得 不错。
   Zhè ge zì xiěde búcuò.
   This character is quite well written.

3. 不好意思 **bùhǎo yìsi** embarrassed

   让 你 久 等 了, 真 不好意思。
   Ràng nǐ jiǔ děng le, zhēn bùhǎo yìsi.
   I'm sorry to have kept you waiting.

4. 不多不少 **bùduō bùshǎo** just right

   你 买 的 水果 不多 不少, 正 好。
   Nǐ mǎi de shuǐguǒ bùduō bùshǎo, zhèng hǎo.
   You bought just the right amount of fruit—not too much, not too little.

5. 不久 **bùjiǔ** soon

   你 走了 不久, 他 就 来了。
   Nǐ zǒule bùjiǔ, tā jiù lái le.
   He came soon after you left.

Helpful tips: The last stroke ends firmly.											**4 strokes**
不	一	丆	不	不							

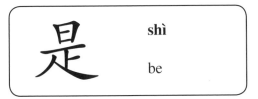

是 shì

be

Radical: 日 # 90 "sun"

Compounds, sentences, and meanings

1. 是 **shì** to be

   她 是 日本人。

   Tā shì Rìběnrén.

   She is Japanese.

2. 是的 **shìde** yes

   是的, 日本人 也 用 汉字。

   Shìde, Rìběnrén yě yòng Hànzì.

   Yes, Japanese people also use Chinese characters.

3. 不是 **búshì** not to be

   他 不是 日本人。

   Tā búshì Rìběnrén.

   He's not Japanese.

4. 是不是 **shìbushì** to be or not to be

   他 是不是 日本人?

   Tā shìbushì Rìběnrén?

   Is he Japanese?

5. 还是 **háishi** or

   她是 日本人, 还是 韩国人?

   Tā shì Rìběnrén, háishi Hánguórén?

   Is she Japanese, or Korean?

Helpful tips: Make sure that the last stroke is not too flat.   **9 strokes**

是	丿	口	日	旦	旱	昺	昰	昰	是			

的 **de**

[particle]

Radical: 白 # 125 "white"

Compounds, sentences, and meanings

1. 的 **de** particle

   她 有 一 双 大大的 眼睛。

   Tā yǒu yì shuāng dàdà de yǎnjing.

   She has big eyes (literally, a pair of big eyes).

2. 辣的 **là de** spicy hot

   我爱 吃辣的。

   Wǒ ài chī là de.

   I love spicy food.

3. 昨天的 **zuótiān de** yesterday's

   这是 昨天 的 报。

   Zhè shì zuótiān de bào.

   This is yesterday's newspaper.

4. 有的 **yǒude** some

   有的 是 新 的, 有的 是 旧的。

   Yǒude shì xīn de, yǒude shì jiù de.

   Some are new, some are old.

Helpful tips: Write the final stroke firmly.								**8 strokes**

的 ⺍¹ 亻² 𠂉³ 自⁴ 自⁵ 白⁶ 的⁷ 的⁸

朋

péng

friend

Radical: 月 # 103 "flesh/moon"

Compounds, sentences, and meanings

1. 朋 **péng** friend

   昨晚 亲朋 戚友聚在一起 真 高兴。

   Zuówǎn qīn-péng qī-yǒu jù zài yìqǐ zhēn gāoxìng.

   It was very happy to have relatives and friends gathered together last night.

2. 朋友 **péngyou** friend

   你有 中国 朋友 吗?

   Nǐ yǒu Zhōngguó péngyou ma?

   Do you have any Chinese friends?

3. 男朋友 **nánpéngyou** boyfriend

   她跟 男朋友 住在一起。

   Tā gēn nánpéngyou zhù zài yìqǐ.

   She lives with her boyfriend.

4. 女朋友 **nǚpéngyou** girlfriend

   你有 女朋友 了 没有?

   Nǐ yǒu nǚpéngyou le méiyou?

   Do you have a girlfriend?

5. 老朋友 **lǎopéngyou** old friend

   难得 有机会跟 老朋友 聚在一起。

   Nándé yǒu jīhuì gēn lǎopéngyou jù zài yìqǐ.

   Old friends don't often get the chance to meet.

Helpful tips: The right component is written slightly wider.　　　　**8 strokes**

朋	丿¹	刀²	月³	月⁴	朋⁵	朋⁶	朋⁷	朋⁸				

友　yǒu

friend

Radical: 又 # 24 "again"

Compounds, sentences, and meanings

1. 友 **yǒu** friend
   他是我十多年的好友。
   Tā shì wǒ shí duō nián de hǎo yǒu.
   He has been my good friend for over ten years.

2. 友情 **yǒuqíng** friendship
   他很重友情。
   Tā hěn zhòng yǒuqíng.
   He values friendship greatly.

3. 友谊 **yǒuyì** friendship
   友谊第一, 比赛第二。
   Yǒuyì dìyī, bǐsài dì'èr.
   Friendship first, competition second.

4. 友好 **yǒuhǎo** friendly
   他对人很友好。
   Tā duì rén hěn yǒuhǎo.
   He's a friendly person.

5. 走亲访友 **zǒu-qīn fǎng-yǒu** visiting relatives and friends
   中国 普通 的 老百姓 走亲 访友
   Zhōngguó pǔtōng de lǎobǎixìng zǒu-qīn fǎng-yǒu
   都 是 骑 自行车。
   dōu shì qí zìxíngchē.
   Ordinary people in China use bicycles to visit their relatives and friends.

Helpful tips: The long horizontal stroke covers 又.							**4 strokes**
友	一	ナ	方	友			

Lesson 2: Review Activities

A. Identification and Pronunciation

Please write out in *pinyin* the phrases that follow. Then practice reciting aloud the phrases in Mandarin Chinese.

1. 我是 _____
2. 你是 _____

3. 她是 _____
4. 我们不是 _____

5. 你们是 _____
6. 他们不是 _____

7. 我的朋友 _____
8. 你的朋友 _____

9. 她们的朋友 _____
10. 他的女朋友 _____

B. Answer the Questions

Please answer the following questions appropriately in Chinese characters.

1. 她是不是你的朋友？

_____

2. 我是不是你的朋友？

_____

3. 你是不是他的朋友？

_____

4. 他们是不是我们的朋友？

_____

5. 她们是不是你们的朋友？

_____

C. Diagram

For each group below, please create a small diagram that demonstrates the differences between basic pronouns in Mandarin Chinese. For example, you might choose to sketch simple stick-figure people in various positions in relation to each other, with arrows showing how each pronoun applies.

我 / 你 / 她 / 他

我们 / 你们 / 他们

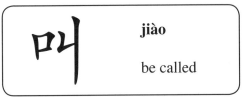

jiào

be called

叫

Radical: 口 # 50 "mouth"

Compounds, sentences, and meanings

1. 叫 **jiào** be called

她 叫 什么 名字?

Tā jiào shénme míngzi?

What's her name?

2. 叫做 **jiàozuò** be called

这 种 汽油 叫做 含铅 汽油。

Zhè zhǒng qìyóu jiàozuò hánqiān qìyóu.

This type of gasoline is called leaded gasoline.

3. 叫门 **jiàomén** call at the door

有 人 在 叫门。

Yǒu rén zài jiàomén.

Someone is at the door.

4. 叫喊 **jiàohǎn** shout

请 别 在 这里 高声 叫喊。

Qǐng bié zài zhèlǐ gāoshēng jiàohǎn.

Please don't shout here.

5. 叫座 **jiàozuò** draw a large audience

这 个 电影 很 叫座。

Zhè ge diànyǐng hěn jiàozuò.

This movie is a box-office hit.

Helpful tips: Write 口 halfway down the left strokes of 丩.											5 strokes
叫	刂¹	卩²	口³	叫⁴	叫⁵						

什   shén

what?

甚

Radical: 亻 # 19 "upright person"

Compounds, sentences, and meanings

1. 什么 **shénme** what

你 叫 什么 名字?

Nǐ jiào shénme míngzi?

What's your given name / first name?

2. 什么? **shénme** Pardon me?

什么? 请 再 说 一 遍。

Shénme? Qǐng zài shuō yí biàn.

Pardon? Please say that again.

3. 什么的 **shénmede** etcetera

我 要 买鱼、肉、鸡蛋、什么的。

Wǒ yào mǎi yú, ròu, jīdàn, shénmede.

I have to buy fish, meat, eggs etc.

Helpful tips: The left and right components do not join up.				**4 strokes**

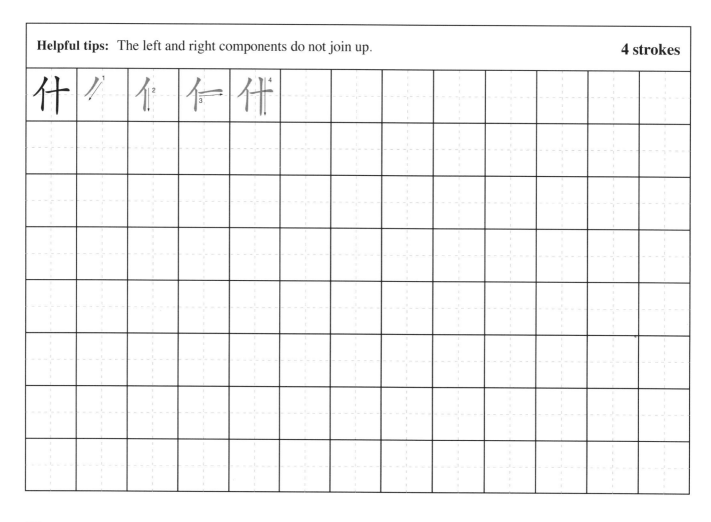

么   me

[particle]

麼

Radical: ノ # 4 "downward-left stroke" or ㄙ # 56 "private"

Compounds, sentences, and meanings

1. 这么 **zhème** so, such

    这么 做 就 行 了。

    Zhème zuò jiù xíng le.

    It should be fine if you do it this way.

2. 那么 **nàme** in that way

    别 走得 那么 快，好不好？

    Bié zǒude nàme kuài, hǎobuhǎo?

    Don't walk so fast, okay?

3. 怎么 **zěnme** how

    这个 词儿 英语 怎么 说？

    Zhè ge cír Yīngyǔ zěnme shuō?

    How do you say this word in English?

4. 多么 **duōme** to what extent

    多么 新鲜 的 水果 啊！

    Duōme xīnxiān de shuǐguǒ a!

    What fresh fruits!

5. 要么 **yàome** either or

    要么 他来，要么 我 去，我们 总 得见

    Yàome tā lái, yàome wǒ qù, wǒmen zǒng děi jiàn

    个 面。

    ge miàn.

    Either he comes here or I go there; either way we've got to meet.

Helpful tips: The first stroke only comes halfway down.											**3 strokes**
么	ノ	幺	么								

ma

[particle]

嗎

Radical: 口 # 50 "mouth"

Compounds, sentences, and meanings

1. 吗 **ma** question particle

   你 找 我 吗?

   Nǐ zhǎo wǒ ma?

   Are you looking for me?

2. 好吗 **hǎo ma** good?

   你 好 吗?

   Nǐ hǎo ma?

   How are you?

3. 忙吗 **máng ma** busy?

   你 忙 吗?

   Nǐ máng ma?

   Are you busy?

4. 干吗 **gàn ma** what are you doing?

   你 晚上 干 吗?

   Nǐ wǎnshang gàn ma?

   What will you be doing in the evening?

Helpful tips: 马 should be upright.											**6 strokes**
吗	丨¹	口²	口³	吗⁴	吗⁵	吗⁶					

名 **míng**

name

Radical: 口 # 50 "mouth" or 夕 # 56 "sunset"

Compounds, sentences, and meanings

1. 名 **míng** name
   他 名 叫 王 刚。
   Tā míng jiào Wáng Gāng.
   His name is Wang Gang.

2. 名字 **míngzi** name
   我 有 中文 名字。
   Wǒ yǒu Zhōngwén míngzi.
   I have a Chinese name.

3. 名牌 **míngpái** brand name
   北京 大学 是 名牌 大学。
   Běijīng Dàxué shì míngpái dàxué.
   Beijing University is a prestigious university.

4. 名片 **míngpiàn** business card
   这 是 我的 名片。
   Zhè shì wǒde míngpiàn.
   This is my business card.

5. 名胜 **míngshèng** famous scenic spot
   南京 有 很多 名胜。
   Nánjīng yǒu hěnduō míngshèng.
   Nanjing has many famous scenic spots.

Helpful tips: The third stroke does not cross through the second stroke.							6 strokes

名 丿 夕 夕 夕 名 名

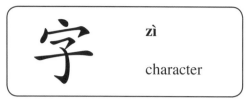

字　**zì**

character

Radical: 宀 # 34 "roof"

Compounds, sentences, and meanings

1. 字 **zì** character, word

   你 这 个 字 写得 不对。

   Nǐ zhè ge zì xiěde búduì.

   You wrote this character incorrectly.

2. 字典 **zìdiǎn** dictionary

   你 有 汉英 字典 吗?

   Nǐ yǒu Hàn-yīng zìdiǎn ma?

   Do you have a Chinese-English dictionary?

3. 字母 **zìmǔ** alphabet

   汉语 拼音 用 的 是 拉丁 字母。

   Hànyǔ Pīnyīn yòng de shì Lādīng zìmǔ.

   Pinyin uses the Latin alphabet.

4. 字幕 **zìmù** subtitles, captions

   这 个 电影 有 中文 字幕。

   Zhè ge diànyǐng yǒu Zhōngwén zìmù.

   This movie has Chinese subtitles.

5. 汉字 **Hànzì** characters

   我 学了 十五 个 汉字。

   Wǒ xuéle shíwǔ ge Hànzì.

   I've learned 15 Chinese characters.

Helpful tips: The fifth stroke ends with a hook.											**6 strokes**
字	丶	丷	宀	宁	宁	字					

姓

xìng

surname

Radical: 女 # 65 "female"

Compounds, sentences, and meanings

1. 姓 **xìng** to be surnamed

   我 姓 李, 名 叫 恩华。

   Wǒ xìng Lǐ, míng jiào Ēnhuá.

   My surname is Li, my given name is Enhua.

2. 姓名 **xìngmíng** full name

   请 写下 你的 姓名。

   Qǐng xiěxià nǐde xìngmíng.

   Please write down your full name.

3. 姓氏 **xìngshì** surname

   以 姓氏 笔划 为 序。

   Yǐ xìngshì bǐhuà wéi xù.

   Arranged by surname in the order of the number of strokes.

4. 老百姓 **lǎobǎixìng** common people (literally, the 100 old names)

   中国 一般 老百姓 很 穷。

   Zhōngguó yìbān lǎobǎixìng hěn qióng.

   In general, people in China are poor.

5. 同姓 **tóngxìng** having the same surname

   以前 中国人 同姓 不 通婚。

   Yǐqián Zhōngguórén tóngxìng bù tōnghūn.

   In the past, people would not marry someone with the same surname.

Helpful tips: The bottom horizontal stroke on the right-hand side is longer.							**8 strokes**			
姓	〈¹	〈²	女³	女⁴	妒⁵	妒⁶	姓⁷	姓⁸		

很　hěn
very

Radical: 彳 # 54 "double person"

Compounds, sentences, and meanings

1. 很 **hěn** very

   他 这 个 人 好得 很。

   Tā zhè ge rén hǎode hěn.

   He's a very good man.

2. 很好 **hěn hǎo** very good/well

   这 个 汉字 你 写得 很 好。

   Zhè ge Hànzì nǐ xiěde hěn hǎo.

   You've written this Chinese character very nicely.

3. 很坏 **hěn huài** very bad

   当心, 这 个 人 很 坏。

   Dāngxīn, zhè ge rén hěn huài!

   Look out! This person is no good.

4. 很多 **hěnduō** a lot of

   你 认识 很多 汉字。

   Nǐ rènshi hěnduō Hànzì.

   You recognize lots of characters.

5. 很近 **hěn jìn** very near

   我 家离 火车站 很 近。

   Wǒ jiā lí huǒchēzhàn hěn jìn.

   I live quite near the train station.

Helpful tips: The last stroke tapers off.								9 strokes		
很	彳	彳	彳	彳	彳	很	很	很		

好 **hǎo**

good

Radical: 女 # 65 "female"

Compounds, sentences, and meanings

1. 好 **hǎo** good

   今天 天气 真 好。
   Jīntiān tiānqì zhēn hǎo.
   The weather is really lovely today.

2. 好办 **hǎobàn** easy to handle

   这 件 事 好办。
   Zhè jiàn shì hǎobàn.
   This matter can be settled.

3. 好吃 **hǎochī** delicious

   我 觉得 中餐 很 好吃。
   Wǒ juéde Zhōngcān hěn hǎochī.
   I think Chinese food is delicious.

4. 好处 **hǎochù** good points

   学 拼音 对 学 汉字 有 好处。
   Xué Pīnyīn duì xué Hànzì yǒu hǎochù.
   Learning pinyin helps you learn Chinese characters.

5. 好看 **hǎokàn** pretty

   你 说 这 条 裙子 好 不 好看?
   Nǐ shuō zhè tiáo qúnzi hǎo bu hǎokàn?
   Do you think this dress is pretty?

Helpful tips: The first stroke travels down, turns and ends firmly.						6 strokes
好	ㄑ	女	女	女	奵	好

再 **zài**

again

Radical: 一 # 2 "horizontal stroke"

Compounds, sentences, and meanings

1. 再 **zài** again

有 工夫, 请 再来玩儿。

Yǒu gōngfu, qǐng zài lái wánr.

Please come again whenever you're free.

2. 再次 **zàicì** once more

再次 感谢 你们的 帮助。

Zàicì gǎnxiè nǐmende bāngzhù.

Thanks once again for your help.

3. 再见 **zàijiàn** see you again, goodbye

下 星期天 再见。

Xià Xīngqītiān zàijiàn.

I'll see you next Sunday.

4. 再三 **zàisān** again and again

希望 你 再三 考虑 才 决定。

Xīwàng nǐ zàisān kǎolǜ cái juédìng.

I hope that you consider carefully before you make your decision.

5. 再说 **zàishuō** what's more, besides

现在 去 找 他太 晚 了, 再 说 我 路

Xiànzài qù zhǎo tā tài wǎn le, zài shuō wǒ lù

也不 熟。

yě bù shú.

It's too late to go and see him now; besides, I don't quite know the way.

Helpful tips: The bottom horizontal stroke is the longest.　　　　　　**6 strokes**

再	一	一	冂	冃	再	再					

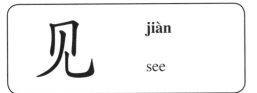

見

Radical: 见 # 93 "see"

Compounds, sentences, and meanings

1. 见 **jiàn** see

   下午 他要来 见 你。

   Xiàwǔ tā yào lái jiàn nǐ.

   He's coming to see you this afternoon.

2. 见面 **jiànmiàn** meet, see

   他们 经常 见面。

   Tāmen jīngcháng jiànmiàn.

   They see a lot of each other.

3. 见识 **jiànshi** experience, knowledge

   多 旅游, 长 见识。

   Duō lǚyóu, zhǎng jiànshi.

   More travels will broaden your experience.

4. 见笑 **jiànxiào** laugh at (me or us)

   我 刚 开始 学, 您 别 见笑。

   Wǒ gāng kāishǐ xué, nín bié jiànxiào.

   Don't laugh at me, I'm only a beginner.

5. 再见 **zàijiàn** see you again

   下 星期天 再见。

   Xià Xīngqītiān zàijiàn.

   I'll see you next Sunday.

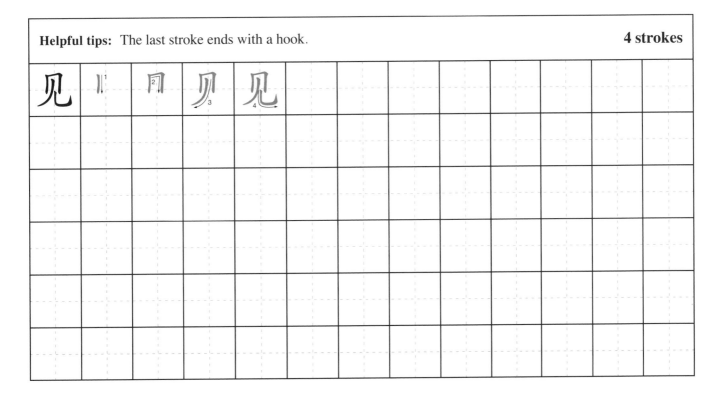

Helpful tips: The last stroke ends with a hook.

4 strokes

Lesson 3: Review Activities

A. Character Identification

Please identify the following characters by writing the *pinyin* for each character. Then continue by illustrating the stroke order for each character. For example:

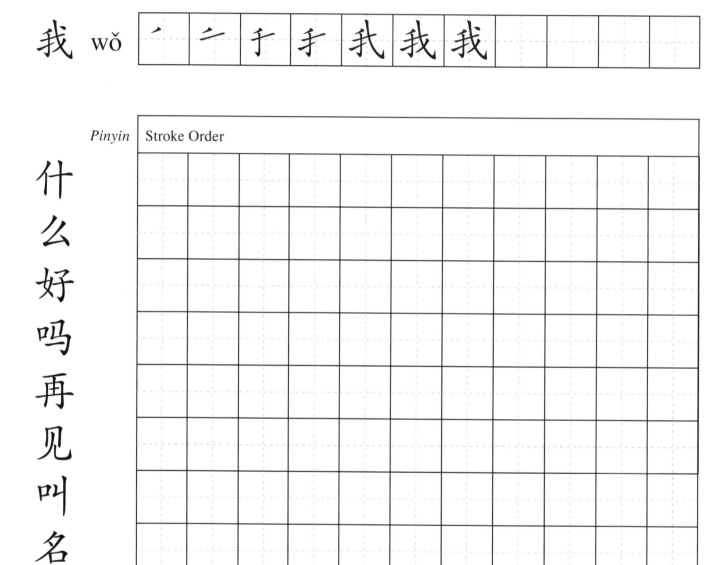

B. Reading Comprehension

Please read the following description of the friend of the speaker. Answer the questions in English based on the information in the description.

我要介绍介绍我的好朋友。我的朋友叫李春花。她是很好的朋友。她姓李，她的名字叫春花。她二十二岁。我们是小学的同学。大家说老朋友就是好朋友。李春花是我的老朋友。

1. What is the friend's name?

   _____

2. What is the friend's family name?

   _____

3. What is the friend's personal name?

   _____

4. What is the age of the friend?

   _____

5. Any other interesting information?

   _____

   _____

C. Creating a Conversation

Please create a conversation between two people. Write out and practice responding to both parts of the conversation (person A and person B). The conversation should cover the following topics: greeting, names, age, friendship, and partings. Question clues are given below.

A: _____

B: _____

A: _____

B: _____

A: _____

B: _____

A: _____

B: _____

(Question clues:)
你好吗？
你是不是他的朋友？
你叫什么名字？
我们是不是好朋友？
再见！

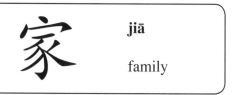

家

jiā

family

Radical: 宀 # 34 "roof"

Compounds, sentences, and meanings

1. 家 **jiā** family, home

   我 今天 晚上 不在家。

   Wǒ jīntiān wǎnshang bú zài jiā.

   I won't be home tonight.

2. 家庭 **jiātíng** family

   我 有 一个 幸福 的 家庭。

   Wǒ yǒu yí ge xìngfú de jiātíng.

   I have a happy family.

3. 家常菜 **jiāchángcài** home cooking

   我 喜欢 吃 家常菜。

   Wǒ xǐhuan chī jiāchángcài.

   I'm fond of home cooking.

4. 家务事 **jiāwùshì** housework

   家务事 总 做不完。

   Jiāwùshì zǒng zuòbuwán.

   Housework is never done.

5. 人家 **rénjia** other people

   人家 的 事情 我们 用不着 管。

   Rénjia de shìqing wǒmen yòngbuzháo guǎn.

   We needn't concern ourselves with others' affairs.

Helpful tips: The sixth stroke ends with a hook.									**10 strokes**
家									

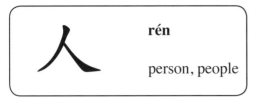

人 **rén**

person, people

Radical: 人 # 18 "person"

Compounds, sentences, and meanings

1. 人 **rén** person, people

   房间 里 没有 人。

   Fángjiān li méiyǒu rén.

   There is no one in the room.

2. 人们 **rénmen** people

   人们 都 说 她不错。

   Rénmen dōu shuō tā búcuò.

   People all speak well of her.

3. 中国人 **Zhōngguórén** Chinese (person)

   中国人 跟 日本人 不 一样。

   Zhōngguórén gēn Rìběnrén bù yíyàng.

   Chinese people are different from Japanese.

4. 人口 **rénkǒu** population

   中国 的 人口 众多。

   Zhōngguó de rénkǒu zhòngduō.

   China has a large population.

5. 人山人海 **rénshān-rénhǎi** sea of people (literally, a mountain of people, a sea of people)

   广场 上 人山人海。

   Guǎngchǎng shang rénshān-rénhǎi.

   The square was crowded with many people.

Helpful tips: Note the difference between 人 and 入.											2 strokes

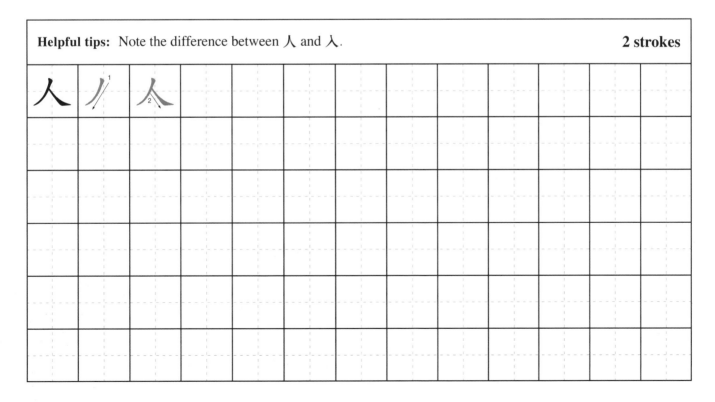

kǒu

[measure word]; mouth

Radical: 口 # 50 "mouth"

Compounds, sentences, and meanings

1. 口 **kǒu** measure word

   你 家 有 几 口 人?

   Nǐ jiā yǒu jǐ kǒu rén?

   How many are there in your family?

2. 口福 **kǒufú** gourmet's luck

   我 今天 口福 可 不浅。

   Wǒ jīntiān kǒufú kě bùqiǎn.

   I'm really in luck today where food is concerned.

3. 口味 **kǒuwèi** taste of food

   今天 换换 口味, 吃 西餐 吧。

   Jīntiān huànhuan kǒuwèi, chī Xīcān ba.

   Let's have a change today and have Western food.

4. 口气 **kǒuqì** tone of voice

   她 说话 有 埋怨 的 口气。

   Tā shuōhuà yǒu mányuàn de kǒuqì.

   There was a note of complaint in what she said.

5. 口音 **kǒuyīn** accent

   她 说 英语 带 美国 口音。

   Tā shuō Yīngyǔ dài Měiguó kǒuyīn.

   She speaks English with an American accent.

Helpful tips: The last horizontal stroke travels from left to right.										3 strokes
口	丨	冂	口							

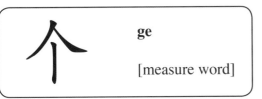

个 ge

[measure word]

個

Radical: 人 # 18 "person"

Compounds, sentences, and meanings

1. 个 **ge** measure word

洗个澡, 休息休息。

Xǐ ge zǎo, xiūxi xiūxi.

Have a shower and then rest.

2. 两个 **liǎng ge** a couple of

请 给 我 两 个。

Qǐng gěi wǒ liǎng ge.

Please give me two.

3. 个个 **gègè** each

你的孩子个个 都 很 聪明。

Nǐde háizi gègè dōu hěn cōngmíng.

All your children are very bright.

4. 个人 **gèrén** individual

我 个人 认为 这样 做 不对。

Wǒ gèrén rènwéi zhèyàng zuò búduì.

In my opinion this is not the way to do it.

5. 个别 **gèbié** individual (adjective)

我 喜欢 个别 辅导。

Wǒ xǐhuan gèbié fǔdǎo.

I prefer individual tuition.

Helpful tips: The second stroke joins the first stroke at the top.

3 strokes

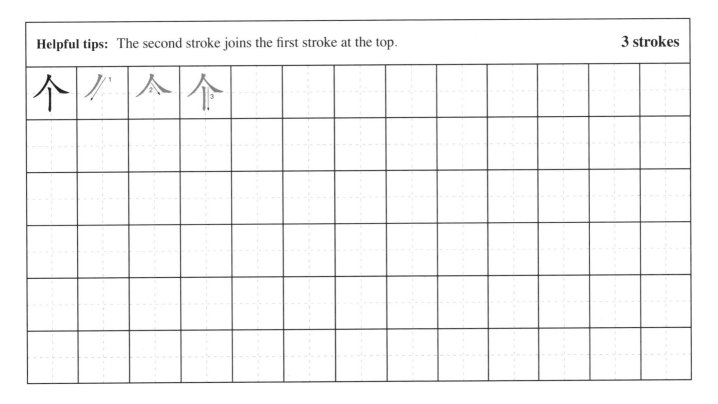

liǎng

two

两

Radical: 一 # 2 "horizontal stroke"

Compounds, sentences, and meanings

1. 两 **liǎng** two

   这 件 事 过 两 天 再 说。

   Zhè jiàn shì guò liǎng tiān zài shuō.

   Let's leave this matter for a couple of days.

2. 两个 **liǎng ge** two (of something)

   那 两 个 人 是 谁?

   Nà liǎng ge rén shì shéi?

   Who are those two people?

3. 两次 **liǎng cì** twice

   我 去 过 两次 中国。

   Wǒ qùguo liǎng cì Zhōngguó.

   I've been to China twice.

4. 两岁 **liǎng suì** two years (age)

   我 姐 姐 比 我 大 两 岁。

   Wǒ jiějie bǐ wǒ dà liǎng suì.

   My older sister is 2 years older than me.

5. 两半儿 **liǎngbànr** two halves

   把 苹 果 切 成 两 半 儿。

   Bǎ píngguǒ qiēchéng liǎngbànr.

   Cut the apple into halves.

Helpful tips: 从 joins the horizontal stroke.　　　　　　　　**7 strokes**

两	一	一	币	两	两	两	两				

多

duō

many, much

Radical: 夕 # 56 "evening"

Compounds, sentences, and meanings

1. 多 **duō** many

   里面 有 很多 人。

   Lǐmiàn yǒu hěnduō rén.

   There are many people inside.

2. 多少 **duōshao** how many

   你 认识 多少 汉字？

   Nǐ rènshi duōshao Hànzì?

   How many Chinese characters do you know?

3. 多半 **duōbàn** more often than not

   星期天 他 多半 上 这儿来。

   Xīngqītiān tā duōbàn shàng zhèr lái.

   He comes over on Sundays quite often.

4. 多数 **duōshù** majority

   我们 是 多数。

   Wǒmen shì duōshù.

   We are in the majority.

5. 多么 **duōme** how, what

   多么 新鲜 的 水果 啊！

   Duōme xīnxiān de shuǐguǒ a!

   How fresh the fruit is!

Helpful tips: The top component rides on top of the lower one.											**6 strokes**
多	夕	夕	夕	多	多	多					

少   **shǎo/shào**
few, less;
young

Radical: 小 # 49 "small"

Compounds, sentences, and meanings

1. 少 **shao** few

    上海 很少 下雪。

    Shànghǎi hěnshǎo xiàxuě.

    It seldom snows in Shanghai.

2. 不少 **bùshǎo** quite a lot

    这次旅行 花了 不少 钱。

    Zhè cì lǚxíng huāle bùshǎo qián.

    I spent quite a lot of money on this trip.

3. 少数 **shǎoshù** minority

    少数 服从 多数。

    Shǎoshù fúcóng duōshù.

    The minority is subordinate to the majority.

4. 多少 **duōshao** how many

    你认识 多少 汉字?

    Nǐ rènshi duōshao Hànzì?

    How many Chinese characters do you know?

5. 少年 **shàonián** juvenile

    西方 国家 的 少年 犯罪 比较 多。

    Xīfāng guójiā de shàonián fànzuì bǐjiào duō.

    Juvenile delinquency is more common in Western countries.

Helpful tips: The last stroke tapers off.   **4 strokes**

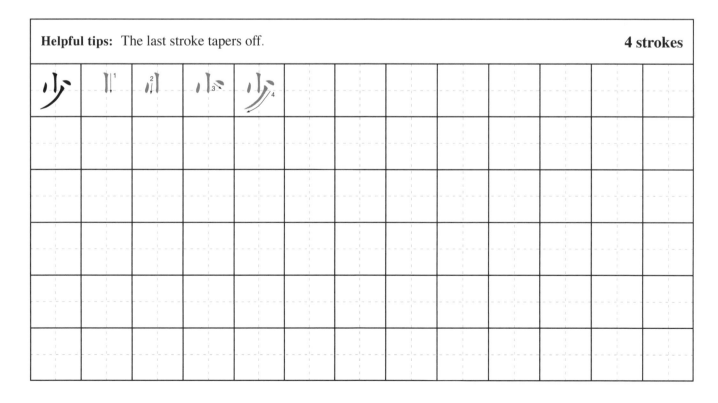

请　**qǐng**

please; invite

请

Radical: 讠 # 9 "word"

Compounds, sentences, and meanings

1. 请 **qǐng** please
   请 安静。
   Qǐng ānjìng.
   Please be quiet.

2. 请 **qǐng** invite
   今晚 我 请了 几个 朋友 回家 吃饭。
   Jīnwǎn wǒ qǐngle jǐge péngyou huíjiā chīfàn.
   I invited some friends home to dinner tonight.

3. 请问 **qǐngwèn** excuse me
   请问, 你叫 什么 名字?
   Qǐngwen, nǐ jiào shénme míngzi?
   May I ask your name?

4. 请进来 **qǐng jìnlai** please come in
   不要 站 在 门口, 请 进来。
   Búyào zhàn zài ménkǒu, qǐng jīnlai.
   Don't stand at the door, please come in.

5. 请教 **qǐngjiào** seek advice
   我可以 请教 你一个 问题 吗?
   Wǒ kěyǐ qǐngjiào nǐ yí ge wèntí ma?
   Can I get some advice from you?

Helpful tips: The second stroke is a horizontal-bend-tick.　　**10 strokes**

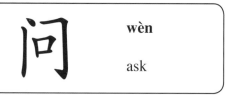

问	wèn
	ask

問

Radical: 门 # 37 "door"

Compounds, sentences, and meanings

1. 问 **wèn** ask

   不 懂 就 问。

   Bù dǒng jiù wèn.

   Ask when you don't understand.

2. 问答 **wèndá** questions and answers

   我 现在 做 问答 练习。

   Wǒ xiànzài zuò wèndá liànxí.

   I'm doing questions and answers drills at present.

3. 问题 **wèntí** question

   没有 问题。

   Méiyǒu wèntí.

   There are no problems.

4. 问好 **wènhǎo** say hello to

   请 代我 向 你父亲 问好。

   Qǐng dài wǒ xiàng nǐ fùqin wènhǎo.

   Please give my regards to your father.

5. 学问 **xuéwèn** learning

   他 是一 位 学问 高深 的人。

   Tā shì yí wèi xuéwèn gāoshēn de rén.

   He is a very learned person.

Helpful tips: The first stroke is a downward dot.　　　　　**6 strokes**

问	丶	门	问	问	问	问					

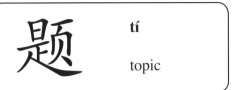

題　　tí

　　　topic

題

Radical: 頁 # 140 "page"

Compounds, sentences, and meanings

1. 題 **tí** problem

这 道题我 没 回答 对。

Zhè dào tí wǒ méi huídá duì.

I didn't give the correct answer to the problem.

2. 问题 **wèntí** question

我 提个问题,可以吗?

Wǒ tí ge wèntí, kěyǐ ma?

Can I ask a question?

3. 题材 **tícái** subject matter

这是写 小说 的 好题材。

Zhè shì xiě xiǎoshuō de hǎo tícái.

This is good material for a novel.

4. 题目 **tímù** topic

你 刚 发表 的那篇　文章　叫

Nǐ gāng fābiǎo de nà biān wénzhāng jiào

什么 题目?

shénme tímù?

What's the topic of the article you just published?

5. 话题 **huàtí** topic of conversation

我们　换 个话题好 不 好?

Wǒmen huàn ge huàtí hǎo bù hǎo?

Why don't we change the topic of conversation?

Helpful tips: The last stroke of 頁 ends firmly.											**15 strokes**
題	丨¹	口²	日³	旦⁴	旦⁵	早⁶	昰⁷	昰⁸	是⁹	是¹⁰	是¹¹	題¹²
題¹³	題¹⁴	題¹⁵									

hé

and

Radical: 口 # 50 "mouth" or 禾 # 124 "grain"

Compounds, sentences, and meanings

1. 和 **hé** and

   他和我 一样 高。

   Tā hé wǒ yíyàng gāo.

   He's as tall as me.

2. 和好 **héhǎo** become reconciled

   他们 吵过架, 现在 和好了。

   Tāmen chǎoguojià, xiànzài héhǎo le.

   They had a quarrel, but have made it up now.

3. 和平 **hépíng** peace

   我们 应该 和平 解决 问题。

   Wǒmen yīnggāi hépíng jiějué wèntí.

   We should resolve problems peacefully.

4. 和睦 **hémù** harmonious

   我们 一家 人 和睦 相处, 是个

   Wǒmen yì jiā rén hémù xiāngchù, shì ge

   幸福 的 家庭。

   xìngfú de jiātíng.

   My family gets along well together, ours is a happy family.

5. 和气 **héqì** amiable

   父亲 对 人 很 和气。

   Fùqin duì rén hěn héqì.

   My father is very friendly.

Helpful tips: 口 is slightly larger when written on the right. **8 strokes**

和 一 二 千 禾 禾 和 和 和

Lesson 4: Review Activities

A. Pronunciation and *Pinyin* Practice

Please write out the pronunciation of the following phrases in *pinyin*. Then practice reciting the phrases, with careful attention paid to the measure in each phrase.

一个人	_____	两个人	_____
三个人	_____	四个人	_____
五个人	_____	六个人	_____
七个人	_____	八个人	_____
九个人	_____	十个人	_____

十个问题	_____	二十个问题	_____
三十个问题	_____	四十个问题	_____
五十个问题	_____	六十个问题	_____
七十个问题	_____	八十个问题	_____
九十个问题	_____	一百个问题	_____

十一口人	_____	十二口人	_____
十三口人	_____	十四口人	_____
十五口人	_____	十六口人	_____
十七口人	_____	十八口人	_____
十九口人	_____	二十口人	_____

51

B. How Many?

Please look at the following illustrations and then write in Chinese characters how many of the noun provided is depicted in each illustration. Please be aware of measure choice with each noun.

人 家人 问题 朋友

C. Sentence Completion

Please complete the following sentences with appropriate nouns in Chinese characters. Each sentence begins with an amount that you have; you supply an appropriate noun for each.

我有一个＿＿＿＿＿＿＿＿＿＿＿＿＿＿＿＿＿＿＿＿＿

我有两个＿＿＿＿＿＿＿＿＿＿＿＿＿＿＿＿＿＿＿＿＿

我有三个＿＿＿＿＿＿＿＿＿＿＿＿＿＿＿＿＿＿＿＿＿

我有四个＿＿＿＿＿＿＿＿＿＿＿＿＿＿＿＿＿＿＿＿＿

我有五个＿＿＿＿＿＿＿＿＿＿＿＿＿＿＿＿＿＿＿＿＿

我有十个＿＿＿＿＿＿＿＿＿＿＿＿＿＿＿＿＿＿＿＿＿

我有五十个＿＿＿＿＿＿＿＿＿＿＿＿＿＿＿＿＿＿＿＿

我有九十九个＿＿＿＿＿＿＿＿＿＿＿＿＿＿＿＿＿＿

我有两百个＿＿＿＿＿＿＿＿＿＿＿＿＿＿＿＿＿＿＿

我有五百五十个＿＿＿＿＿＿＿＿＿＿＿＿＿＿＿＿＿

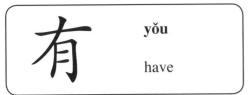

yǒu

have

Radical: 月 # 103 "flesh/moon"

Compounds, sentences, and meanings

1. 有 **yǒu** have, has

   我 有 一个 哥哥。

   Wǒ yǒu yí ge gēge.

   I have an older brother.

2. 有名 **yǒumíng** famous

   这 个 演员 很 有名。

   Zhè ge yǎnyuán hěn yǒumíng.

   This actor is very famous.

3. 有钱 **yǒuqián** rich

   很多 有钱 人 住在 这里。

   Hěnduō yǒuqián rén zhù zài zhèlǐ.

   Many rich people live here.

4. 有意思 **yǒu yìsi** interesting

   今天 的 晚会 很 有意思。

   Jīntiān de wǎnhuì hěn yǒu yìsi.

   The performance tonight was enjoyable.

5. 有害 **yǒuhài** harmful

   吸烟 对 身体 有害。

   Xīyān duì shēntǐ yǒuhài.

   Smoking is harmful to one's health.

Helpful tips: The stroke ends with a hook.											**6 strokes**
有	一	ナ	ナ	有	有	有					

méi

not have

没

Radical: 氵 # 32 "3 drops of water"

Compounds, sentences, and meanings

1. 没 **méi** not have, did not

   昨天 银行 没 开门。

   Zuótiān yínháng méi kāimén.

   Banks were closed yesterday.

2. 没有 **méiyǒu** not have

   里面 没有 人。

   Lǐmiàn méiyǒu rén.

   There's no one inside.

3. 没关系 **méi guānxi** it doesn't matter

   他来不来都 没 关系。

   Tā lái bu lái dōu méi guānxi.

   It doesn't matter if he comes or not.

4. 没意思 **méiyìsi** boring

   这 本 书 没意思。

   Zhè běn shū méiyìsi.

   This book is boring.

5. 没完没了 **méiwán-méiliǎo** endless

   她 这么 没完没了 的 唠叨, 烦死

   Tā zhème méiwán-méiliǎo de láodao, fánsǐ

   人 了。

   rén le.

   Her endless chattering is really driving me up the wall.

Helpful tips: The third stroke lifts with no bend.										**7 strokes**
没	丶	氵	氵	沙	沙	没				

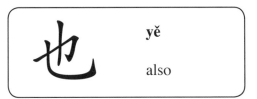

也   **yě**

also

Radical: ㇆ # 5 "horizontal-bend-hook"

Compounds, sentences, and meanings

1. 也 **yě** also

   我 妈妈 也是 老师。

   Wǒ māma yě shì lǎoshī.

   My mother is also a teacher.

2. 也... 也... **yě ... yě** ...either ... or ...

   他 也不 抽烟, 也 不喝酒。

   Tā yě bù chōuyān, yě bù hējiǔ.

   He neither smokes nor drinks.

3. 也许 **yěxǔ** perhaps

   也许我 不 该 告诉她。

   Yěxǔ wǒ bù gāi gàosu tā.

   Perhaps I shouldn't have told her.

4. ... 也罢 ...也罢 **...yěbà ... yěbà** whether ... or

   你去也罢, 不去也罢, 反正 是 一样。

   Nǐ qù yěba, bú qù yěbà, fǎnzhèng shì yíyàng.

   It makes no difference whether you go or not.

5. 也好 **yěhǎo** may as well

   你 说明 一下也 好。

   Nǐ shuōmíng yíxià yě hǎo.

   Maybe you'd better give an explanation.

Helpful tips: The first stroke is a horizontal-bend-hook.   **3 strokes**

也	㇆	也	也						

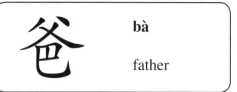

爸 **bà**

father

Radical: 父 # 94 "father"

Compounds, sentences, and meanings

1. 爸 **bà** father

   我 爸 是 医生。

   Wǒ bà shì yīshēng.

   My father is a doctor.

2. 爸爸 **bàba** father

   我 爸爸 是 医生。

   Wǒ bàba shì yīshēng.

   My father is a doctor.

3. 后爸 **hòubà** stepfather

   后爸 也 叫 后爹。

   Hòubà yě jiào hòudiē.

   *Another name for stepfather is **hòudiē**.*

Helpful tips: The last stroke ends with a hook.											8 strokes
爸	⺀¹	�ハ²	少³	父⁴	爷⁵	爷⁶	爸⁷	爸⁸			

妈 **mā** mother

媽

Radical: 女 # 65 "female"

Compounds, sentences, and meanings

1. 妈 **mā** mother

   妈 最 疼 我。

   Mā zuì téng wǒ.

   Mom loves me most.

2. 妈妈 **māma** mother

   妈妈 常常 给 我 补衣服。

   Māma chángcháng gěi wǒ bǔ yīfu.

   Mom often mends my clothes.

3. 后妈 **hòumā** stepmother

   后妈 也 叫 后母。

   Hòumā yě jiào hòumǔ.

   *Another name for stepmother is **hòumǔ**.*

4. 姨妈 **yímā** aunt (mother's married sister)

   姨妈 是 妈妈 已婚的 姐姐 或 妹妹。

   Yímā shì māma yǐhūn de jiějie huò mèimei.

   Yímā refers to a married maternal aunt.

5. 姑妈 **gūmā** aunt (father's married sister)

   姑妈 是 爸爸 已婚的 姐姐 或 妹妹。

   Gūmā shì bàba yǐhūn de jiějie huò mèimei.

   Gūmā refers to a married paternal aunt.

Helpful tips: The fifth stroke ends with a hook.　　　　　**6 strokes**

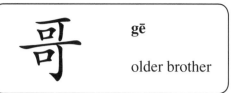

gē

older brother

Radical: 一 # 2 "horizontal stroke" or 口 # 50 "mouth"

Compounds, sentences, and meanings

1. 哥 **gē** older brother

   我 哥 去年 结婚 了。

   Wǒ gē qùnián jiéhūn le.

   My older brother married last year.

2. 哥哥 **gēge** older brother

   我 有 两 个 哥哥。

   Wǒ yǒu liǎng ge gēge.

   I have two older brothers.

3. 大哥 **dàgē** eldest brother

   今天 是 我 大哥的 生日。

   Jīntiān shì wǒ dàgē de shēngrì.

   Today is my oldest brother's birthday.

4. 二哥 **èrgē** second oldest brother

   二哥 出国 读书 了。

   Èrgē chūguó dúshū le.

   My second older brother has gone abroad to study.

5. 哥儿们 **gērmen** buddies

   朋友 之间 分得 太 清 就 不够

   Péngyou zhījiān fēnde tài qīng jiù búgòu

   哥儿们了。

   gērmen le.

   If friends become too calculating, then there's not much friendship between them.

Helpful tips: The bottom vertical stroke ends with a hook.										10 strokes
哥	一	丁	可	豆	叮	豆	哥	哥	哥	哥

姐

jiě

older sister

Radical: 女 # 65 "female"

Compounds, sentences, and meanings

1. 姐 **jiě** older sister

   我 姐 快 三十 岁了。

   Wǒ jiě kuài sānshí suì le.

   My older sister is nearly thirty.

2. 姐姐 **jiějie** older sister

   我 姐姐比我 大 十 岁。

   Wǒ jiějie bǐ wǒ dà shí suì.

   My older sister is 10 years older than me.

3. 小姐 **xiǎojie** Miss

   王 小姐 今天 休假。

   Wáng xiǎojie jīntiān xiūjià.

   Miss Wang is off work today.

4. 二姐 **èrjiě** second oldest sister

   我 二姐 大学 快 毕业了。

   Wǒ èrjiě dàxué kuài bìyè le.

   My second oldest sister will soon graduate from university.

5. 姐夫 **jiěfu** older sister's husband, brother-in-law

   我 姐夫 很 照顾 我。

   Wǒ jiěfu hěn zhàogu wǒ.

   My brother-in-law looks after me very well.

Helpful tips: The last horizontal stroke is longer.								**8 strokes**

姐 ⟨ 女 女 奴 如 姐 姐 姐

dì

younger brother

Radical: ⸯ # 17 "eight"

Compounds, sentences, and meanings

1. 弟 **dì** younger brother

   三弟 今年 刚 进 中学。

   Sāndì jīnnián gāng jìn zhōngxué.

   My third youngest brother has just started secondary school.

2. 弟弟 **dìdi** younger brother

   你 有 没有 弟弟?

   Nǐ yǒu méiyǒu dìdi?

   Do you have a younger brother?

3. 弟兄 **dìxiōng** brothers

   他 就 弟兄 一个。

   Tā jiù dìxiōng yí ge.

   He's the only son of the family.

4. 弟媳 **dìxí** wife of younger brother, sister-in-law

   我弟媳是 中国人。

   Wǒ dìxí shì Zhōngguórén.

   My younger brother's wife is Chinese.

5. 徒弟 **túdì** disciple, follower

   他们 是师父徒弟关系。

   Tāmen shì shīfu túdì guānxi.

   Theirs is a master-disciple relationship.

Helpful tips: The fifth stroke ends with a hook.   **7 strokes**

弟	丶	丷	丷	弟	弟	弟	弟				

妹

mèi

younger sister

Radical: 女 # 65 "female"

Compounds, sentences, and meanings

1. 妹 **mèi** younger sister

   我 妹 还 很 小。

   Wǒ mèi hái hěn xiǎo.

   My younger sister is still quite small.

2. 三妹 **sānmèi** third youngest sister

   我 三妹 在 中学 学习。

   Wǒ sānmèi zài zhōngxué xuéxí.

   My third youngest sister is in high school.

3. 小妹 **xiǎomèi** youngest sister

   我 小妹 在 小学 学习。

   Wǒ xiǎomei zài xiǎoxué xuéxí.

   My youngest sister is in primary school.

4. 妹夫 **mèifu** younger sister's husband, brother-in-law

   我 妹夫 在 小学 教书。

   Wǒ mèifu zài xiǎoxué jiāoshū.

   My younger sister's husband teaches in a primary school.

5. 姐妹 **jiěmèi** sisters

   她 没有 姐妹，只 有 一个 哥哥。

   Tā méiyǒu jiěmèi, zhǐ yǒu yí ge gēge.

   She has no sisters, only an older brother.

Helpful tips: The horizontal stroke on the right-hand side is longer than the one above.　　**8 strokes**

妹	ㄣ¹	ㄠ²	女³	奸⁴	奸⁵	妌⁶	妹⁷	妹⁸				

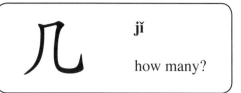

几　**jǐ**

how many?

幾

Radical: 几 # 22 "how many"

Compounds, sentences, and meanings

1. 几 **jǐ** how many (for a small number)

   几点了?

   Jǐ diǎn le?

   What's the time?

2. 几个 **jǐ ge** how many

   你有几个 中国 朋友?

   Nǐ yǒu jǐ ge Zhōngguó péngyou?

   How many Chinese friends do you have?

3. 几次 **jǐ cì** how many times

   你去过 中国 几次?

   Nǐ qùguo Zhōngguó jǐ cì?

   How many times have you been to China?

4. 几时 **jǐshí** what time

   你们 几时走?

   Nǐmen jǐshí zǒu?

   What time are you leaving?

5. 几分 **jǐfēn** somewhat

   他说 的有几分道理。

   Tā shuō de yǒu jǐfēn dàoli.

   There's something in what he said.

Helpful tips: The character is closed at the top.

2 strokes

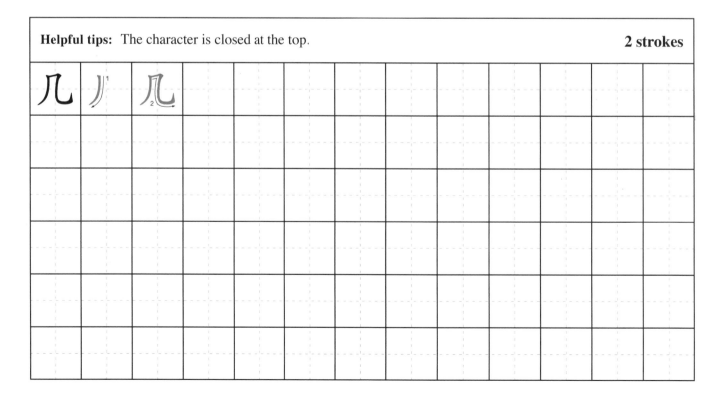

suì

age in years

歲

Radical: 山 # 53 "hill" or 夕 # 56 "sunset"

Compounds, sentences, and meanings

1. 岁 **suì** age in years

   李老师 今年 五十七 岁。

   Lǐ lǎoshī jīnnián wǔshíqī suì.

   Teacher Li is 57 years old.

2. 岁数 **suìshu** age (used in question)

   您 今年 多 大 岁数 了?

   Nín jīnnián duō dà suíshu le?

   How old are you? [question directed at older people as a sign of respect]

3. 年岁 **niánsuì** age

   他 是 上了 年岁 的 人。

   Tā shì shàngle niánsuì de rén.

   He is a person who is getting on in years.

4. 岁月 **suìyuè** years

   岁月 不 居。

   Suìyuè bú jū.

   Time and tide wait for no one.

Helpful tips: The dot is written last.   **6 strokes**

岁	丨¹	²山	山³	岁⁴	岁⁵	岁⁶						

A. Pronunciation and *Pinyin* Practice

Please write the following questions written in Chinese characters in *pinyin*. Then construct an answer for each of the questions. For extra practice, ask the question aloud and then respond to the question with your answer.

1. 你有五个家人吗？

_____

2. 你是不是我的好朋友？

_____

3. 你有没有姐姐？

_____

4. 你有多少个问题？

_____

5. 你的爸爸几岁？

_____

6. 你叫什么名字？

_____

B. Family Members

For each of the following family members, please write a sentence describing your family. Include numbers and measure words to accurately describe your family, including those family members that you do not have.

1. （家人）_____

2. （朋友）_____

3. （哥哥）_____

4. （姐姐）_____

5.（弟弟）_____

6.（妹妹）_____

C. Paragraph Describing a Family

Please write a short paragraph describing the family of a friend as shown in the family tree below. Create and add additional information in order to create a complete description of the family. Both having given family members and not having other family members can be part of the paragraph.

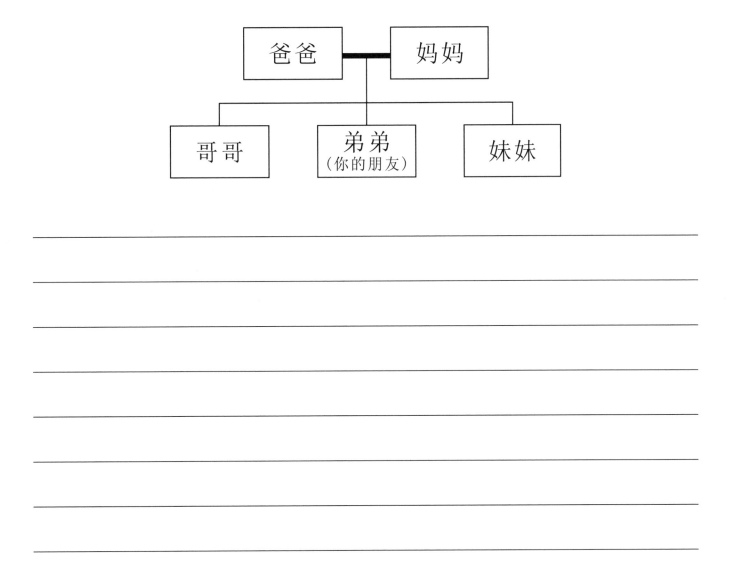

_____

_____

_____

_____

_____

_____

_____

Section 1 Review (Lessons 1–5)

A. Numbers and Sentence Construction

Please write each of the numbers given in Chinese characters. Then in the four sentence-length spaces below, select one of the numbers for each sentence and create a 有 sentence utilizing the number chosen.

2 _____   7 _____   14 _____

25 _____   63 _____   89 _____

105 _____   250 _____   580 _____

999 _____

1. _____

2. _____

3. _____

4. _____

B. Grammatical Particles and Translation

Please complete each of the following sentences with one grammatical particle from the list provided. Then translate your sentence into English, paying careful attention to the particular particle chosen.

吗　的　几　很　不　没

1. 对不起, 你姓王____?

_____

2. 你的妹妹____岁?

_____

3. 我的好朋友____有两个弟弟。

_____

4. 她的问题也____好。

_____

5. 请问：你____家有多少人？

_____

C. Family Description

Please utilize the space provided to fully describe your family. This free writing exercise should demonstrate the range of expression possible about a known topic. Attempt to explore the topic with vocabulary and construction that show both an ability to speak on the topic with depth and the awareness of the cultural concerns that surround the topic.

_____

_____

_____

_____

_____

_____

_____

D. Reflective Questions

Use these questions to both check the expressiveness of the previous section and to confirm your understanding of the previous topic. For additional practice, say and then respond to these questions aloud.

你有几个家人？

你叫什么名字？

你的妈妈叫什么名字？

你有哥哥, 弟弟, 姐姐, 还是妹妹？

他们做什么？

他们姓什么？

你的爸爸叫什么名字？

你们的名字一样吗？

他们几岁？

你喜欢你的家人吗？

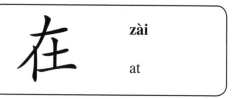

在 zài

at

Radical: 土 # 40 "earth"

Compounds, sentences, and meanings

1. 在 **zài** at

   你 住 在 哪里?

   Nǐ zhù zài nǎlǐ?

   Where do you live?

2. 在家 **zài jiā** at home

   我 今天　晚上　不 在 家。

   Wǒ jīntiān wǎnshang bú zài jiā.

   I won't be home tonight.

3. 在内 **zàinèi** included

   连 我 在内 一共 是 八个 人。

   Lián wǒ zàinèi yígòng shì bā ge rén.

   Including me, there are altogether eight people.

4. 在外 **zàiwài** excluded

   这 是 饭钱, 服务费 在 外。

   Zhè shì fànqián, fúwùfèi zàiwài.

   That's the price of the meal exclusive of service charge.

5. 实在 **shízài** really

   我 实 在 不 知道。

   Wǒ shízài bù zhīdao.

   I really don't know.

Helpful tips: The bottom horizontal stroke is slightly longer.						**6 strokes**					
在	一	大	右	右	在	在					

哪　　**nǎ**

which

Radical: 口 # 50 "mouth"

Compounds, sentences, and meanings

1. 哪 **nǎ** which one?

    你 喜欢 哪个 玩具?

    Nǐ xǐhuan nǎ ge wánjù?

    Which toy would you like?

2. 哪儿 **nǎr** where?

    你 上 哪儿去?

    Nǐ shàng nǎr qù?

    Where are you going?

3. 哪里 **nǎli** where?

    你 上 哪里去?

    Nǐ shàng nǎli qù?

    Where are you going?

4. 哪些 **nǎxiē** which ones?

    你 去过 北京 哪些 地方?

    Nǐ qùguo Běijīng nǎxiē dìfang?

    Where have you been to in Beijing?

5. 哪国人 **nǎguórén** which nationality?

    你 是 哪国人?

    Nǐ shì nǎguórén?

    What nationality are you?

Helpful tips: The eighth stroke is written like the figure 3.									**9 strokes**		
哪	丨	口	口	叮	叧	吲	哪	哪	哪			

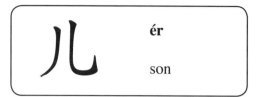

兒

儿　ér

son

Radical: 儿 # 21 "son"

Compounds, sentences, and meanings

1. 儿 **ér** suffix (transcribed as **r**)

   你去哪儿?

   Nǐ qù nǎr?

   Where are you going?

2. 儿子 **érzi** son

   我的大儿子 今年 二十六 岁了。

   Wǒde dà érzi jīnnián èrshíliù suì le.

   My eldest son is 26 this year.

3. 儿女 **érnǚ** sons and daughters

   我的儿女 都 长大 成人 了。

   Wǒde érnǚ dōu zhǎngdà chéngrén le.

   My children have all grown up.

4. 儿歌 **érgē** children's song

   今天 我 学了一 首 儿歌。

   Jīntiān wǒ xuéle yì shǒu érgē.

   I learned a nursery rhyme today.

5. 儿童 **értóng** children

   这 是 儿童 医院。

   Zhè shì értóng yīyuàn.

   This is a children's hospital.

| Helpful tips: Note the difference between 儿 and 儿. | | | | | | | | | | 2 strokes |

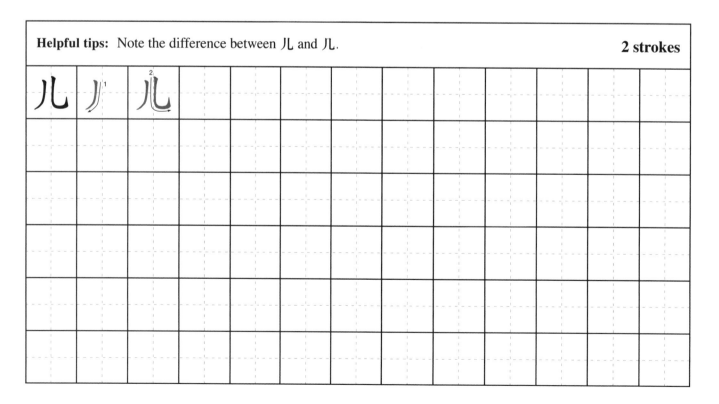

里 **lǐ**
inside

裡 / 裏

Radical: 里 # 163 "inside"

Compounds, sentences, and meanings

1. 里 **lǐ** inside
   家里没人。
   Jiāli méi rén.
   There is no one home.

2. 哪里 **nǎli** where?
   你 上 哪里去?
   Nǐ shàng nǎli qù?
   Where are you going?

3. 这里 **zhèlǐ** here
   我们 这里的 东西 很 便宜。
   Wǒmen zhèlǐ de dōngxi hěn piányi.
   Our merchandise is inexpensive.

4. 里边 **lǐbian** inside
   这个 箱子 里边 有 什么?
   Zhè ge xiāngzi lǐbiān yǒu shénme?
   What's inside this box?

5. 里头 **lǐtou** inside
   这个 箱子 里头 有 什么?
   Zhè ge xiāngzi lǐtou yǒu shénme?
   What's inside this box?

Helpful tips: The bottom horizontal stroke is slightly longer.											**7 strokes**
里	⼁	⺆	日	旦	旦	里	里				

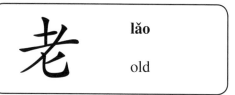

老   **lǎo**

old

Radical: 老 # 136 "old"

Compounds, sentences, and meanings

1. 老 **lǎo** old

   他老了,走路走不快了。

   Tā lǎo le, zǒulù zǒu bú kuài le.

   He's getting old, he can no longer walk fast.

2. 老大 **lǎodà** oldest sibling

   我家三兄弟,我是老大。

   Wǒ jiā sān xiōngdì, wǒ shì lǎodà.

   Of the three brothers in my family, I'm the eldest.

3. 老婆 **lǎopo** wife

   他 说 他老婆 不会 做饭。

   Tā shuō tā lǎopo búhuì zuòfàn.

   He says his wife can't cook.

4. 老外 **lǎowài** foreigner

   很多 老外 说 汉语 都 说得 很 好。

   Hěnduō lǎowài shuō Hànyǔ dōu shuōde hěn hǎo.

   Many foreigners can speak Mandarin very well.

5. 老实 **lǎoshi** frank, honest

   老实 说,我 不 赞成 这个意见。

   Lǎoshi shuō, wǒ bú zànchéng zhè ge yìjiàn.

   Frankly speaking, I don't like the idea at all.

Helpful tips: The next-to-last stroke is a downward left stroke.   **6 strokes**

老	一	十	土	耂	耂	老					

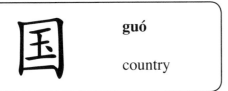

CHARACTER 61

Traditional Form

国 guó country

國

Radical: 囗 # 51 "4-sided frame"

Compounds, sentences, and meanings

1. 国 **guó** nation

《一国 两 制》这个 政策 是
"Yī guó liǎng zhì" zhè ge zhèngcè shì
邓 小平 提出的。
Dèng Xiǎopíng tíchū de.
It was Deng Xiaoping who proposed the policy of "One country, two systems."

2. 国家 **guójiā** nation

美国 是 民主 国家。
Měiguó shì mínzhǔ guójiā.
The United States is a democratic country.

3. 德国 **Déguó** Germany

德国 在 欧洲。
Déguó zài Ōuzhōu.
Germany is in Europe.

4. 国庆 **guóqìng** National Day

十月 一号 是 中国 国庆节。
Shíyuè-yīhào shì Zhōngguó Guóqìngjié.
October 1st is Chinese National Day.

5. 国际 **guójì** international

中国 的国际 地位 提高了。
Zhōngguó de guójì dìwèi tígāo le.
China's international status has improved.

Helpful tips: The last stroke seals the enclosure.								8 strokes			
国	丨	冂	冂	冃	用	囯	国	国			

73

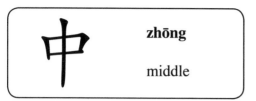

CHARACTER 62

中   **zhōng**

       middle

Radical: ｜ # 3 "vertical stroke"

Compounds, sentences, and meanings

1. 中 **zhōng** middle

   我 穿 中 号 的。

   Wǒ chuān zhōng hào de.

   I wear medium size.

2. 中级 **zhōngjí** intermediate level

   这 是 中级 课程。

   Zhè shì zhōngjí kèchéng.

   This is an intermediate course.

3. 中国 **Zhōngguó** China

   中国 是世界第三 大国。

   Zhōngguó shì shìjiè dìsān dàguó.

   China is the world's third largest country.

4. 中文 **Zhōngwén** Chinese language

   我 看不懂 中文 报。

   Wǒ kànbudǒng Zhōngwén bào.

   I can't read Chinese newspapers.

5. 中餐 **Zhōngcān** Chinese food

   我爸爸 喜欢 吃 中餐。

   Wǒ bàba xǐhuan chī Zhōngcān.

   My father loves Chinese food.

Helpful tips: The vertical stroke is in the middle of the rectangle.												**4 strokes**
中	中	口	口	中								

美 **měi**

beautiful

Radical: 羊 # 133 "sheep" or 大 # 43 "big"

Compounds, sentences, and meanings

1. 美 **měi** good, satisfactory

   这里的 东西 物美 价廉。

   Zhèlǐ de dōngxi wùměi-jiàlián.

   The things here are good and inexpensive.

2. 美丽 **měilì** beautiful

   这里的 风景 很 美丽。

   Zhèlǐ de fēngjǐng hěn měilì.

   The scenery here is beautiful.

3. 美好 **měihǎo** fine, happy

   我的 童年 是一个 美好 的回忆。

   Wǒde tóngnián shì yí ge měihǎo de huíyì.

   I have good memories of my childhood.

4. 美化 **měihuà** beautify

   我们 应该 尽 可能 美化 环境。

   Wǒmen yīnggāi jìn kěnéng měihuà huánjìng.

   We should try our best to beautify the environment.

5. 美国 **Měiguó** USA

   美国 在北 美洲。

   Měiguó zài Běi Měizhōu.

   The United States is in North America.

Helpful tips: The last two strokes taper off.										**9 strokes**	
美	丶¹	丷²	兰₃	兰₄	芉₅	美₆	美₇	美₈	美₉		

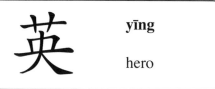

英 **yīng**

hero

Radical: 艹 # 42 "grass"

Compounds, sentences, and meanings

1. 英 **yīng** hero

   学校 开了一个 群英会 庆祝
   Xuéxiào kāile yí ge qúnyīnghuì qìngzhù
   运动会 的 结束。
   yùndònghuì de jiéshù.
   The school organized a celebration for the participants at the end of the sports meet.

2. 英俊 **yīngjùn** handsome

   这 个 小伙子 长得 很 英俊。
   Zhè ge xiǎohuǒzi zhǎngde hěn yīngjùn.
   This young lad is quite handsome.

3. 英国 **Yīngguó** England

   每年 去 英国 的人 很多。
   Měinián qù Yīngguó de rén hěnduō.
   Many people travel to the UK every year.

4. 英语 **Yīngyǔ** English language

   中国 有 很多 人 学 英语。
   Zhōngguó yǒu hěnduō rén xué Yīngyǔ.
   Many people in China study English.

5. 英里 **yīnglǐ** mile

   美国 还 用 英里, 不用 公里。
   Měiguó hái yòng yīnglǐ, búyòng gōnglǐ.
   The United States still uses miles, not kilometers.

Helpful tips: The seventh stroke crosses the fifth stroke. **8 strokes**

英	一	艹	艹	艹	苩	芇	英	英			

Traditional Form

谁 shuí/shéi

who

誰

Radical: 讠 # 9 "word"

Compounds, sentences, and meanings

1. 谁 shuí/shéi who

   有 谁 能 帮助 我 就 好 了!
   Yǒu shuí/shéi néng bāngzhù wǒ jiù hǎo le!
   If only someone could help me!

2. 谁的 shuí/shéi de whose

   这 是 谁 的 中文 课本?
   Zhè shì shuí/shéi de Zhōngwén kèběn?
   Whose Chinese textbook is this?

3. 谁知道 shuí/shéi zhīdao no one knows

   我 本 是 跟 她 开 玩笑, 谁 知道 她
   Wǒ běn shì gēn tā kāi wánxiào, shéi zhīdao tā
   生气 了。
   shēngqì le.
   I was only joking with her, I didn't expect her to get angry.

Helpful tips: There is equal spacing between the horizontal lines.   **10 strokes**

A. Pronunciation and *Pinyin* Practice

Please write the following questions written in Chinese characters in *pinyin*. Then construct an answer for each of the questions. If possible, ask the question aloud and then respond to the question with your answer.

1. 你在什么国家？

   _____

2. 你的好朋友在什么国家？

   _____

3. 你的老家在什么国家？

   _____

4. 什么人在美国？

   _____

5. 什么人在中国？

   _____

6. 什么人在英国？

   _____

B. Hometown Description

Please refer to the illustration to help construct answers to the following questions. Please answer the questions completely in Chinese characters introducing detail as appropriate.

你朋友的老家：

1. 你朋友的老家在哪儿？

   _____

2. 你的朋友跟谁在她的老家？

   _____

3. 你也在她的老家吗？

   _____

4. 你的老家在哪儿？

   _____

5. 你老家的国家人口很多吗？

   _____

C. Different Countries

Please describe with some specific detail the similarities and differences between the following backgrounds. If possible, demonstrate awareness both of patterns and general observations along with exceptions to those general observations.

美国人, 中国人, 跟英国人有什么一样? 也有什么不一样?
(Possible topics: 名字, 姓, 家人, 人口, 等等。)

您 nín

you (polite)

Radical: 心 # 76 "heart"

Compounds, sentences, and meanings

1. 您 **nín** you (polite)

您 贵姓?

Nín guìxìng?

May I ask your name (surname)?

2. 您好 **Nín hǎo!** How are you!

老师，您 好!

Lǎoshī, nín hǎo!

How are you, sir/ma'am (teacher)?

3. 您早 **Nín zǎo!** Good morning!

老师，您 早!

Lǎoshī, nín zǎo!

Good morning, sir/ma'am (teacher)!

Helpful tips: Note the position of the three dots in 心.   **11 strokes**

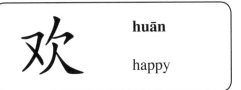

欢   **huān**

happy

歡

Radical: 欠 # 104 "owe" or 又 # 24 "again"

Compounds, sentences, and meanings

1. 欢 **huān** joyous

   大家 欢天 喜地地 过 圣诞节。

   Dàjiā huāntiān-xǐdì de guò Shèngdànjié.

   Everyone was having a very happy Christmas.

2. 欢喜 **huānxǐ** joyful

   一家人 欢欢喜喜 地过 春节。

   Yì jiā rén huānhuānxǐxǐ de guò Chūnjié.

   The whole family spent a joyful Chinese New Year.

3. 欢聚 **huānjù** happy reunion

   难得 有机会跟 老朋友 欢聚。

   Nánde yǒu jīhuì gēn lǎopéngyou huānjù.

   Old friends don't often get the chance to meet.

4. 欢乐 **huānlè** happy

   国庆 的 时候, 北京 一 片 欢乐 的

   Guóqìng de shíhou, Běijīng yí piàn huānlè de

   景象。

   jǐngxiàng.

   On National Day, Beijing is a scene of great joy.

5. 欢迎 **huānyíng** welcome

   欢迎 你到 北京 来。

   Huānyíng nǐ dào Běijīng lái.

   Welcome to Beijing.

Helpful tips: Note the difference between 久 and 欠.													6 strokes
欢	丿	又	对	欢	欢	欢							

迎　**yíng**

to welcome, to greet

Radical: 辶 # 38 "movement"

Compounds, sentences, and meanings

1. 欢迎 **huānyíng** welcome

   欢迎　欢迎　到　我们　的　家!
   Huānyíng huānyíng dào wǒmen de jiā!
   Welcome to our home!

2. 迎新 **yíngxīn** to celebrate the new year

   每年　我　跟　我　的　家人　喜欢　送旧
   Měinián wǒ gēn wǒ de jiārén xǐhuan sòngjiù
   迎新。
   yíngxīn.
   Every year my family and I enjoy ringing in the new year.

3. 迎宾 **yíngbīn** to host, to welcome guests

   每个　星期天　我　的　父母　要　迎宾。
   Měige Xīngqītiān wǒ de fùmǔ yào yíngbīn.
   Every Sunday my mother and father want to host guests.

4. 迎接 **yíngjiē** to meet, to greet

   在　马路　上　迎接　客人　的　习惯　是　好
   Zài mǎlù shàng yíngjiē kèrén de xíguàn shì hǎo
   客气。
   kèqi.
   Meeting guests when they arrive while they are still at the road is very respectful.

Helpful tips: The middle vertical stroke is longer.									**7 strokes**
迎	𠄌¹	㇉²	卬³	卬⁴	卬⁵	迎⁶	迎⁷		

对

duì

opposite; correct

對

Radical: 又 # 24 "again" or 寸 # 46 "inch"

Compounds, sentences, and meanings

1. 对 **duì** correct

   这 件 事 你 做得 很 对。

   Zhe jiàn shì nǐ zuòde hěn duì.

   You did the right thing.

2. 对面 **duìmiàn** opposite

   他 家 就 在 我 家 对面。

   Tā jiā jiù zài wǒ jiā duìmiàn.

   His house is opposite mine.

3. 对不起 **duìbuqǐ** I'm sorry

   对不起, 给你 添 麻烦 了。

   Duìbuqǐ, gěi nǐ tiān máfan le.

   Sorry to have given you so much trouble.

4. 对手 **duìshǒu** opponent

   他 不是 你的 对手。

   Tā búshì nǐde duìshǒu.

   He's no match for you.

5. 对于 **duìyú** with regard to, about

   对于 他的 工作 我 没有 什么 意见。

   Duìyú tāde gōngzuò wǒ méiyǒu shénme yìjiàn.

   Regarding his work, I have no complaints.

Helpful tips: End the second stroke firmly.											**5 strokes**
对	丁	又	对	对	对						

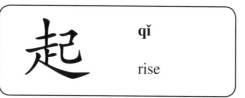

CHARACTER 70

起   **qǐ**

rise

Radical: 走 # 156 "walk"

Compounds, sentences, and meanings

1. 起 **qǐ** get out of bed

    早睡 早起 对 身体 好。
    Zǎo-shuì zǎo-qǐ duì shēntǐ hǎo.
    Early to bed and early to rise is good for the health.

2. 起床 **qǐchuáng** get out of bed

    今天 我 六点半 起床。
    Jīntiān wǒ liùdiǎnbàn qǐchuáng.
    I got up at 6:30 today.

3. 起动 **qǐdòng** start

    汽车 起动，请 抓好 扶手。
    Qìchē qǐdòng, qǐng zhuāhǎo fúshǒu.
    The bus is starting, please hold on to the handrail.

4. 起码 **qǐmǎ** at least

    这 个 工作 起码要 三 个 月 才 能
    Zhè ge gōngzuò qǐmǎ yào sān ge yuè cái néng
    完成。
    wánchéng.
    This job will take at least three months.

5. 一起 **yìqǐ** together

    跟 我一起去 看 电影 吧。
    Gēn wǒ yìqǐ qù kàn diànyǐng ba.
    Let's see a movie together.

Helpful tips: The last stroke is a vertical-bend-hook.   **10 strokes**

| 起 | 一₁ | 土² | 土₃ | 丰₄ | 丰₅ | 走₆ | 走₇ | 走₈ | 起₉ | 起₁₀ | | |

84

谢

xiè

thank

謝

Radical: 讠 # 9 "word"

Compounds, sentences, and meanings

1. 谢 xiè thank

   不用 谢。

   Búyòng xiè.

   Don't mention it. (literally, no need to thank)

2. 谢谢 xièxie thanks

   谢谢 你。

   Xièxie nǐ.

   Thank you.

3. 多谢 duōxiè many thanks

   多谢, 再见!

   Duōxiè, zàijiàn!

   Thanks a lot, goodbye!

4. 感谢 gǎnxiè thank

   非常 感谢。

   Fēicháng gǎnxiè.

   Many thanks.

5. 谢天谢地 xiètiān-xièdì thank heavens (literally, thank heaven and earth)

   谢天谢地, 没 发生 事故。

   Xiètiān-xièdì, méi fāshēng shìgù.

   Thank goodness, there was no accident.

Helpful tips: The ninth stroke is downward-left.

12 strokes

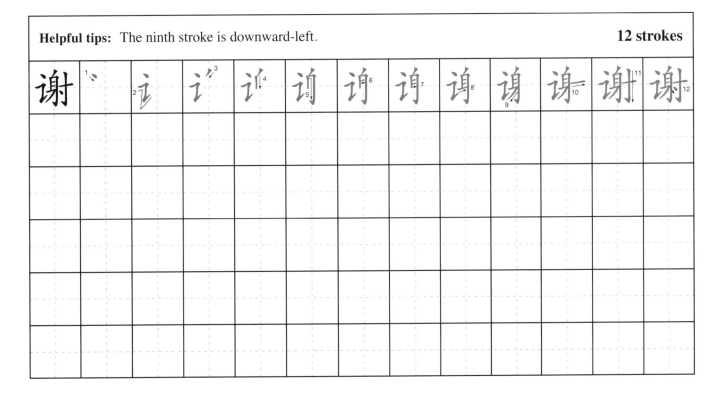

客 kè

guest

Radical: 宀 # 34 "roof"

Compounds, sentences, and meanings

1. 客 **kè** guest

家里来客了。

Jiālǐ lái kè le.

We have a guest.

2. 客观 **kèguān** objective

她看问题比较客观。

Tā kàn wèntí bǐjiào kèguān.

She looks at problems objectively.

3. 客气 **kèqi** polite

他对人很客气。

Tā duì rén hěn kèqi.

He is very polite.

4. 客套话 **kètàohuà** polite expressions

"劳驾"是客套话。

"Láojià" shì kètàohuà.

The phrase "Excuse me" is a polite expression.

5. 顾客 **gùkè** customer

顾客至上。

Gùkè zhìshàng.

The customer is always right.

Helpful tips: Note the difference between 客 and 容.   **9 strokes**

客	丶	宀	宀	灾	宛	客	客	客			

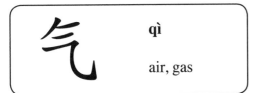

气　qì

air, gas

氣

Radical: 气 #98 "air"

Compounds, sentences, and meanings

1. 气 **qì** air

   自行车　前带　没 气了。

   Zìxíngchē qiándài méi qì le.

   The front tire of the bike is flat.

2. 气候 **qìhòu** climate

   他不　适应　北京 的　气候。

   Tā bú shìyìng Běijīng de qìhòu.

   He's not used to the climate in Beijing.

3. 气味 **qìwèi** smell

   这是　什么　气味?

   Zhè shì shénme qìwèi?

   What kind of smell is this?

4. 气色 **qìsè** complexion

   她气色不 好，脸上　没　什么　血色。

   Tā qìsè bù hǎo, liǎnshàng méi shénme xuèsè.

   She's very pale, there isn't much color in her face.

5. 气力 **qìlì** strength

   学　外国语　要 用　很大的气力才

   Xué wàiguóyǔ yào yòng hěndà de qìlì cái

   能　学好。

   néng xuéhǎo.

   It takes a lot of effort to learn a foreign language well.

Helpful tips: The last stroke ends with a hook.　　　　**4 strokes**

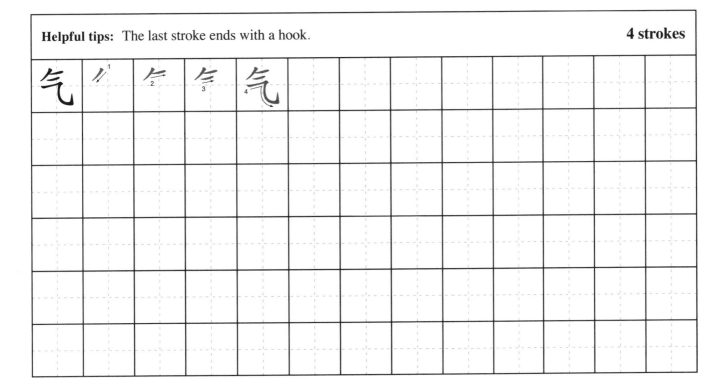

慢   **màn**

slow

Radical: 忄 # 33 "upright heart"

Compounds, sentences, and meanings

1. **慢 màn** slow

   我的 表 慢 一 分钟。

   Wǒde biǎo màn yī fēnzhōng.

   My watch is one minute slow.

2. **慢镜头 mànjìngtóu** slow motion

   我可以 看 慢镜头 吗?

   Wǒ kěyǐ kàn mànjìngtóu ma?

   Can I see it in slow motion?

3. **慢慢 mànmàn** slowly

   别急，慢慢 来。

   Bié jí, mànmàn lái.

   Calm down. Easy does it.

4. **慢腾腾 màntēngtēng** at a leisurely pace

   你 这么 慢腾腾 的, 什么 时候

   Nǐ zhème màntēngtēng de, shénme shíhou

   能 做完?

   néng zuòwán?

   How will you ever finish the job at this pace?

5. **慢条斯理 màntiáo-sīlǐ** unhurriedly

   他 说话 做事 总是 慢条斯理 的。

   Tā shuōhuà zuòshì zǒngshì màntiáo-sīlǐ de.

   He always speaks slowly and acts unhurriedly.

Helpful tips: The top part of 曼 is squarish; the middle section is rectangular.   **14 strokes**

慢	1	2	3	4	5	6	7	8	9	10	11	12
13	14											

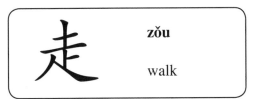

CHARACTER 75

走   zǒu

walk

Radical: 走 # 156 "walk"

Compounds, sentences, and meanings

1. 走 **zǒu** walk

一直 往 前 走。

Yìzhí wǎng qián zǒu.

Go straight ahead.

2. 走路 **zǒulù** go on foot

你们 是 坐车 去 还是 走路 去?

Nǐmen shì zuòchē qù háishi zǒulù qù?

Will you go there by bus or on foot?

3. 走运 **zǒuyùn** be in luck

祝 你 走运!

Zhù nǐ zǒuyùn!

Good luck!

4. 走失 **zǒushī** wander away

我们 一起 出去 的, 半路 上 她 走失 了。

Wǒmen yìqǐ chūqu de, bànlù shàng tā zǒushī le.

We went out together and she got lost on the way.

5. 走动 **zǒudòng** stretch one's legs

坐了 一 整天 了, 出去 走动

Zuòle yì zhěngtiān le, chūqu zǒudòng

走动 吧。

zǒudòng ba.

We've been sitting all day long. Let's go out and stretch our legs.

Helpful tips: The second horizontal stroke is longer.

7 strokes

走　一　士　土　卡　走　走　走

Lesson 7: Review Activities

A. Response and *Pinyin*

Please respond appropriately to each of the following phrases in Chinese characters. Then, next to your response, utilize *pinyin* to write the sounds of your response. For extra practice, say each aloud.

你好　　(_____) _____　　谢谢 (_____) _____

欢迎　　(_____) _____　　慢走 (_____) _____

你好吗 (_____) _____

B. Politeness Crossword

Please complete the following crossword by responding the statement or question given in the entry across. For example, the response to 1 **across** is written in 1 **down**. Altogether, the entries combine to form one conversation. Please pay attention to appropriate polite responses. Also, only characters (not punctuation) are counted in the down entries.

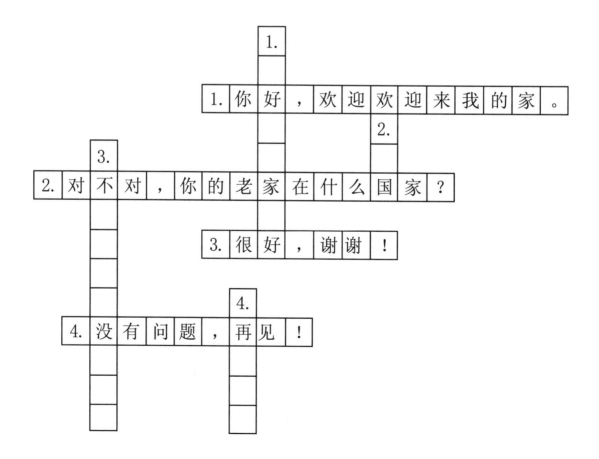

C. New Friend

Please imagine a conversation with a person you just met. Create 5 questions that you would want to ask someone in order to get to know them better. Please pay attention to politeness as an aspect of the conversation and how different questions can lead to other possibilities in a conversation. There are examples of question possibilities in the answer key.

1. 对不起, _____ ?

2. _____ ?

3. _____ ?

4. _____ ?

5. _____ ?

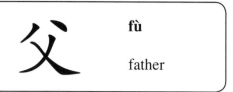

父

fù

father

Radical: 父 # 94 "father"

Compounds, sentences, and meanings

1. 父 **fù** father

   以前 在 中国, 长兄 当 父。

   Yǐqián zài Zhōngguó, zhǎngxiōng dāng fù.

   Formerly in China, the oldest brother assumed the authority of the father.

2. 父亲 **fùqin** father

   我 父亲 对 中国 很 有 兴趣。

   Wǒ fùqin duì Zhōngguó hěn yǒu xìngqù.

   My father is very interested in China.

3. 父母 **fùmǔ** parents

   下 个 月 我 父母 要 去 旅行。

   Xià ge yuè wǒ fùmǔ yào qù lǚxíng.

   Next month my parents are going on a trip.

4. 祖父 **zǔfù** paternal grandfather

   他的祖父去世了。

   Tāde zǔfù qùshì le.

   His paternal grandfather has passed away.

5. 继父 **jìfù** stepfather

   他的继父对他不错。

   Tāde jìfù duì tā búcuò.

   His stepfather is quite nice to him.

Helpful tips: The last stroke tapers off.										**4 strokes**
父	⺌	⺍	少	父						

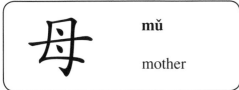

母　mǔ

mother

Radical: 母 # 108 "mother"

Compounds, sentences, and meanings

1. 母 **mǔ** female (animal)

   你的狗 是 公 的 还是 母 的?

   Nǐde gǒu shì gōng de háishi mǔ de?

   Is your dog male or female?

2. 母亲 **mǔqin** mother

   我 母亲 做 的 饭菜 最 好吃。

   Wǒ mǔqin zuò de fàncài zuì hǎochī.

   My mother cooks the best meals.

3. 父母 **fùmǔ** parents

   下 个 月 我 父母 要 去 旅行。

   Xià ge yuè wǒ fùmǔ yào qù lǚxíng.

   Next month my parents are going on a trip.

4. 母语 **mǔyǔ** mother tongue

   英语 是 我的母语。

   Yīngyǔ shì wǒde mǔyǔ.

   English is my mother tongue.

5. 外祖母 **wàizǔmǔ** maternal grandmother

   他的 外祖母 每天 打 太极拳。

   Tāde wàizǔmǔ měitiān dǎ tàijíquán.

   His grandmother practices tai chi every day.

Helpful tips: The second stroke ends with a hook.　　　　　**5 strokes**

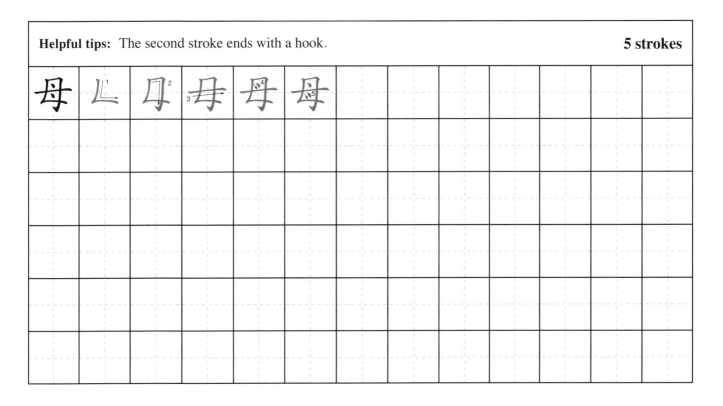

亲 **qīn**

kin

親

Radical: 立 # 111 "erect"

Compounds, sentences, and meanings

1. 亲 **qīn** close, intimate

   我 和 姐姐 最 亲。

   Wǒ hé jiějie zuì qīn.

   I'm very close to my older sister.

2. 亲人 **qīnrén** kin

   你在 中国 有 没有 亲人?

   Nǐ zài Zhōngguó yǒu méiyǒu qīnrén?

   Do you have any relatives in China?

3. 父亲 **fùqin** father

   我 父亲 对 中国 很 有 兴趣。

   Wǒ fùqin duì Zhōngguó hěn yǒu xìngqù.

   My father is very interested in China.

4. 母亲 **mǔqin** mother

   我 母亲 做 的 饭菜 最 好吃。

   Wǒ mǔqin zuò de fàncài zuì hǎochī.

   My mother cooks the best meals.

5. 亲戚 **qīnqi** relatives

   我们 两家 是 亲戚。

   Wǒmen liǎng jiā shì qīnqi.

   Our two families are related.

Helpful tips: The middle horizontal stroke is the longest.										**9 strokes**	
亲	丶	二	亠	立	立	音	辛	亲	亲		

做　zuò

do

Radical: 亻 # 19 "upright person"

Compounds, sentences, and meanings

1. **做 zuò** do, make

这 是 你 自己 做 的 吗?

Zhè shì nǐ zìjǐ zuò de ma?

Did you do/make this yourself?

2. **做菜 zuòcài** cook

她 丈夫 很 会 做菜。

Tā zhàngfu hěn huì zuòcài.

Her husband is very good at cooking.

3. **做事 zuòshì** work

他 做事 做得 很 认真。

Tā zuòshì zuòde hěn rènzhēn.

He does his work conscientiously.

4. **做生意 zuò shēngyì** do business

我 爸爸 做 生意 的。

Wǒ bàba zuò shēngyì de.

My father is a businessman.

5. **做梦 zuòmèng** dream

昨晚 我 做了 一个 可怕 的 梦。

Zuówǎn wǒ zuòle yí ge kěpà de mèng.

I had a terrible dream last night.

Helpful tips: The last stroke tapers off.　　**11 strokes**

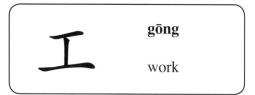

CHARACTER 80

工　gōng

work

Radical: 工 # 39 "work"

Compounds, sentences, and meanings

1. 工 **gōng** work

   假期的 时候,他去 打工 挣 零花钱。

   Jiàqī de shíhou, tā qù dǎgōng zhèng línghuāqián.

   During the holidays, he does menial work to earn some pocket money.

2. 工作 **gōngzuò** work

   你做 什么 工作?

   Nǐ zuò shénme gōngzuò?

   What work do you do?

3. 工资 **gōngzī** wage or salary

   一个 月 的 工资 有 多少?

   Yí ge yuè de gōngzī yǒu duōshao?

   What's the monthly wage?

4. 工业 **gōngyè** industry

   这里 工业 污染 很 严重。

   Zhèlǐ gōngyè wūrǎn hěn yánzhòng.

   Industrial pollution is quite serious here.

5. 工厂 **gōngchǎng** factory

   这家 工厂 生产 运动鞋。

   Zhè jiā gōngchǎng shēngchǎn yùndòngxié.

   This factory manufactures sport shoes.

Helpful tips: The second horizontal stroke is slightly longer.											**3 strokes**
工	一	丁	工								

作

zuò

do, make

Radical: 亻 # 19 "upright person"

Compounds, sentences, and meanings

1. 作 **zuò** work

   这 本 小说 是她的 成名 之 作。

   Zhè běn xiǎoshuō shì tāde chéngmíng zhī zuò.

   This novel is the work that made her famous.

2. 作家 **zuòjiā** writer

   我 从小 就 想 当 作家。

   Wǒ cóngxiǎo jiù xiǎng dāng zuòjiā.

   I've wanted to be a writer since I was small.

3. 作文 **zuòwén** essay

   这 是一 篇 小学生 的 作文。

   Zhè shì yì piān xiǎoxuésheng de zuòwén.

   This is an essay by a school child.

4. 作业 **zuòyè** assignment

   今天 的 作业 还 没 做 呢。

   Jīntiān de zuòyè hái méi zuò ne.

   I haven't done today's assignment yet.

5. 作用 **zuòyòng** intention

   他 说 那 句 话 有 什么 作用?

   Tā shuō nà jù huà yǒu shénme zuòyòng?

   What was his intention in saying that?

Helpful tips: The top horizontal stroke is longer than those below it.   **7 strokes**

师　shī　teacher

師

Radical: 丨 # 3 "vertical stroke" or 巾 # 52 "napkin"

Compounds, sentences, and meanings

1. 师 **shī** teacher

   我们 是 师生 关系。
   Wǒmen shì shīshēng guānxi.
   We have a teacher-student relationship.

2. 老师 **lǎoshī** teacher

   他 以前 是 老师, 现在 退休了。
   Tā yǐqián shì lǎoshī, xiànzài tuìxiū le.
   He used to be a teacher, now he has retired.

3. 师父 **shīfu** master/teacher

   他 是 我的 师父, 我 是 他的 徒弟。
   Tā shì wǒde shīfu, wǒ shì tā de túdì.
   He's my master, I'm his disciple.

4. 师母 **shīmǔ** wife of master/teacher

   师母 很 好客, 经常 请 学生
   Shīmǔ hěn hàokè, jīngcháng qǐng xuésheng

   到家里吃饭。
   dào jiālǐ chīfàn.
   Our teacher's wife is very hospitable, she often invites students to dinner at her home.

5. 律师 **lùshī** lawyer

   她 是 一个 很 有名 的 律师。
   Tā shì yí ge hěn yǒumíng de lùshī.
   She's a very famous lawyer.

Helpful tips: Note the difference between 师 and 帅.　　　　**6 strokes**

师	丨¹	丿²	厂³	师⁴	师⁵	师⁶					

学 xué

learn

Traditional Form

學

Radical: 子 # 67 "child"

Compounds, sentences, and meanings

1. 学 xué study, learn

只要 努力, 一定 能 学会。

Zhǐyào nǔlì, yídìng néng xuéhuì.

If you work hard, you will master it.

2. 学生 xuésheng student

中国 学生 很 认真 学习。

Zhōngguó xuésheng hěn rènzhēn xuéxí.

Chinese students are very studious.

3. 学习 xuéxí learn

应该 学习 别人 的 长处。

Yīnggāi xuéxí biéren de chángchù.

One should learn from others' strong points.

4. 学校 xuéxiào school

这 个 学校 有 点儿 名气。

Zhè ge xuéxiào yǒu diǎnr míngqì.

This school has a good reputation.

5. 学费 xuéfèi tuition fees

念 大学 一 年 的 学费 是 多少?

Niàn dàxué yì nián de xuéfèi shì duōshao?

How much are the annual university tuition fees?

Helpful tips: The first two dots slant to the right.

8 strokes

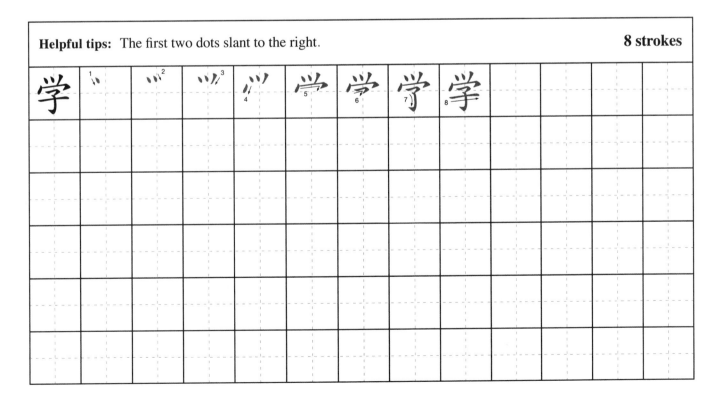

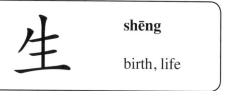

生　　shēng

birth, life

Radical: 丿 # 4 "downward-left stroke"

Compounds, sentences, and meanings

1. 生 **shēng** give birth to

   我 家 的 猫　生了 三 只　小猫。

   Wǒ jiā de māo shēngle sān zhī xiǎomāo.

   Our cat gave birth to three kittens.

2. 生日 **shēngrì** birthday

   今天 是 谁的　生日?

   Jīntiān shì shéide shēngrì?

   Whose birthday is it today?

3. 生词 **shēngcí** new word

   我 今天 学了 五个　生词。

   Wǒ jīntiān xuéle wǔ ge shēngcí.

   I've learned five new words today.

4. 大学生 **dàxuésheng** university student

   美国　大学生　很 自由。

   Měiguó dàxuésheng hěn zìyóu.

   American students have a lot of freedom.

5. 生产 **shēngchǎn** manufacture

   这家　工厂　生产　运动鞋。

   Zhè jiā gōngchǎng shēngchǎn yùndòngxié.

   This factory manufactures sport shoes.

Helpful tips: The bottom horizontal stroke is the longest.

5 strokes

生	丿	仁	仨	牛	生						

医　yī

cure, treat

Radical: ⊏ # 13 "3-sided frame (open at the right)"

Compounds, sentences, and meanings

1. 医 **yī** cure, treat

中医 把他的 病 医好。

Zhōngyī bǎ tāde bìng yīhǎo.

The Chinese doctor cured him.

2. 医生 **yīshēng** doctor

他 是内科 医生, 不做 手术。

Tā shì nèikē yīshēng, bú zuò shǒushù.

He's a physician, he does not operate.

3. 医务所 **yīwùsuǒ** clinic

今天 医务所 有 很多 人。

Jīntiān yīwùsuǒ yǒu hěnduō rén.

There are lots of people in the clinic today.

4. 医院 **yīyuàn** hospital

请问, 到 医院 怎么 走?

Qǐngwèn, dào yīyuàn zěnme zǒu?

Excuse me, how do you get to the hospital?

5. 医科 **yīkē** medical science

她 在 大学 念 医科。

Tā zài dàxué niàn yīkē.

She studies medicine at the university.

Helpful tips: The second stroke is made up of vertical and horizontal lines.　　**7 strokes**

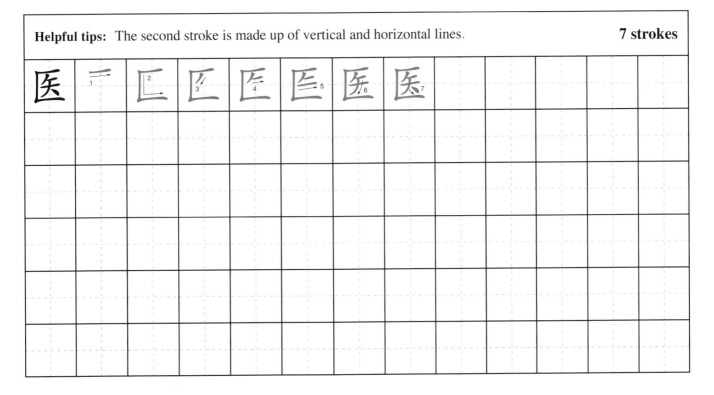

Lesson 8: Review Activities

A. Sentence Creation

For each of the individuals indicated please provide an occupation for each of those people. Then create a complete sentence that expresses the occupation that each person has.

我 _____   我的父亲 _____   我的母亲 _____

1. _____

2. _____

3. _____

B. Reading Comprehension

Please read the following description of the mother of a friend. Create a small illustration of your friend and her mother based on the information in the passage. Then answer the questions provided in English based on the information in the passage.

我的朋友是一个很有意思的美国人。她的老家不是美国，是德国。她是医生。她喜欢她的工作。她的母亲是老师，而且在医学院教课。我的朋友原来要也做律师，可是她母亲要她做医生。我想医生的工作很有意思。

1. What is the occupation of your friend?

_____

2. Does she enjoy her work?

_____

3. What is the occupation of her mother?

_____

4. Is that occupation interesting?

_____

5. Is there a connection between their jobs?

_____

C. Short Description

For each of the spaces provided, please write a sentence that describes your own mother or father. Please be mindful of demonstrating the range of effective expression possible when describing a family member. Example questions, based on describing one's mother, are given in the answer key.

1. _____

2. _____

3. _____

4. _____

5. _____

6. _____

孩

hái

child

Radical: 子 # 67 "child"

Compounds, sentences, and meanings

1. 孩 **hái** child (usually used with suffix **zi** or **ér**)

   这 个 孩子 很 淘气。

   Zhè ge háizi hěn táoqì.

   This child is very naughty.

2. 男孩儿 **nánháir** boy

   男孩儿 比较 淘气。

   Nánháir bǐjiào táoqì.

   Boys are more mischievous.

3. 女孩子 **nǚháizi** girl

   这 个 女孩子 很   聪明。

   Zhè ge nǚháizi hěn cōngmíng.

   This girl is very clever.

4. 孩子气 **háiziqì** childish

   你已经 十六 岁了, 别 那么孩子气!

   Nǐ yǐjīng shíliù suì le, bié nàme háiziqì!

   You shouldn't be so childish, you're 16 now!

5. 孩子话 **háizihuà** childish talk

   你已经 十六 岁了, 别 说 孩子话!

   Nǐ yǐjīng shíliù suì le, bié shuō haizihuà!

   You shouldn't talk like a child, you're 16 now!

Helpful tips: The last stroke ends firmly.												9 strokes
孩	了	了	子	孑	孩	孩	孩	孩				

子 **zǐ**

[noun suffix]; child

Radical: 子 # 67 "child"

Compounds, sentences, and meanings

1. 子 **zǐ** noun suffix

   桌子 是旧的, 椅子是新的。

   Zhuōzi shì jiùde, yǐzi shì xīnde.

   The desk is old but the chair is new.

2. 孩子 **háizi** child

   这 个孩子 很 淘气。

   Zhè ge háizi hěn táoqì.

   This kid is very naughty.

3. 子女 **zǐnǚ** sons and daughters

   五十年代 的 人大 都子女 成群。

   Wǔshíniándài de rén dà dōu zǐnǚ chéngqún.

   In the 50s, most people had lots of children.

4. 子孙 **zǐsūn** descendants

   中国人 叫自己 炎黄 子孙。

   Zhōngguórén jiào zìjǐ Yánhuáng zǐsūn.

   The Chinese people call themselves descendants of the Yellow Emperor.

5. 妻子 **qīzi** wife

   我来 介绍, 这是 我妻子。

   Wō lái jièshào, zhè shì wǒ qīzi.

   Let me introduce my wife.

Helpful tips: The second stroke is a vertical hook.　　　　　**3 strokes**

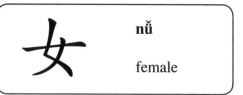

女 nǔ female

Radical: 女 # 65 "female"

Compounds, sentences, and meanings

1. 女 **nǔ** female

   中国 的女 运动员 都 很 出色。

   Zhōngguó de nǔ yùndòngyuán dōu hěn chūsè.

   The female Chinese athletes are outstanding.

2. 女儿 **nǔ'ér** daughter

   我 女儿 在 上海 教 英语。

   Wǒ nǔ'ér zài Shànghǎi jiāo Yīngyǔ.

   My daughter teaches English in Shanghai.

3. 女强人 **nǔqiángrén** a strong woman

   现在 女孩子 喜欢 当 女强人。

   Xiànzài nǔháizi xǐhuan dāng nǔqiángrén.

   These days girls want to be strong women.

4. 女生 **nǔshēng** female student

   学 语言 的 女生 比 男生 多。

   Xué yǔyán de nǔshēng bǐ nánshēng duō.

   Female language students outnumber male students.

5. 妇女 **fùnǔ** woman

   我 母亲 是 家庭 妇女。

   Wǒ mǔqin shì jiātíng fùnǔ.

   My mother is a housewife.

Helpful tips: End the first stroke firmly.									

3 strokes

女 乚 女 女

男 **nán**

male

Radical: 田 # 119 "field" or 力 # 31 "strength"

Compounds, sentences, and meanings

1. 男 **nán** man

   我们 家里 男女 平等。

   Wǒmen jiāli nán nǚ píngděng.

   In our household, we have equality of the sexes.

2. 男孩儿 **nánháir** boy

   男孩儿 比较 淘气。

   Nánháir bǐjiào táoqì.

   Boys are more mischievous.

3. 男朋友 **nánpéngyou** boy friend

   她 跟 男朋友 住 在一起。

   Tā gēn nánpéngyou zhù zài yìqǐ.

   She lives with her boyfriend.

4. 男高音 **nán'gāoyīn** tenor

   他的 声音 是 男 高音。

   Tāde shēngyīn shì nán'gāoyīn.

   He's a tenor.

5. 男厕所 **náncèsuǒ** men's toilet

   那边 有 男厕所。

   Nàbiān yǒu náncèsuǒ.

   There's a men's toilet over there.

Helpful tips: Finish the top component first.												7 strokes
男	丨	冂	曰	田	田	罗	男					

狗

gǒu

dog

Radical: 犭 # 58 "animal"

Compounds, sentences, and meanings

1. 狗 **gǒu** dog

   我们 家的 狗是 公 的。
   Wǒmen jiā de gǒu shì gōng de.
   Our dog is a male.

2. 小狗 **xiǎogǒu** puppy

   这只 小狗 真 可爱。
   Zhè zhī xiǎogǒu zhēn kě'ài.
   This puppy is really cute.

3. 母狗 **mǔgǒu** female dog, bitch

   这只 母狗 已经 很 老 了。
   Zhè zhī mǔgǒu yǐjīng hěn lǎo le.
   This female dog is quite old.

4. 狗熊 **gǒuxióng** black bear

   狗熊 有 时候 吃 人。
   Gǒuxióng yǒu shíhou chī rén.
   Black bears sometimes eat people.

5. 狗屁 **gǒupì** bullshit, rubbish (literally, dog fart)

   这 篇 文章 写得狗屁 不通。
   Zhè piān wénzhāng xiěde gǒupì bùtōng.
   The article is mere rubbish.

Helpful tips: The second stroke finishes with a hook.								**8 strokes**			
狗	⺈	⺘	犭	犭	狗	狗	狗	狗			

猫 **māo**

cat

貓

Radical: 犭 # 58 "animal"

Compounds, sentences, and meanings

1. 猫 **māo** cat

这 只 猫 是 公 的。
Zhè zhī māo shì gōng de.
This is a tomcat.

2. 母猫 **mǔmāo** female cat

这 母猫 很 老 了。
Zhè mǔmāo hěn lǎo le.
This female cat is quite old.

3. 小猫 **xiǎomāo** kitten

这些 小猫 太可爱了!
Zhèxiē xiǎomāo tài kě'ài le!
These kittens are so cute!

4. 大熊猫 **dàxióngmāo** panda

我 要 去 中国 看 大熊猫。
Wǒ yào qù Zhōngguó kàn dàxióngmāo.
I want to go to China to see the panda.

5. 猫头鹰 **māotóuyīng** owl

猫头鹰 吃 老鼠。
Māotóuyīng chī lǎoshǔ.
Owls eat rats.

Helpful tips: The second stroke is a curving hook.　　　**11 strokes**

猫

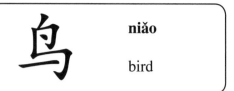

鳥

Radical: 鸟 #127 "bird"

Compounds, sentences, and meanings

1. 鸟 **niǎo** bird

有些 人 很 喜欢 看 鸟。

Yǒuxiē rén hěn xǐhuan kàn niǎo.

There are some people who enjoy bird watching.

2. 鸟窝 **niǎowō** bird nest

树 上 有 鸟窝。

Shù shàng yǒu niǎowō.

There is a bird nest in the tree.

Helpful tips: The horizontal stroke does not cross any other stroke.					5 strokes

鸟

馬

Radical: 马 # 69 "horse"

Compounds, sentences, and meanings

1. 马 **mǎ** horse
   二零零二年 是马年。
   Èrlínglíng'èrnián shì mǎ nián.
   2002 was the Year of the Horse.

2. 马路 **mǎlù** road
   过马路要 小心 车辆。
   Guò mǎlù yào xiǎoxīn chēliàng.
   Be careful of vehicles when crossing the road.

3. 马虎 **mǎhu** careless
   他 这 个人 做事 比较 马虎。
   Tā zhè ge rén zuòshì bǐjiào mǎhu.
   He's a rather careless fellow.

4. 马上 **mǎshàng** at once
   你 马上 就 走 吗?
   Nǐ mǎshàng jiù zǒu ma?
   Are you leaving right away?

5. 马拉松 **Mǎlāsōng** marathon
   去年 我 参加了 马拉松 赛跑。
   Qùnián wǒ cānjiāle Mǎlāsōng sàipǎo.
   Last year I took part in the marathon race.

Helpful tips: The last stroke ends in a straight line.										**3 strokes**
马	马	马 马								

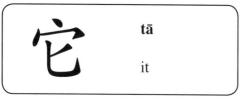

它 tā

it

Radical: 宀 # 34 "roof"

Compounds, sentences, and meanings

1. 它 **tā** it (animal/thing)

   这 杯 牛奶 你 喝完 它。
   Zhè bēi niúnǎi nǐ hēwán tā.
   Drink up this glass of milk.

2. 它的 **tāde** its (animals/things)

   这 裙子 很 好看, 我 喜欢 它的 颜色。
   Zhè qúnzi hěn hǎokàn, wǒ xǐhuan tāde yánsè.
   This skirt is pretty. I like its color.

3. 它们 **tāmen** they (animals/things)

   猫 狗 虽然 可爱, 但 它们 不会 说话。
   Māo gǒu suīrán kě'ài, dàn tāmen búhuì shuōhuà.
   Although cats and dogs are cute, they can't speak.

4. 其它 **qítā** other; else

   还有 什么 其它 事情 要 我们 做 吗?
   Háiyǒu shénme qítā shìqing yào wǒmen zuò ma?
   Is there anything else you want us to do?

Helpful tips: The last stroke sweeps from left to right.											**5 strokes**
它	丶	宀	宁	宁	它						

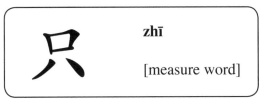

隻

只 zhī

[measure word]

Radical: 口 # 50 "mouth" or 八 # 17 "eight"

Compounds, sentences, and meanings

1. 只 **zhī** measure word

这 只 猫 是 公 的。

Zhè zhī māo shì gōng de.

This is a tomcat.

两只老虎 **Liǎng zhī lǎohu** (Two Tigers) is a well-known children's song.

两 只老虎，两 只 老虎;
Liǎng zhī lǎohu, liǎng zhī lǎohu;
Two tigers, two tigers;

跑得 快, 跑得 快,
Pǎode kuài, pǎode kuài;
They run fast, they run fast;

一 只 没有 眼睛,
Yì zhī méiyǒu yǎnjing,
One has no eyes,

一 只 没有 尾巴;
Yì zhī méiyǒu wěiba;
One has no tail;

真 奇怪! 真 奇怪!
Zhēn qíguài! Zhēn qíguài!
It's really strange! It's really strange!

Helpful tips: The last stroke finishes firmly. **5 strokes**

只 丨 口 口 只 只

A. Vocabulary Classification

Please write each of the following vocabulary items into the correct one of the two groups given below. Then write four sentences in Chinese characters that express the classification chosen for different possible subjects.

我　　孩子　　女朋友　　男朋友　　狗　　猫　　马　　我的父母

有工作	没有工作

（有工作）

1. _____

2. _____

（没有工作）

3. _____

4. _____

B. Answering Questions

Please answer the following questions in Chinese characters. For each response, please utilize both numbers and measure words for each noun and also the adverb 只 to emphasize the number in the statement. Then, if possible, ask and respond to the questions in speaking with attention paid to using vocal emphasis as appropriate.

1. 你有没有狗?

_____

2. 你有没有鸟?

_____

3. 你有没有音乐老师?

_____

4. 你有没有孩子？

_____

5. 你的猫有没有朋友？

_____

C. Expressing Opinion

Please consider the following questions and construct an opinion in response. Consider possible examples and exceptions to your thoughts. Then, write in connected discussion your opinion concerning the topic in Chinese characters. Keep in mind that these forms of questions offer strong opportunities to imagine, construct, and create in language in order to accurately express your thinking.

孩子应不应该有小动物（宠物）？ 孩子应该有什么样的宠物？

_____

_____

_____

_____

_____

_____

_____

_____

知 zhī

know

Radical: 矢 # 123 "arrow" or 口 # 50 "mouth"

Compounds, sentences, and meanings

1. 知 **zhī** be aware of, know

   这 话 不 知 是 谁 说 的。

   Zhè huà bù zhī shì shéi/shuí shuō de.

   I don't know who said this.

2. 知道 **zhīdao** know

   你 知道 邮局 在 哪儿 吗?

   Nǐ zhīdao yóujú zài nǎr ma?

   Do you know where the post office is?

3. 知识 **zhīshi** knowledge

   王 老师 的 知识 渊博。

   Wáng lǎoshī de zhīshi yuānbó.

   Teacher Wang is very knowledgeable.

4. 知己 **zhījǐ** bosom friend

   人生 难得 有 个 知己。

   Rénshēng nándé yǒu ge zhījǐ.

   It is difficult to find a true friend.

5. 知音 **zhīyīn** an understanding friend

   难得 有 个 知音。

   Nándé yǒu ge zhīyīn.

   It is difficult to find someone who really understands you.

Helpful tips: The fifth stroke ends firmly.　　　　　**8 strokes**

知	ノ	丨	丨	矢	矢	知	知	知

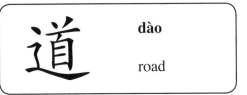

道 dào road

Radical: 辶 # 38 "movement"

Compounds, sentences, and meanings

1. 道 **dào** way, method

   他 对　养生　之 道 很 有 研究。

   Tā duì yǎngshēng zhī dào hěn yǒu yánjiū.

   He's very knowledgeable about staying healthy.

2. 道路 **dàolù** road

   走　前人　没有　走过　的道路。

   Zǒu qiánrén méiyǒu zǒuguo de dàolù.

   Explore paths none have taken before.

3. 道理 **dàoli** reason

   你的话　很 有 道理。

   Nǐde huà hěn yǒu dàoli.

   What you said is quite reasonable.

4. 道歉 **dàoqiàn** apologize

   我 得 向 你 道歉。

   Wǒ děi xiàng nǐ dàoqiàn.

   I owe you an apology.

5. 道义 **dàoyì** morality and justice

   我们　应该 给他 道义 上　的支持。

   Wǒmen yīnggāi gěi tā dàoyì shang de zhīchí.

   We should give him moral support.

Helpful tips: The top horizontal stroke is longer.											**12 strokes**
道	丷¹	丷²	兰³	半⁴	首⁵	首⁶	首⁷	首⁸	首⁹	首¹⁰	道¹¹	道¹²

Traditional Form

会

huì

able to

會

Radical: 人 # 18 "person"

Compounds, sentences, and meanings

1. 会 **huì** be able to

   我 会 英语, 不会 法语。

   Wǒ huì Yīngyǔ, búhuì Fǎyǔ.

   I speak English but I don't speak French.

2. 会 **huì** be likely to

   明天 会 下雨 吗?

   Míngtiān huì xiàyǔ ma?

   Will it rain tomorrow?

3. 一会儿 **yíhuìr** a moment

   请 你 等 一会儿。

   Qǐng nǐ děng yíhuìr.

   Please wait for a while.

4. 会议 **huìyì** meeting

   会议 进行 中, 请 勿 打搅。

   Huìyì jìnxíng zhōng, qǐng wù dǎjiǎo.

   Meeting in progress, please do not disturb.

5. 会话 **huìhuà** conversation

   学 语言 应该 多 听 会话。

   Xué yǔyán yīnggāi duō tīng huìhuà.

   You should listen to lots of conversation when learning a language.

Helpful tips: The last stroke ends firmly.

6 strokes

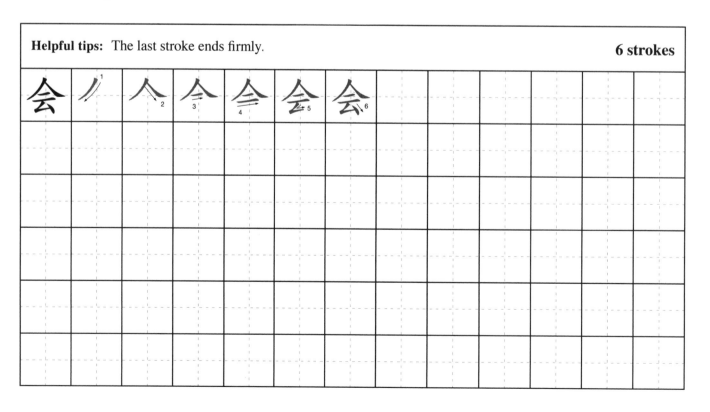

说　shuō

speak

說

Radical: 讠 # 9 "word"

Compounds, sentences, and meanings

1. 说 **shuō** speak

   请 听 我 说。

   Qǐng tīng wǒ shuō.

   Please listen to what I have to say.

2. 说话 **shuōhuà** speak

   我 爸爸 不 太 爱 说话。

   Wǒ bàba bú tài ài shuōhuà.

   My father doesn't like to talk much.

3. 说谎 **shuōhuǎng** tell a lie

   小孩子 不 要 学 说谎。

   Xiǎoháizi búyào xué shuōhuǎng.

   Children should learn not to tell lies.

4. 说不定 **shuōbudìng** maybe

   说不定 他 已经 走 了。

   Shuōbudìng tā yǐjīng zǒu le.

   Maybe he's already left.

5. 说服 **shuōfú** convince

   她 说服了 我。

   Tā shuōfúle wǒ.

   She has convinced me.

Helpful tips: The last stroke ends with a hook.　　**9 strokes**

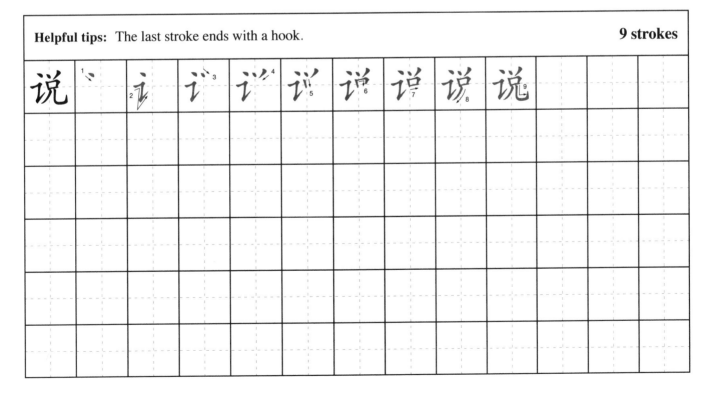

写 xiě

write

寫

Radical: 宀 # 8 "flat roof"

Compounds, sentences, and meanings

1. 写 xiě write

   这 个 字 写得 很 好。

   Zhè ge zì xiěde hěn hǎo.

   This character is well-written.

2. 写作 xiězuò writing

   我 觉得 写作 最 难 学。

   Wǒ juéde xiězuò zuì nán xué.

   I think writing is the hardest thing to learn.

3. 大写 dàxiě upper case/capital letter

   名字 缩写 应该 用 大写。

   Míngzi suōxiě yīnggāi yòng dàxiě.

   Initials for names should be written in capital letters.

4. 小写 xiǎoxiě lower case

   一般 的 词 应该 用 小写。

   Yìbān de cí yīnggāi yòng xiǎoxiě.

   Ordinary words should be written in lower case.

5. 书写 shūxiě hand-written

   书写 没有 打印 好看。

   Shūxiě méiyǒu dǎyìn hǎokàn.

   Handwriting doesn't look as good as printing.

Helpful tips: The fourth stroke has two bends ending with a hook.													**5 strokes**
写	冖	冖	写	写	写								

汉

Hàn

ethnic Han Chinese

漢

Radical: 氵 # 32 "3 drops of water"

Compounds, sentences, and meanings

1. 汉 **hàn** person

   不 到　长城　非 好汉。

   Bú dào Chángchéng fēi hǎohàn.

   You are not a true person if you haven't been to the Great Wall of China.

2. 汉语 **Hànyǔ** Chinese language

   你的 汉语 说得　很 不错。

   Nǐde Hànyǔ shuōde hěn búcuò.

   You speak Chinese very well.

3. 汉字 **Hànzì** Chinese characters

   我 觉得 汉字 很 有意思。

   Wǒ juéde Hànzì hěn yǒu yìsi.

   I think Chinese characters are very interesting.

4. 汉族 **Hànzú** ethnic Han Chinese

   汉族 在 新疆　占　少数。

   Hànzú zài Xīnjiāng zhàn shǎoshù.

   Ethnic Hans are in the minority in Xinjiang.

5. 汉学 **Hànxué** Chinese studies

   她 研究　汉学。

   Tā yánjiū Hànxué.

   She is doing research in Chinese studies.

Helpful tips: The third stroke simply lifts with no bend.

5 strokes

汉	丶	氵	沪	汉							

语   yǔ

language

語

Radical: 讠 # 9 "word"

Compounds, sentences, and meanings

1. 语 **yǔ** language

   你的法语 说得 很 好。

   Nǐde Fǎyǔ shuōde hěn hǎo.

   You speak French very well.

2. 外语 **wàiyǔ** foreign language

   我 没 学过 外语。

   Wǒ méi xuéguo wàiyǔ.

   I have never studied a foreign language.

3. 语法 **yǔfǎ** grammar

   中文 语法不太 难。

   Zhōngwén yǔfǎ bú tài nán.

   Chinese grammar is not too difficult.

4. 语言 **yǔyán** language

   北京 语言 文化 大学

   Běijīng Yǔyán Wénhuà Dàxué

   Beijing Language and Culture University

5. 语气 **yǔqì** manner of speaking

   她 用 婉转 的语气 说。

   Tā yòng wǎnzhuǎn de yǔqì shuō.

   She speaks in a tactful manner.

Helpful tips: 语 is easily confused with 话.									**9 strokes**		
语	丶	讠	订	订	语	语	语	语	语		

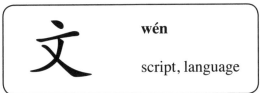

文　wén

script, language

Radical: 文 # 73 "script"

Compounds, sentences, and meanings

1. 文 **wén** language, script

这 篇 文章 写得 文 不 对题。

Zhè piān wénzhāng xiěde wén bú duì tí.

This essay was irrelevant to the topic.

2. 英文 **Yīngwén** English language

你的 英文 说得 很 好。

Nǐde Yīngwén shuōde hěn hǎo.

You speak English very well.

3. 文字 **wénzì** written language

这 是 有 文字 可考 的 历史。

Zhè shì yǒu wénzì kěkǎo de lìshǐ.

This is a documented history.

4. 文化 **wénhuà** civilization

我 想 研究 中国 文化。

Wǒ xiǎng yánjiū Zhōngguó wénhuà.

I want to study Chinese civilization.

5. 文学 **wénxué** literature

我 想 研究 中国 文学。

Wǒ xiǎng yánjiū Zhōngguó wénxué.

I want to study Chinese literature.

Helpful tips: The third stroke sweeps left.　　　**4 strokes**

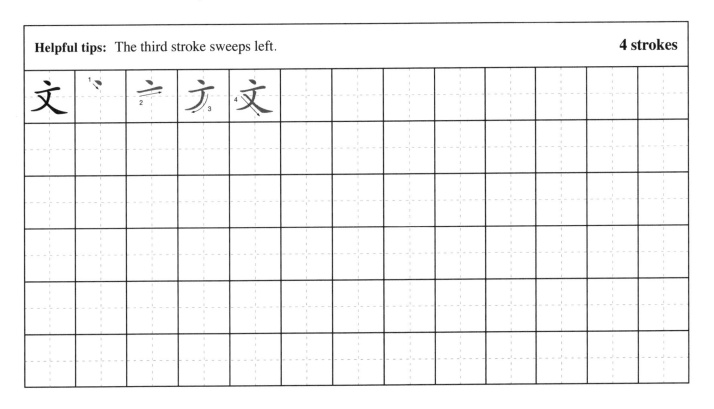

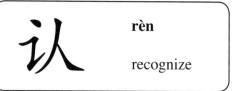

認

Radical: 讠 # 9 "word"

Compounds, sentences, and meanings

1. 认 **rèn** recognize

   你 变 多 了, 都 认不出 你 了。

   Nǐ biàn duō le, dōu rènbuchū nǐ le.

   You've changed so much that I hardly recognized you.

2. 认识 **rènshi** be acquainted with

   认识 你, 很 高兴。

   Rènshi nǐ, hěn gāoxìng.

   I'm pleased to meet you.

3. 认字 **rènzì** read characters

   我 现在 学 认字。

   Wǒ xiànzài xué rènzì.

   I'm learning to read characters.

4. 认得 **rènde** know, recognize

   你 还 认得 我 吗?

   Nǐ hái rènde wǒ ma?

   Do you still recognize me?

5. 认真 **rènzhēn** conscientious

   她 工作 很 认真。

   Tā gōngzuò hěn rènzhēn.

   She is conscientious in her work.

Helpful tips: The last stroke joins the previous stroke midway down.			**4 strokes**

认 认 认 认

识   **shí**   know

識

Radical: 讠 # 9 "word"

Compounds, sentences, and meanings

1. 识 **shí** know

   这 个 农民 一字不识。

   Zhè ge nóngmín yízì-bùshí.

   This peasant is completely illiterate (literally, knows not one word).

2. 识别 **shíbié** distinguish

   他 不能 识别 真假 朋友。

   Tā bùnéng shíbié zhēnjiǎ péngyou.

   He cannot distinguish true friends from false ones.

3. 识货 **shíhuò** able to tell value in goods

   买 东西 要 识货。

   Mǎi dōngxi yào shíhuò.

   You need to know the value of things when shopping.

4. 识字 **shízì** become literate

   这 是 识字课本。

   Zhè shì shízì kèběn.

   This is a reading primer.

5. 学识 **xuéshí** knowledge

   这 位 老先生 的 学识 很 广。

   Zhè wèi lǎoxiānsheng de xuéshí hěn guǎng.

   This old gentleman is very learned.

Helpful tips: The last stroke finishes firmly.   **7 strokes**

识 | 丶 | 讠 | 讥 | 识 | 识 | 识 | 识

Lesson 10: Review Activities

A. Character Recognition

Please write out the *pinyin* transcription for each of the following characters. Then write a two-character word that utilizes that character.

	Pinyin	2-Character Word
汉		
中		
英		
字		
人		

	Pinyin	2-Character Word
知		
生		
国		
文		
语		

B. Sentence Completion and Translation

Please complete each of the following sentences by adding one of the following words. Then translate the resulting sentence into effective English statements.

会　　认识　　知道　　写　　有

1. 我的朋友不＿＿＿＿＿＿我的哥哥。

_____

2. 我也＿＿＿＿＿＿两只猫。

_____

3. 你的同学＿＿＿＿＿＿说汉语吗？

_____

4. 他喜欢＿＿＿＿＿＿汉字, 他也喜欢说汉语。

_____

5. 我不能回答你的问题, 我不＿＿＿＿＿＿。

_____

C. Expressing Opinion

Please consider the following questions and construct an opinion in response. Consider possible examples and exceptions to your thoughts. Then, write in connected discussion your opinion concerning the topic in Chinese characters. Keep in mind that these forms of questions offer strong opportunities to imagine, construct, and create in language in order to accurately express your thinking.

什么工作要会汉语，什么工作要会英语？ 这个工作在哪儿？

Section 2 Review (Lessons 6–10)

A. Word Completion

For each empty box, please write a character that creates an effective two-character word.

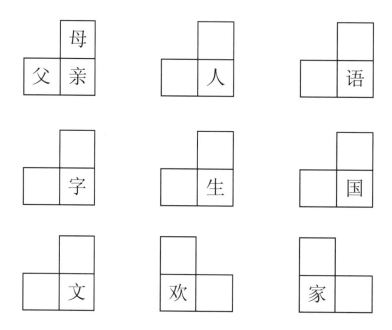

B. Occupation Description

Based on the illustration provided below, please describe the occupation that is depicted and express your opinion about the particular occupation. Demonstrate your understanding of the different functions and roles of the occupation. A stronger description will also include your own experiences with this occupation.

C. Describing a Place

Please utilize the space provided to fully describe your hometown. This free writing exercise should demonstrate the range of expression possible about a known topic. Attempt to explore the topic with vocabulary and construction that show both an ability to speak on the topic with depth and the awareness of the cultural concerns that surround the topic.

_____

_____

_____

_____

_____

_____

_____

_____

D. Reflective Questions

Use these questions to both check the expressiveness of the previous section and to confirm your understanding of the previous topic. For additional practice, say and then respond to these questions aloud.

你好, 对不起你叫什么名字?

你是什么国家的人?

你的老家在哪里?

你住在你的老家吗?

你有什么家人还住在你的老家?

你作什么工作?

你喜不喜欢你的工作?

你的父母作什么工作?

你有没有孩子?

你说汉语说得很好, 你会写汉字吗?

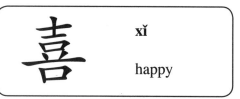

喜　xǐ

happy

Radical: 士 # 41 "scholar" or 口 # 50 "mouth"

Compounds, sentences, and meanings

1. 喜 **xǐ** be happy

   笑 在 脸上，喜在心里。

   Xiào zài liǎnshang, xǐ zài xīnli.

   With a smile on your face and joy in your heart.

2. 喜爱 **xǐ'ài** be fond of

   我喜爱 户外 活动。

   Wǒ xǐ'ài hùwài huódòng.

   I'm fond of outdoor activities.

3. 喜欢 **xǐhuan** enjoy, like

   我 喜欢 听 中国 音乐。

   Wǒ xǐhuan tīng Zhōngguó yīnyuè.

   I like Chinese music.

4. 欢喜 **huānxǐ** joyful

   一家 人 欢欢喜喜地 过 春节。

   Yì jiā rén huānhuānxǐxǐde guò Chūnjié.

   The whole family spent a joyful Chinese New Year.

5. 喜事 **xǐshì** happy event

   你 这么 高兴，有 什么 喜事?

   Nǐ zhème gāoxìng, yǒu shénme xǐshì?

   You look so happy. What's the good news?

Helpful tips: The short strokes in the middle do not protrude.										**12 strokes**	

喜　二　卄　吉　吉　吉　吉　吉　吉　壴　壴　喜　喜

要   yào

want

Radical: 西 # 139 "west" or 女 # 65 "female"

Compounds, sentences, and meanings

1. 要 **yào** want

   您要买 什么?

   Nǐ yào mǎi shénme?

   What would you like to buy?

2. 要不 **yàobù** otherwise

   你可以坐 船 去,要不 坐 火车 也行。

   Nǐ kěyi zuò chuán qù, yàobù zuò huǒchē yě xíng.

   You can go there by boat or by train.

3. 要好 **yàohǎo** be close friends

   他们 从小 就 很 要好。

   Tāmen cóngxiǎo jiù hěn yàohǎo.

   They have been close friends since childhood.

4. 要紧 **yàojǐn** important

   我 有 件 要紧 的事儿跟他 商量。

   Wǒ yǒu jiàn yàojǐn de shìr gēn tā shāngliang.

   I have an important matter to discuss with him.

5. 首要 **shǒuyào** of the first importance

   首要 的事 先 办。

   Shǒuyào de shì xiān bàn.

   First things first.

Helpful tips: The two vertical strokes are parallel.									9 strokes	
要	一	一	一	西	西	西	要	要	要	

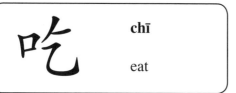

chī

eat

Radical: 口 # 50 "mouth"

Compounds, sentences, and meanings

1. 吃 **chī** eat

   我 每天 都 吃个 苹果。
   Wǒ měitiān dōu chī ge píngguó.
   I eat an apple every day.

2. 吃饭 **chīfàn** have a meal

   我们 什么 时候 吃饭?
   Wǒmen shénme shíhou chīfàn?
   When do we eat?

3. 吃得下 **chīdexià** be able to eat

   我 吃得下 两 碗 饭。
   Wǒ chīdexià liǎng wǎn fàn.
   I can eat two bowls of rice.

4. 吃不下 **chībuxià** not able to eat

   我 吃不下 两 碗 饭。
   Wǒ chībuxià liǎng wǎn fàn.
   I can't eat two bowls of rice.

5. 吃苦 **chīkǔ** bear hardships (literally, eat bitterness)

   他 小时候 吃了 不少 苦。
   Tā xiǎoshíhou chīle bùshǎo kǔ.
   He suffered a great deal in his childhood.

Helpful tips: The last stroke is a horizontal-bend-hook.　　　　**6 strokes**

吃	一	口	口	吃	吃	吃					

饭

fàn

meal

饭

Radical: 饣 # 59 "food"

Compounds, sentences, and meanings

1. 饭 **fàn** meal

   饭 前 洗手。

   Fàn qián xǐshǒu.

   Wash your hands before meals.

2. 饭菜 **fàncài** food

   这个 饭馆 的 饭菜 做得 不错。

   Zhè ge fànguǎn de fàncài zuòde búcuò.

   The food in this restaurant is quite good.

3. 饭馆儿 **fànguǎnr** restaurant

   学校 对面 有一家 饭馆儿。

   Xuéxiào duìmian yǒu yì jiā fànguǎnr.

   There's a restaurant opposite the school.

4. 饭店 **fàndiàn** hotel

   我 住 在 北京 饭店。

   Wǒ zhù zài Běijīng Fàndiàn.

   I'm staying at Beijing Hotel.

5. 米饭 **mǐfàn** boiled rice

   我 平常 吃 两 碗 米饭。

   Wǒ píngcháng chī liǎng wǎn mǐfàn.

   I usually eat two bowls of rice.

Helpful tips: The second stroke is a horizontal hook.　　　**7 strokes**

CHARACTER 110

kàn

see, watch

Radical: 目 # 118 "eyes"

Compounds, sentences, and meanings

1. 看 **kàn** see, look at

   你 对 这 件 事 怎么 看?

   Nǐ duì zhè jiàn shì zěnme kàn?

   What's your view on this matter?

2. 看电影 **kàn diànyǐng** see a movie

   今晚 我 去 看 电影。

   Jīnwǎn wǒ qù kàn diànyǐng.

   I'm going to see a movie tonight.

3. 看书 **kànshū** read books

   我 喜欢 看书。

   Wǒ xǐhuan kànshū.

   I like to read.

4. 看见 **kànjiàn** see

   我 今天 在 车站 看见 她。

   Wǒ jīntiān zài chēzhàn kànjiàn tā.

   I saw her at the bus stop today.

5. 看来 **kànlái** it seems

   看来 他 还 没 拿定 主意。

   Kànlái tā hái méi nádìng zhǔyi.

   It looks as if he hasn't made up his mind.

Helpful tips: The first stroke travels from right to left.										**9 strokes**

看 一¹ 二² 三³ 手⁴ 看⁵ 看⁶ 看⁷ 看⁸ 看⁹

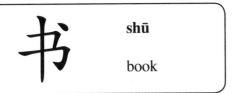

书 shū

book

書

Radical: 乛 # 5 "horizontal-bend"

Compounds, sentences, and meanings

1. 书 shū book

这 是 一 本 教科书。

Zhè shì yì běn jiàokēshū.

This is a textbook.

2. 书包 shūbāo school bag

小孩 背着 书包 上学。

Xiǎohái bēizhe shūbāo shàngxué.

The children carry their school bags on their backs to go to school.

3. 书店 shūdiàn bookstore

马路 对面 有 一家 书店。

Mǎlù duìmian yǒu yì jiā shūdiàn.

There is a bookstore across the road.

4. 书架 shūjià bookshelf

我 刚 买了 一个 书架。

Wǒ gāng mǎile yí ge shūjià.

I just bought a bookshelf.

5. 书法 shūfǎ calligraphy

我 觉得 中国 书法 很 好看。

Wǒ juéde Zhōngguó shūfǎ hěn hǎokàn.

I think Chinese calligraphy is beautiful.

Helpful tips: The second stroke ends with a hook.   **4 strokes**

书　乛　马　书　书

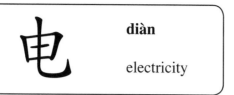

電

Radical: ㄴ # 5 "vertical-bend-hook"

Compounds, sentences, and meanings

1. 电 **diàn** electricity

电门 有 毛病， 电了 我 一下。

Diànmén yǔ máobìng, diànle wǒ yíxià.

There was something wrong with the switch and I got a shock.

2. 电影 **diànyǐng** movie

我 喜欢 看 中国 电影。

Wǒ xǐhuan kàn Zhōngguó diànyǐng.

I like to see Chinese movies.

3. 电视 **diànshì** television

今晚 电视 有 什么 好 节目?

Jīnwǎn diànshì yǒu shénme hǎo jiémù?

Are there any good programs on TV tonight?

4. 电脑 **diànnǎo** computer

现在 电脑 在 中国 很 普及。

Xiànzài diànnǎo zài Zhōngguó hěn pǔjí.

Computers are now common in China.

5. 电话 **diànhuà** telephone

今晚 请 给 我 回 个 电话。

Jīnwǎn qǐng gěi wǒ huí ge diànhuà.

Please give me a call tonight.

Helpful tips: The horizontal lines are equally spaced.										**5 strokes**
电	丨	冂	日	日	电					

shì

to see, to look

視

Radical: 礻 (示) # 78 "show"

Compounds, sentences, and meanings

1. 电视 **diànshì** television

   每个 星期六 早上 小 孩子 喜欢 看
   Měige Xīngqīliù zǎoshàng xiǎo háizi xǐhuan kàn
   电视。
   diànshì.
   Every Saturday morning, small children enjoy watching television.

2. 视力 **shìlì** vision, sight

   他 不 需要 眼镜，他的视力 很 好。
   Tā bù xūyào yǎnjìng, tā de shìlì hěn hǎo.
   He doesn't need glasses, his eyesight is good.

3. 视点 **shìdiǎn** view, perspective

   每 人 都 有 自己的 视点。
   Měi rén dōu yǒu zìjǐ de shìdiǎn.
   All people have individual perspectives.

4. 视而不见 **shìérbújiàn** overlook, turn a blind eye towards

   父母 常常 对 孩子的 缺点
   Fùmǔ chángcháng duì háizi de quēdiǎn
   视而不见。
   shìérbújiàn.
   Parents often overlook their child's shortcomings.

Helpful tips: The two parts are evenly balanced and the last stroke ends in a hook.												**8 strokes**

视 丶 ﻁ 礻 礻 礻 初 视 视

影

yǐng

shadow

Radical: 彡 # 55 "feathery"

Compounds, sentences, and meanings

1. 影 **yǐng** shadow

   听说 他是 回来了，可是 还没 看见
   Tīngshuō tā shì huílai le, kěshì hái méi kànjiàn
   他的影儿。
   tāde yǐngr.
   I heard that he's back, but I haven't seen any sign of him yet.

2. 合影 **héyǐng** take a photo together

   我们 照个 合影 留念，好 吗？
   Wǒmen zhào ge héyǐng liúniàn, hǎo ma?
   Let's take a photo together to mark the occasion, shall we?

3. 影迷 **yǐngmí** movie fan

   他 喜欢 看 电影，是 个 影迷。
   Tā xǐhuan kàn diànyǐng, shì ge yǐngmí.
   He's fond of movies, he's a movie fan.

4. 影印 **yǐngyìn** photocopy

   请 给我 影印 两份。
   Qǐng gěi wǒ yǐngyìn liǎng fèn.
   Please photocopy two copies for me.

5. 影响 **yǐngxiǎng** influence, effect

   吸烟 影响 健康。
   Xīyān yǐngxiǎng jiànkāng.
   Smoking affects health.

Helpful tips: The last three strokes slant downward, then left.　　　**15 strokes**

影	丿 ¹	口 ²	日 ³	旦 ⁴	旦 ⁵	旦 ⁶	昜 ⁷	景 ⁸	景 ⁹	景 ¹⁰	景 ¹¹	景 ¹²
影 ¹³	影 ¹⁴	影 ¹⁵										

打 dǎ

hit

Radical: 扌 # 48 "hand"

Compounds, sentences, and meanings

1. 打 **dǎ** hit, strike

   现在 父母也 不能 打孩子了。

   Xiànzài fùmǔ yě bùnéng dǎ háizi le.

   Nowadays parents can't hit their children.

2. 打电话 **dǎ diànhuà** phone someone

   你 应该 先 给他打个 电话。

   Nǐ yīnggāi xiān gěi tā dǎ ge diànhuà.

   You should telephone him first.

3. 打扫 **dǎsǎo** sweep, clean

   请 打扫 一下 房间。

   Qǐng dǎsǎo yíxià fángjiān.

   Please clean my room.

4. 打听 **dǎtīng** find out

   跟 您 打听一件 事。

   Gēn nín dǎtīng yí jiàn shì.

   I'd like to ask you about something.

5. 打字 **dǎzì** type

   她打字比我 打得 快。

   Tā dǎzì bǐ wǒ dǎde kuài.

   She types faster than me.

Helpful tips: The last stroke ends with a hook.   **5 strokes**

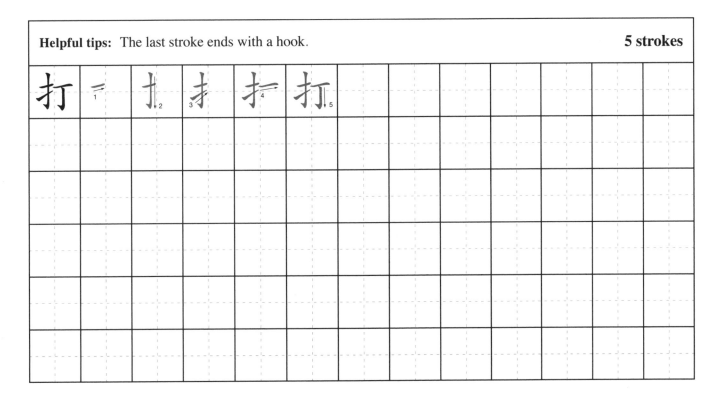

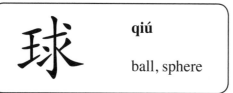

CHARACTER 116

球　qiú

ball, sphere

Radical: 王 # 79 "king"

Compounds, sentences, and meanings

1. 打球 **dǎqiú** to play (sport)

   我 的 朋友 喜欢 天天 打球。

   Wǒ de péngyou xǐhuan tiāntiān dǎqiú.

   My friend likes to play sports every day.

2. 球赛 **qiúsài** athletic contest

   你 喜欢 看 哪一 种 球赛?

   Nǐ xǐhuan kàn nǎyī zhǒng qiúsài?

   What sort of sporting contest do you like to watch?

3. 半球 **bànqiú** hemisphere

   中国 和日本 都 在 东 半球。

   Zhōngguó hé Rìběn dōu zài dōng bànqiú.

   China and Japan are in the Eastern Hemisphere.

4. 环球 **huánqiú** the world, the earth

   二十一世纪的问题　常常　是 环球 的

   Èrshíyī shìjì de wèntí chángcháng shì huánqiú de

   问题。

   wèntí.

   Problems in the 21st century often are global problems.

5. 球员 **qiúyuán** player

   每个足球队 需要 有 十一个 球员

   Měi ge zúqiúduì xūyào yǒu shíyī ge qiúyuán

   参加 比赛。

   cānjiā bǐsai.

   Every soccer team needs 11 players to participate in a match.

Helpful tips: The last stroke appears at the top right corner.　　**11 strokes**

球 | 二₁ | 三₂ | 王₃ | 王₄ | 王₅ | 玎₆ | 玎₇ | 球₈ | 球₉ | 球₁₀ | 球₁₁ |

Lesson 11: Review Activities

A. Pronunciation and *Pinyin* Practice

Please write the following questions written in Chinese characters in pinyin. Then construct an answer for each of the questions. For additional practice, say and then respond to these questions aloud.

1. 你是不是学生?　　　　　(*Pinyin*) _____

_____

2. 你要不要看电视?　　　　(*Pinyin*) _____

_____

3. 你要做什么?　　　　　　(*Pinyin*) _____

_____

4. 你喜不喜欢看书?　　　　(*Pinyin*) _____

_____

5. 你的家人喜欢做什么?　　(*Pinyin*) _____

_____

B. Verb Object Matching

Please match an object to each of the following verbs. Then, in the space provided, write a complete sentence demonstrating context for the verb-object relationship.

吃_____　　　　打_____　　　　看_____　　　　喜欢_____　　　　是_____

1. _____

2. _____

3. _____

4. _____

5. _____

C. Comparative Discussion

Please consider the following topic which asks for two related concepts to be described and compared. In two paragraphs create a discussion that connects and compares the two components. A strong demonstration of understanding will express both immediate differences and similarities and also engage the extended implications of those features.

老人喜欢做什么？ 你喜欢做什么？ 什么运动一样？ 什么不一样？ 这些不一样有什么原因？

_____

_____

_____

_____

_____

_____

_____

_____

_____

_____

_____

练 liàn

practice

練

Radical: 纟 # 68 "silk"

Compounds, sentences, and meanings

1. 练 **liàn** practice

   我 下定 决心 练好 身体。

   Wǒ xiàdìng juéxīn liànhǎo shēntǐ.

   I've made up my mind to get fit.

2. 练习 **liànxí** practice

   我 每天 练习写 汉字。

   Wǒ měitiān liànxí xiě Hànzì.

   I practice writing Chinese characters every day.

3. 练习本 **liànxíběn** workbook

   这 是 汉字 读写 练习本。

   Zhè shì Hànzì dú-xiě liànxíběn.

   This is a Chinese character reading workbook.

4. 练习题 **liànxítí** exercise problems

   今天 的 作业 有 两 条 练习题我

   Jīntiān de zuòyè yǒu liǎng tiáo liànxítí wǒ

   不会 做。

   búhuì zuò.

   There are two exercise problems that I can't do in today's homework.

5. 练武 **liànwǔ** practice martial arts

   我 每天 早晨 都 练武。

   Wǒ měitiān zǎochén dōu liànwǔ.

   I practice martial arts every morning.

Helpful tips: Note the difference between 东 and 东.   **8 strokes**

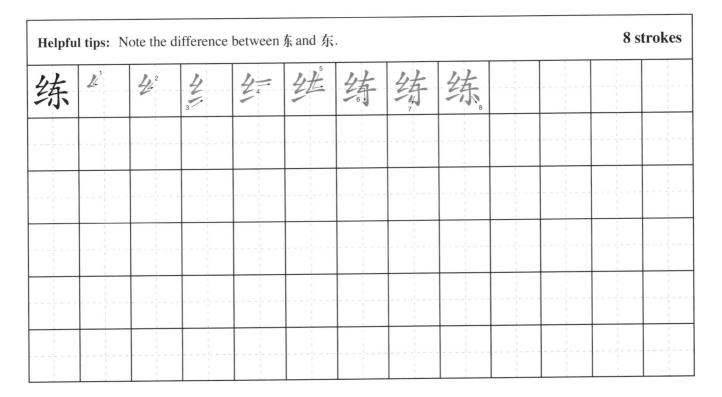

复　fù

to review

復／複／覆

Radical: ノ # 4 "downward-left stroke"

Compounds, sentences, and meanings

1. 复习 **fùxí** to review

考试　以前　学生　复习复习。

Kǎoshì yǐqián xuésheng fùxí fùxí.

Prior to an exam students review.

2. 复杂 **fùzá** complex, complicated

你的 问题　很复杂。

Nǐ de wèntí hěn fùzá.

Your question is very complicated.

3. 复印 **fùyìn** to photocopy, to duplicate

请　帮 我的　忙 复印 这　张　文章。

Qǐng bāng wǒde máng fùyìn zhè zhāng wénzhāng.

Please help me photocopy this article.

4. 复信 **fùxìn** to reply (by letter)

你 收 到　老朋友　的信, 你 得复信。

Nǐ shòu dào lǎopéngyou de xīn, nǐ děi fùxìn.

When you receive a letter from an old friend, you must reply.

5. 复原 **fùyuán** to return to health, to recover

去年 你　生了 一　场　很 利害的 病,

Qùnián nǐ shēngle yì chǎng hěn lìhai de bìng,

现在 你　完全　复原 了吗?

xiànzài nǐ wánquán fùyuán le ma?

Last year you had a really serious illness, have you fully recovered?

Helpful tips:	Each horizontal stroke is evenly spaced. There are multiple traditional forms: 復習, 複雜, 複印, 覆信, and 復原.	**9 strokes**

复　ノ　ケ　午　自　自　自　复　复　复

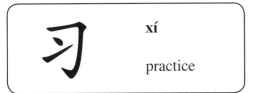

习 xí practice

習

Radical: 乛 # 5 "horizontal-vertical-hook"

Compounds, sentences, and meanings

1. 习 **xí** practice
   习非 成 是。
   Xí fēi chéng shì.
   Accept what is wrong as right.

2. 习惯 **xíguàn** habit
   我 习惯 早起。
   Wǒ xíguàn zǎoqǐ.
   I'm used to getting up early.

3. 习气 **xíqì** bad habit
   中国 的 官僚 习气很 严重。
   Zhōngguó de guānliáo xíqì hěn yánzhòng.
   Bad bureaucratic habits prevail in China.

4. 习染 **xírǎn** fall into a bad habit of
   青年人 很 容易 习染 抽烟。
   Qīngniánrén hěn róngyì xírǎn chōuyān.
   It's easy for young people to pick up the bad habit of smoking.

5. 习俗 **xísú** custom
   中国人 有 赏月 的习俗。
   Zhōngguórén yǒu shǎngyuè de xísú.
   The Chinese people have the custom of enjoying the full moon.

Helpful tips: The first stroke ends with a hook.　　**3 strokes**

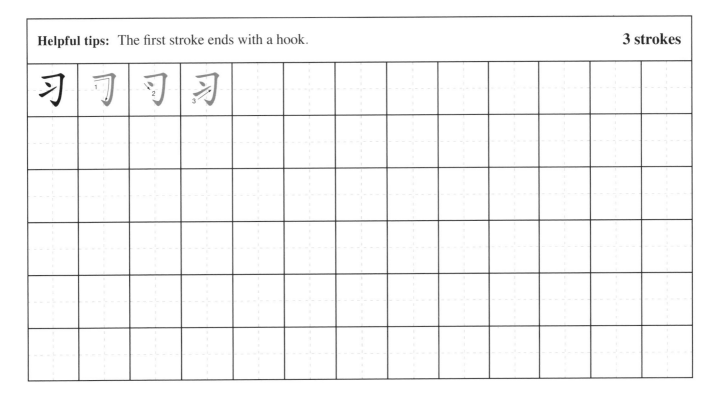

课 **kè** class

課

Radical: 讠(言) # 9 "word"

Compounds, sentences, and meanings

1. 课堂 **kètáng** classroom

   对不起，二十三 号 课堂 在哪里？

   Duìbuqǐ, èrshísān hào kètáng zài nǎlǐ?

   Excuse me, where is classroom 23?

2. 课本 **kèběn** textbook

   这 本 课本 一百 多 块钱，太 贵 啊！

   Zhè běn kèběn yībǎi duō kuàiqián, tài guì a!

   This textbook is more than a hundred dollars, too expensive!

3. 课文 **kèwén** text

   学生 常常 念 课文 练习 课。

   Xuésheng chángcháng niàn kèwén liànxí kè.

   Students often recite texts for practice.

4. 课程 **kèchéng** curriculum

   每种 课 都 需要特色的 课程。

   Měizhǒng kè dōu xūyào tèsè de kèchéng.

   Every sort of class needs a special curriculum.

Helpful tips: The straight vertical stroke continues through all parts of the character.　　**10 strokes**

课	丶	讠	讠¹	讲	误	误	误	误	课	课		

kǎo

to test, to examine

Radical: 老 # 136 "old"

Compounds, sentences, and meanings

1. 考试 **kǎoshì** test, examination

   人们 都有 考 考试 的 经历。
   Rénmen dōuyǒu kǎo kǎoshì de jīnglì.
   Everyone has had the experience of taking an examination.

2. 考虑 **kǎolǜ** to consider, to examine

   有 机会的 时候, 你 应该 考虑 考虑。
   Yǒu jīhuìde shíhou, nǐ yīnggāi kǎolǜ kǎolǜ.
   When you have an opportunity, you should think it over.

3. 考验 **kǎoyàn** to test, to trial

   这 个 很 复杂的 问题, 考验 人 的 能力。
   Zhè ge hěn fùzá de wèntí, kǎoyàn rén de nénglì.
   This is a complicated question, it will test a person's abilities.

4. 大考 **dàkǎo** college entrance examination

   每年 夏天 中国 年轻 人 考
   Měinián xiàtiān Zhōngguó niánqīng rén kǎo

   中国 的大考。
   Zhōngguó de dàkǎo.
   Every summer the young people of China take the college entrance examination.

5. 考上 **kǎoshàng** to test into, to achieve
   (by examination)

   每个 高中 学生 都 希望 考上
   Měige gāozhōng xuésheng dōu xīwàng kǎoshàng

   大学。
   dàxué.
   Every high school student desires to gain admission to college.

Helpful tips: The last stroke begins at the previous stroke and ends in a hook.　　　　**6 strokes**

考	=	#	土	少	考	考					

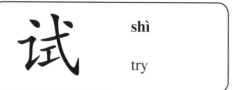

Traditional Form

試

试 **shì** try

Radical: 讠 # 9 "word"

Compounds, sentences, and meanings

1. 试 **shì** try

让 我 试一试。

Ràng wǒ shìyishì.

Let me try.

2. 试探 **shìtàn** sound out

试探 一下他 对 这 个 问题 的 看法。

Shìtàn yíxià tā duì zhè ge wèntí de kànfǎ.

Sound him out about it.

3. 试行 **shìxíng** try out

先 试行，后 推广。

Xiān shìxíng, hòu tuīguǎng.

Test it before general use.

4. 试用 **shìyòng** try out (a product)

我 想 试用 一下。

Wǒ xiǎng shìyòng yíxià.

I'd like to try it out.

5. 考试 **kǎoshì** exam

他 这次考试 的 成绩 很 好。

Tā zhè cì kǎoshì de chéngjī hěn hǎo.

He got excellent grades in this exam.

Helpful tips: Note the difference between 弋 and 戈.

8 strokes

试

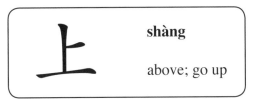

上　　shàng

above; go up

Radical: 一 # 2 "horizontal stroke"

Compounds, sentences, and meanings

1. 上 **shàng** most recent, last

   上　星期三　我　有事儿。

   Shàng Xīngqīsān wǒ yǒu shìr.

   I was busy last Wednesday.

2. 上 **shàng** go to

   你　上　哪儿去?

   Nǐ shàng nǎr qù?

   Where are you going?

3. 上面 **shàngmian** above

   书　　上面　有我的　名字。

   Shū shàngmian yǒu wǒde míngzi.

   My name is written on the book.

4. 上午 **shàngwǔ** A.M.

   今天　上午　风　很　大。

   Jīntiān shàngwǔ fēng hěn dà.

   It's quite windy this morning.

5. 上学 **shàngxué** go to school

   小孩　已经　五　岁了,该　上学　了。

   Xiǎohái yǐjīng wǔ suì le, gāi shàngxué le.

   The child is already five, she/he should be going to school.

Helpful tips: The top horizontal stroke is shorter.　　　　　　**3 strokes**

上	丨	上	上									

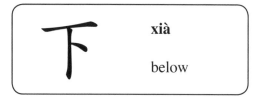

下 xià

below

Radical: 一 # 2 "horizontal stroke"

Compounds, sentences, and meanings

1. 下 **xià** next

   下 星期三 我 有 事儿。

   Xià Xīngqīsān wǒ yǒu shìr.

   I'll be busy next Wednesday.

2. 下面 **xiàmian** below

   图表 下面 有 说明。

   Túbiǎo xiàmian yǒu shuōmíng.

   There are captions below the chart.

3. 下班 **xiàbān** get off work

   你 今天 几 点 下班?

   Nǐ jīntiān jǐ diǎn xiàbān?

   When will you be finishing work today?

4. 下午 **xiàwǔ** afternoon

   下午 有 雷阵雨。

   Xiàwǔ yǒu léizhènyǔ.

   There'll be thunderstorms in the afternoon.

5. 下雨 **xiàyǔ** rain

   外面 下雨。

   Wàimian xiàyǔ.

   It's raining outside.

Helpful tips: End the last stroke firmly.											**3 strokes**
下	一	丁	下								

历 **lì**
experience, calendar, almanac

歷／曆

Radical: 厂 # 12 "building"

Compounds, sentences, and meanings

1. 历史 **lìshǐ** history

中国 古代历史 很 有意思。
Zhōngguó gǔdài lìshǐ hěn yǒu yìsi.
Chinese ancient history is very interesting.

2. 日历 **rìlì** calendar

每 个 家 得 有 一 本 日历。
Měi ge jiā děi yǒu yì běn rìlì.
Every house should have a calendar.

3. 历年 **lìnián** over the years

历年 来 我 旅游 很 多 地方 认识 很
Lìnián lái wǒ lǚyóu hěn duō dìfang rènshi hěn
多 人。
duō rén.
Over the years I traveled to many places and met many people.

4. 历书 **lìshū** almanac

家里要 办喜事, 父母 要 查 历书。
Jiālǐ yào bàn xǐshì, fùmǔ yào chǎ lìshū.
When there are auspicious events to plan, parents want to check the almanac.

5. 历次 **lìcì** previous instances, previously

历次我来这个 商店 我买 很 多 东西。
Lìcì wǒ lái zhège shāngdiàn wǒ mǎi hěn duō dōngxi.
The previous time I came to this shop I bought a lot of things.

6. 历代 **lìdài** previous times, previous dynasties

现代 英国 有 总理, 历代有 王。
Xiàndài Yīngguó yǒu zǒnglǐ; lìdài yǒu wáng.
Modern England has a prime minister; in previous times it had a king.

Helpful tips: The first two strokes are separate.								**4 strokes**
历	一	厂	厉	历				

史   shǐ

history

Radical: 口 # 50 "mouth"

Compounds, sentences, and meanings

1. 历史 **lìshǐ** history

    知道自己 国家的 历史很 重要 的。

    Zhīdào zìjǐ guójiā de lìshǐ hěn zhòngyào de.

    Understanding your own country's history is very important.

2. 史册 **shǐcè** a history, annals

    历史家 写 新 的 史册。

    Lìshǐ jiā xiě xīn de shǐcè.

    Great historians write new histories.

3. 史书 **shǐshū** a history, historical writing

    人 喜欢 在 史书里 看到 自己的 名字。

    Rén xǐhuan zài shǐshū lǐ kàndào zìjǐ de míngzi.

    People enjoy reading their own names in history books.

4. 史前 **shǐqián** prehistoric

    考古学者 研究 史前 社会。

    Kǎogǔxuézhě yánjiū shǐqián shèhuì.

    Archaeologists research prehistoric societies.

5. 史无前例 **shǐwúqiánlì** without precedent

    年轻 人 觉得自己的问题 都

    Niánqīng rén juéde zìjǐ de wèntí dōu

    史无前例 的。

    shǐwúqiánlì de.

    Young people feel their problems are all without precedent.

Helpful tips: End the last stroke firmly.   **5 strokes**

史	丿¹	𩂋²	口³	史⁴	史⁵						

数

shù

number, mathematics

數

Radical: 攵 # 99 "tap"

Compounds, sentences, and meanings

5. 数 shù a few, several

我们 只 有 数 分钟 可以 等待。

Wǒmen zhǐ yǒu shù fēnzhōng kěyǐ děngdài.

We only have a few moments that we can wait.

2. 数字 shùzì number

对 华人 来 说,"八" 是 很 吉利 的 数字。

Duì Huárén lái shuō, "bā" shì hēn jílì de shùzì.

For Chinese people, "8" is a very fortuitous number.

3. 数量 shùliàng amount, quantity

在 美国 城市 里 汽车 数量 很大。

Zài Měiguó chéngshì lǐ qìchē shùliàng hěndà.

In American cities the number of cars is very large.

4. 数学 shùxué mathematics

每 个 人 应该 会 数学 的 根本。

Měi ge rén yīnggāi huì shùxué de gēnběn.

Everyone should understand mathematic fundamentals.

5. 数词 shùcí numeral

天文学者 一定 要 会 用 天文 数词。

Tiānwénxuézhě yídìng yào huì yòng tiānwén shùcí.

Astronomers are certainly able to utilize astronomical numbers.

Helpful tips: The two left components are evenly spaced.											**13 strokes**
数	丶1	丷2	兰3	半4	米5	米6	娄7	娄8	娄9	数10	数11	数12
数13											

153

科

kē

science, technology

Radical: 禾 # 124 "grain"

Compounds, sentences, and meanings

1. 科学 **kēxué** science

有 时候 人 觉得 科学 可能 解释 很
Yǒu shíhou rén juéde kēxué kěnéng jiěshì hěn
难 的问题。
nán de wèntí.

There are times people feel that science can solve difficult problems.

2. 科研 **kēyàn** scientific research

在 学院 每个 人 做 科研。
Zài xuéyuàn měi ge rén zuò kēyán.

At an institute everyone engages in scientific research.

3. 文科 **wénkē** liberal arts

大学 有 文科部。
Dàxué yǒu wénkēbù.

Colleges have liberal arts divisions.

4. 理科 **lǐkē** natural sciences

理科是 生物学, 动物学, 生态学,
Lǐkē shì shēngwùxué, dòngwùxué, shēngtàixué,
等等。
děngděng.

Natural sciences are biology, zoology, ecology, etc.

5. 科目 **kēmù** subject of study, branch of study

你有 什么 想法, 什么 科目 最 重要?
Nǐ yǒu shénme xiǎngfǎ, shénme kēmù zuì zhòngyào?

What is your opinion, what subject is most important?

6. 科技 **kējì** technology

在科技 学院 老师 研究 新 的 电脑
Zài kējì xuéyuàn lǎoshī yánjiū xīn de diànnǎo
技术。
jìshù.

At technology institutes teachers research new computer technology.

Helpful tips: End the last vertical stroke firmly.

9 strokes

A. Word Completion

For each empty box, please write a character that creates an effective two-character word.

B. Sentence Completion and Translation

Each of the following sentences is missing a word introduced in the current section. Please supply the missing term to complete the sentence. Then, provide a translation into English for the finished sentence.

1. 我的妹妹喜欢_____数学课。

_____

2. 我们一起_____说中文。

_____

3. 你的母亲是_____, 她也上课。

_____

4. 科学课的_____很难吗?

_____

5. 你跟谁_____汉语生词?

_____

C. Short Description of Examples

For the following general situation there are several component features that can each be described. Please consider the following case and create a specific example or description for each of the components that feature in it. When possible, express connections between the different components to show how each can contribute to the general situation.

想一想很好的历史课，有什么特点？

1.（老师）_____

_____

_____

2.（学生）_____

_____

_____

3.（上课）_____

_____

_____

4.（练习）_____

_____

_____

5.（考试）_____

_____

_____

CHARACTER 129

春 chūn

spring

Radical: 日 # 90 "sun"

Compounds, sentences, and meanings

1. 春 **chūn** spring

   这里的 气候四季如春。

   Zhèlǐ de qìhòu sìjì rú chūn.

   The climate here is like spring all year round.

2. 春天 **chūntiān** spring

   北京 春天 还很 冷。

   Běijīng chūntiān hái hěn lěng.

   Spring is still quite cold in Beijing.

3. 春节 **Chūnjié** Chinese New Year or Spring Festival

   在 中国 过 春节 很 热闹。

   Zài Zhōngguó guò Chūnjié hěn rè'nào.

   Chinese New Year in China is very lively.

4. 春风 **chūnfēng** spring breeze

   他 今天 春风 满面 的, 不知

   Tā jīntiān chūnfēng mǎnmiàn de, bù zhī

   是 为什么。

   shì wèishénme.

   His face is beaming with satisfaction. I wonder what happened.

5. 春药 **chūnyào** aphrodisiac

   有人 说 吃 春药 对身体 有害。

   Yǒu rén shuō chī chūnyào duì shēntǐ yǒuhài.

   People say that taking aphrodisiacs is harmful to health.

Helpful tips: The third horizontal stroke is longer than those above it. **9 strokes**

春 一 二 三 𡗗 夫 表 春 春 春

夏

xià

summer

Radical: 夂 # 57 "top of 冬"

Compounds, sentences, and meanings

1. 夏 **xià** summer

   这 种 树 冬 夏 常 青。

   Zhè zhǒng shù dōng xià cháng qīng.

   This type of tree is evergreen. (Literally, winter summer always green)

2. 夏令时 **xiàlìngshí** daylight-saving

   明天 晚上 要 调 夏令时。

   Míngtiān wǎnshang yào tiáo xiàlìngshí.

   Adjust the clock for daylight-saving time tomorrow night.

3. 夏天 **xiàtiān** summer

   北京 的 夏天 比较 热。

   Běijīng de xiàtiān bǐjiào rè.

   Summer in Beijing is quite hot.

4. 夏令营 **xiàlìngyíng** summer camp

   这 个 暑假 我 参加了 夏令营。

   Zhè ge shǔjià wǒ cānjiāle xiàlìngyíng.

   This summer vacation I went to a summer camp.

5. 夏装 **xiàzhuāng** summer fashion

   今年 的 夏装 很 好看。

   Jīnnián de xiàzhuāng hěn hǎokàn.

   The summer fashions this year are pretty.

Helpful tips: Note the difference between 夂 and 又.									**10 strokes**	

秋 qiū

autumn

Radical: 禾 # 124 "grain"

Compounds, sentences, and meanings

1. 秋 qiū autumn

   二零零一年 秋, 美国 遭到 恐怖
   Èrlínglíngyīnián qiū, Měiguó zāodào kǒngbù

   份子攻击。
   fènzi gōngjī.

   In the autumn of 2001, the United States was attacked by terrorists.

2. 秋季 qiūjì autumn

   广州 每年 秋季有 一个 交易会。
   Guǎngzhōu měinián qiūjì yǒu yí ge jiāoyìhuì.

   There is a trade fair in Guangzhou every autumn.

3. 秋色 qiūsè autumn scenery

   这里 秋色宜人。
   Zhèlǐ qiūsè yírén.

   The autumn scenery here is delightful.

4. 秋收 qiūshōu autumn harvest

   农民 都 忙着 秋收。
   Nóngmín dōu mángzhe qiūshōu.

   The farmers are all busy with the autumn harvest.

5. 秋天 qiūtiān autumn

   秋天 是 北京 最好 的 季节。
   Qiūtiān shì Běijīng zuìhǎo de jìjié.

   Autumn is the loveliest season in Beijing.

Helpful tips: The last stroke tapers off.										9 strokes

秋　　千　二　千　禾　禾　禾　秋　秋

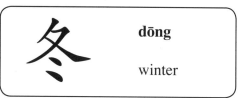

冬 **dōng** winter

Radical: 夂 # 57 "top of 冬"

Compounds, sentences, and meanings

1. 冬 **dōng** winter

   这 种 鸟 在 哪里 过冬?

   Zhè zhǒng niǎo zài nǎli guòdōng?

   Where do these birds go in winter?

2. 冬天 **dōngtiān** winter

   上海 的 冬天 不 下雪。

   Shànghǎi de dōngtiān bú xiàxuě.

   It doesn't snow in Shanghai in winter.

3. 冬季 **dōngjì** winter

   上海 的 冬季 不 下雪。

   Shànghǎi de dōngjì bú xiàxuě.

   It doesn't snow in Shanghai in winter.

4. 冬菇 **dōnggū** dried mushrooms

   我 喜欢 吃 冬菇。

   Wǒ xǐhuan chī dōnggū.

   I like dried mushrooms.

5. 冬装 **dōngzhuāng** winter fashion

   今年 的 冬装 好看极了。

   Jīnnián de dōngzhuāng hǎokànjíle.

   This year's winter fashions are very pretty.

Helpful tips: The last two dots end firmly.											**5 strokes**
冬	⺈	夂	冬	冬	冬						

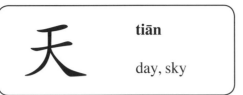

天 **tiān**

day, sky

Radical: 一 # 2 "horizontal stroke" or 大 # 43 "big"

Compounds, sentences, and meanings

1. 天 **tiān** day

   天 不 早 了。

   Tiān bù zǎo le.

   It's getting late.

2. 天才 **tiāncái** genius

   这 孩子 有 音乐 天才。

   Zhè háizi yǒu yīnyuè tiāncái.

   This child has musical talent.

3. 天气 **tiānqì** weather

   今天 天气 真 好。

   Jīntiān tiānqì zhēn hǎo.

   The weather is really good today.

4. 天然 **tiānrán** nature

   我 喜欢 天然 景色。

   Wǒ xǐhuan tiānrán jǐngsè.

   I like natural scenery.

5. 天真 **tiānzhēn** innocent, naive

   你要 相信 这样 的 话, 那就 太

   Nǐ yào xiāngxìn zhèyàng de huà, nà jiù tài

   天真 了。

   tiānzhēn le.

   If you believe that sort of talk, you're really naive.

Helpful tips: The third stroke does not cross the top horizontal stroke.					4 strokes

Traditional Form

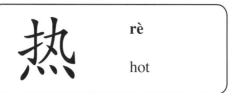

rè

hot

熱

Radical: 灬 # 71 "fire"

Compounds, sentences, and meanings

1. 热 **rè** heat up

   请 把 汤 热一热。

   Qǐng bǎ tāng rèyirè.

   Please heat up the soup.

2. 热带 **rèdài** the tropics

   新加坡 地处 热带。

   Xīnjiāpō dì chǔ rèdài.

   Singapore is situated in the tropics.

3. 热点 **rèdiǎn** hot spot

   那 是个 旅游 热点。

   Nà shì ge lǚyóu rèdiǎn.

   That is a hot spot for tourists.

4. 热情 **rèqíng** enthusiasm

   那个 服务员 对顾客 很 热情。

   Nà ge fúwùyuán duì gùkè hěn rèqíng.

   That waiter is friendly to the customers.

5. ...热 ... **rè** craze, fad

   卡拉OK热 遍及 全 中国。

   Kǎlā'ōukèi-rè biànjí quán Zhōngguó.

   The karaoke craze has spread all over China.

Helpful tips: The first dot goes to the left, the rest go to the right.										**10 strokes**	

热

CHARACTER 135

暖   nuǎn

warm

Radical: 日 # 90 "sun"

Compounds, sentences, and meanings

1. 暖 **nuǎn** warm

    天 暖 了。
    Tiān nuǎn le.
    It's getting warm.

2. 暖呼呼 **nuǎnhūhū** warm

    听了 这 番 话，我们 大家 心里
    Tīngle zhè fān huà, wǒmen dàjiā xīnlǐ
    暖呼呼 的。
    nuǎnhūhū de.
    The words warmed our hearts.

3. 暖和 **nuǎnhuo** nice and warm

    炉子 一 着，屋子 就 暖和 了。
    Lúzi yí zhào, wūzi jiù nuǎnhuo le.
    The room became warm when the fire got going.

4. 暖气 **nuǎnqì** central heating

    北京 不 冷，室内 有 暖气。
    Běijīng bù lěng, shìnèi yǒu nuǎnqì.
    It's not cold in Beijing, there's central heating.

5. 温暖 **wēnnuǎn** warm

    我 喜欢 温暖 的 天气。
    Wǒ xǐhuan wēnnuǎn de tiānqì.
    I like the warm weather.

Helpful tips: There's a horizontal stroke above 友.											13 strokes
暖	丨₁	刀₂	日₃	日₄	日₅	日₆	日₇	日₈	日₉	日₁₀	暖₁₁	暖₁₂
暖₁₃											

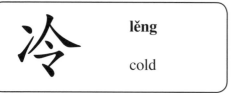

冷

lěng

cold

Radical: 冫 # 7 "ice"

Compounds, sentences, and meanings

1. 冷 **lěng** cold

   今天 真 冷。

   Jīntiān zhēn lěng.

   It's really cold today.

2. 冷静 **lěngjìng** calm (of people)

   请 你 冷静一点儿。

   Qǐng nǐ lěngjìng yìdiǎnr.

   Please calm down.

3. 冷水 **lěngshuǐ** unboiled water

   喝 冷水 容易 得病。

   Hē lěngshuǐ róngyì débìng.

   If you drink unboiled water, you're likely to get sick.

4. 冷落 **lěngluò** treat coldly

   不要 冷落了 客人。

   Búyào lěngluòle kèren.

   Don't leave the guest out in the cold.

5. 冷冰冰 **lěngbīngbīng** cold in manner

   他 对人 冷冰冰 的。

   Tā duì rén lěngbīngbīng de.

   He has a cold manner.

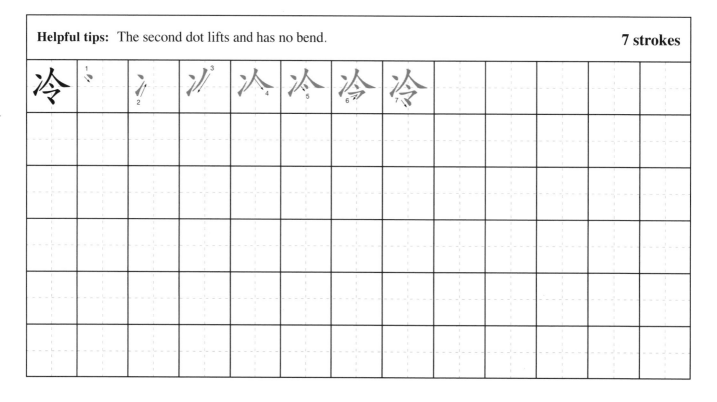

Helpful tips: The second dot lifts and has no bend.　　　　　**7 strokes**

凉

liáng

cool

Radical: 冫 # 7 "ice"

Compounds, sentences, and meanings

1. 凉 **liáng** cool, cold

   天气 忽然 凉 了。

   Tiānqì hūrán liáng le.

   The weather has suddenly turned cold.

2. 凉拌 **liángbàn** (of food) cold and dressed with sauce

   我 喜欢 吃 凉拌面。

   Wǒ xǐhuan chī liángbànmiàn.

   I like cold noodles in sauce.

3. 凉爽 **liángshuǎng** nice and cool

   我 喜欢 凉爽 的 秋天。

   Wǒ xǐhuan liángshuǎng de qiūtiān.

   I like the brisk autumn days.

4. 凉快 **liángkuài** pleasantly cool

   这里 凉快， 坐下来 歇 会儿。

   Zhèlǐ liángkuài, zuòxiàlai xiē huìr.

   It's nice and cool here, let's sit down and have a rest.

5. 凉鞋 **liángxié** sandals

   这 双 凉鞋 很 好看。

   Zhè shuāng liángxié hěn hǎokàn.

   This pair of sandals is very attractive.

Helpful tips: The second stroke of 冫 is a rounded dot that lifts.									**10 strokes**

凉 | 冫 | 冫 | 氵 | 亠 | 亠 | 冫 | 亠 | 凉 | 凉 | 凉

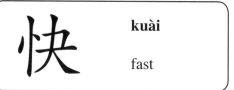

快   kuài

fast

Radical: 忄 # 33 "upright heart"

Compounds, sentences, and meanings

1. 快 **kuài** fast

飞机比火车 快 得多。

Fēijī bǐ huǒchē kuài de duō.

It's much faster to fly than to go by train.

2. 快餐 **kuàicān** fast food

我 喜欢 吃 快餐。

Wǒ xǐhuan chī kuàicān.

I like fast food.

3. 快活 **kuàihuó** merry

孩子们 快活地 打 雪仗。

Háizimen kuàihuóde dǎ xuězhàng.

The children were enjoying a snowball fight.

4. 快乐 **kuàilè** happy

节日过得 很 快乐。

Jiérì guòde hěn kuàilè.

The festival was most enjoyable.

5. 快慢 **kuàimàn** speed

这些 按钮 是 管 快慢 的。

Zhèxiē ànniǔ shì guǎn kuàimàn de.

These buttons control the speed.

Helpful tips: The second horizontal stroke is longer.										**7 strokes**
快	丿	忄	忄	忄コ	忄コ	快	快			

A. Vocabulary Matching

Please write each of the following adjective descriptions in the box with the appropriate season. Each description may apply to more than one season.

春天

夏天

很好

很热

不热

很冷

不冷

很暖

凉快

秋天

冬天

B. Reading Comprehension

Please read the following description of a group of friends. Then answer the question provided in English based on the information in the passage. For each person shown below, write the name of the person underneath his or her picture.

我的朋友们都不一样。他们都有自己喜欢的事情，自己喜欢的运动。我有四个朋友喜欢不一样的天气。我的老朋友，王光仁，喜欢非常冷的天气。他喜欢下雪，喜欢穿很多很多衣服。可是我的朋友郑慧完全不喜欢冷的天气。她喜欢去公园踢球。她很喜欢夏天。我也有两个朋友喜欢凉快的天气。他们喜欢天气不冷也不热。吴东梅喜欢春天，喜欢看花。周正义喜欢秋天，他喜欢上课。这些人是我的好朋友，每个人都不一样。

1. What are the names of the speaker's friends?

_____

2. Which friend enjoys hot weather?

_____

3. Why does she enjoy summer weather?

_____

4. Which friend enjoys cold weather?

_____

5. Who enjoys the weather in the spring and the fall?

_____

6. Why do they enjoy weather during those times?

_____

C. Short Description of Examples

For the following general situation there are several component features that can each be described. Please consider the following case and create a specific example or description for each of the components that feature in it. When possible, express connections between the different components to show how each can contribute to the general situation.

你喜欢做什么? 天气和运动有什么关系？ 在这些时候你要做什么?

1.（春天）_____

_____

_____

2.（夏天）_____

_____

_____

3.（秋天）_____

_____

_____

4.（冬天）_____

_____

_____

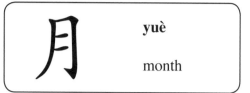

月 yuè

month

Radical: 月 # 103 "moon/flesh"

Compounds, sentences, and meanings

1. 月 **yuè** month

   我的 月 收入 是 五 千 元。

   Wǒde yuè shōurù shì wǔ qiān yuán.

   My monthly income is ¥5000.

2. 这个月 **zhè ge yuè** this month

   这 个 月 我 比较 忙。

   Zhè ge yuè wǒ bǐjiào máng.

   I'm quite busy this month.

3. 上个月 **shàng ge yuè** last month

   我们 上 个 月 去 旅行 了。

   Wǒmen shàng ge yuè qù lǚxíng le.

   We went for a holiday last month.

4. 下个月 **xià ge yuè** next month

   我们 下个月 就 放假 了。

   Wǒmen xià ge yuè jiù fàngjià le.

   We'll be on holiday next month.

5. 月亮 **yuèliang** moon

   今晚 的 月亮 很 圆。

   Jīnwǎn de yuèliang hěn yuán.

   The moon is round tonight.

Helpful tips: The second stroke ends with a hook.											**4 strokes**
月	丿	月	月	月							

星 xīng

star

Radical: 日 # 90 "sun"

Compounds, sentences, and meanings

1. 星 **xīng** star

   今晚 月 明 星 稀。

   Jīnwǎn yuè míng xīng xī.

   The moon is bright and the stars are sparse tonight.

2. 星期 **xīngqī** week

   今天 星期几?

   Jīntiān xīngqījǐ?

   What day of the week is it today?

3. 这个星期 **zhè ge xīngqī** this week

   这 个 星期 工作 比较 轻松。

   Zhè ge xīngqī gōngzuò bǐjiào qīngsōng.

   The workload is easy this week.

4. 上星期 **shàng xīngqī** last week

   上 星期 我 度假 去了。

   Shàng xīngqī wǒ dùjià qù le.

   Last week I was on holiday.

5. 下星期 **xià xīngqī** next week

   下 星期 我 比较 忙。

   Xià xīngqī wǒ bǐjiào máng.

   I'll be rather busy next week.

Helpful tips: The "sun" component 日 should be written squarish.									**9 strokes**		
星											

期

qī

period of time

Radical: 月 # 103 "moon/flesh" or 其 # 171 "secondly"

Compounds, sentences, and meanings

1. 期 **qī** period

   第一期 工程 已经 完成 了。
   Dìyī qī gōngchéng yǐjīng wánchéng le.
   The first phase of the project has been completed.

2. 期间 **qījiān** course

   他 在 住院 期间 看了 很多 小说。
   Tā zài zhùyuàn qījiān kànle hěnduō xiǎoshuō.
   While in the hospital, he read many novels.

3. 假期 **jiàqī** holiday

   假期你有 什么 计划?
   Jiàqī nǐ yǒu shénme jìhuà?
   What plans do you have for your holidays?

4. 学期 **xuéqī** semester

   这 个 学期 功课 比较 轻松。
   Zhè ge xuéqī gōngkè bǐjiào qīngsōng.
   There's not much work this semester.

5. 到期 **dàoqī** expire

   我的 签证 下个 月 到期。
   Wǒde qiānzhèng xià ge yuè dàoqī.
   My visa expires next month.

Helpful tips: The tenth stroke ends with a hook.　　　　　**12 strokes**

期	一	十	卄	甘	甘	其	其	其	朞	期	期	期

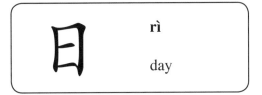

Radical: 日 # 90 "sun"

Compounds, sentences, and meanings

1. 日 **rì** day

   十月 二十五日 是我的 生日。

   Shíyuè-èrshíwǔrì shì wǒde shēngrì.

   October 25th is my birthday.

2. 日期 **rìqī** date

   你 忘了 填上 你的 出生 日期。

   Nǐ wàngle tiánshàng nǐde chūshēng rìqī.

   You forgot to fill in your date of birth.

3. 日记 **rìjì** diary

   我 没有 记日记的 习惯。

   Wǒ méiyǒu jì rìjì de xíguàn.

   I don't have a habit of keeping a diary.

4. 日常 **rìcháng** daily

   这些 都 是 日常 必须用 的 东西。

   Zhèxiē dōu shì rìcháng bìxū yòng de dōngxi.

   These are all the daily needs.

5. 日本 **Rìběn** Japan (literally, rising sun)

   你 去过 日本 没有？

   Nǐ qùguo Rìběn méiyǒu?

   Have you been to Japan?

Helpful tips: The sealing stroke is written last.											**4 strokes**
日	丨	冂	日	日							

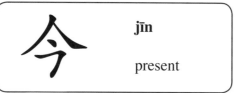

今 **jīn**

present

Radical: 人 # 18 "person"

Compounds, sentences, and meanings

1. 今 **jīn** now, the present

   他 说 从 今 以后 要 认真 学习。

   Tā shuō cóng jīn yǐhòu yào rènzhēn xuéxí.

   He said he will study conscientiously from now on.

2. 今天 **jīntiān** today

   今天 会 下雨 吗?

   Jīntiān huì xiàyǔ ma?

   Will it rain today?

3. 今晚 **jīnwǎn** tonight

   我 今晚 不在家。

   Wǒ jīnwǎn bú zài jiā.

   I won't be home tonight.

4. 今年 **jīnnián** this year

   我 今年 刚 开始 学 中文。

   Wǒ jīnnián gāng kāishǐ xué Zhōngwén.

   I just started learning Chinese this year.

5. 今后 **jīnhòu** from now on

   希望 我们 今后 能 多 交流 经验。

   Xīwàng wǒmen jīnhòu néng duō jiāoliú jīngyàn.

   I hope we can have more exchange of experiences from now on.

Helpful tips: 今 is easily confused with 令.											**4 strokes**

明   **míng**

bright

Radical: 日 # 90 "day"

Compounds, sentences, and meanings

1. 明 **míng** bright, clear

你 有 没有 问明 他的来意？

Nǐ yǒu méiyǒu wènmíng tāde láiyì?

Have you specifically asked him his reasons for coming?

2. 明知 **míngzhī** know perfectly well

你 明知 他不 高兴， 为什么 还

Nǐ míngzhī tā bù gāoxìng, wèishénme hài

要 说？

yào shuō?

You know quite well that he won't be happy to hear this, so why do you still say it?

3. 明白 **míngbai** understand

我 不 明白 你的意思。

Wǒ bù míngbai nǐde yìsi.

I don't understand what you mean.

4. 明天 **míngtiān** tomorrow

对不起 我 明天 没有 空儿。

Duìbuqǐ, wǒ míngtiān méiyǒu kòngr.

Sorry, I'll be busy tomorrow.

5. 明显 **míngxiǎn** obvious

这 很 明显 是一个 借口。

Zhè hěn míngxiǎn shì yí ge jièkǒu.

This is evidently a pretext.

Helpful tips: The sixth stroke ends with a hook.									8 strokes
明	丨	刀	日	日	明	明	明	明	

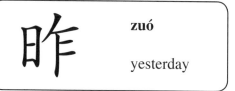

昨   **zuó**

yesterday

Radical: 日 # 90 "sun"

Compounds, sentences, and meanings

1. 昨天 **zuótiān** yesterday

   他 昨天 才 来过。

   Tā zuótiān cái láiguo.

   He came only yesterday.

2. 昨天的 **zuótiān de** yesterday's

   这 是 昨天的 报。

   Zhè shì zuótiān de bào.

   This is yesterday's newspaper.

3. 昨日 **zuórì** yesterday

   他 昨日 才 来过。

   Tā zuórì cái láiguo.

   He came only yesterday.

4. 昨晚 **zuówǎn** last night

   昨晚 雨下得 很 大, 你 知道 吗?

   Zuówǎn yǔ xiàde hěn dà, nǐ zhīdao ma?

   It rained heavily last night, did you know?

5. 昨夜 **zuóyè** last night

   昨夜 雨下得 很 大, 你 知道 吗?

   Zuóyè yǔ xiàde hěn dà, nǐ zhīdao ma?

   It rained heavily last night, did you know?

Helpful tips: The top horizontal stroke is longer than those below it.											**9 strokes**

昨

年   nián

year

Radical: 丿 # 4 "downward-left stroke"

Compounds, sentences, and meanings

1. 年 **nián** year

   你 是 哪 年 去 美国 的?

   Nǐ shì nǎ nián qù Měiguó de?

   Which year did you go to America?

2. 去年 **qùnián** last year

   我 是 去年 开始 学 跳舞 的。

   Wǒ shì qùnián kāishǐ xué tiàowǔ de.

   I started learning to dance last year.

3. 年纪 **niánjì** age

   你 多 大 年纪 了?

   Nǐ duō dà niánjì le?

   How old are you?

4. 年轻 **niánqīng** young

   这 位 教授 看起来 很 年轻。

   Zhè wèi jiàoshòu kànqilai hěn niánqīng.

   This professor looks quite young.

5. 拜年 **bàinián** pay a New Year visit

   去 朋友 家 拜年 最好 别 忘了

   Qù péngyou jiā bàinián zuìhǎo bié wàngle

   带 礼物。

   dài lǐwù.

   When paying New Year visits to friends, don't forget to bring along some gifts.

Helpful tips: The lowest horizontal stroke is the longest.						6 strokes

guā

(of the wind) blow

颳

Radical: 刂 # 15 "upright knife"

Compounds, sentences, and meanings

1. 刮 **guā** blow (of the wind)

   刮 大 风 了。

   Guā dà fēng le.

   There's a gale blowing.

2. 刮破 **guāpò** scratched

   就 刮破 一点 皮。

   Jiù guāpò yìdiǎn pí.

   It's only a scratch.

3. 刮脸 **guāliǎn** shave

   我 天天 早上 刮脸。

   Wǒ tiāntiān zǎoshang guāliǎn.

   I shave every morning.

4. 刮脸刀 **guāliǎndāo** razor

   我 要 买 刮脸刀。

   Wǒ yào mǎi guāliǎndāo.

   I need to buy some razor blades.

5. 刮目相看 **guā mù xiāng kàn** look at someone with new eyes

   她 从 美国 回来 以后, 大家 都

   Tā cóng Měiguó huílai yǐhòu, dàjiā dōu

   刮 目 相 看。

   guā mù xiāng kàn.

   Everyone treats her with increased respect since her return from the United States.

Helpful tips: The first stroke sweeps from right to left.   **8 strokes**

刮	╱¹	二²	千³	千⁴	舌⁵	舌⁶	刮⁷	刮⁸					

风 **fēng**

wind

風

Radical: 风 # 105 "wind"

Compounds, sentences, and meanings

1. 风 **fēng** wind

今天 很 大 风。

Jīntiān hěn dà fēng.

Today is very windy.

2. 风口 **fēngkǒu** a drafty place

别 站 在 风口 上, 小心 着凉。

Bié zhàn zài fēngkǒu shàng, xiǎoxīn zháoliáng.

Don't stand in the draft. You may catch a cold.

3. 风趣 **fēngqù** humor, wit

他 是一个 很 有 风趣 的 人。

Tā shì yí ge hěn yǒu fēngqù de rén.

He is a man of charm and wit.

4. 风俗 **fēngsú** custom

中国 很大, 各地风俗 不同。

Zhōngguó hěn dà, gèdì fēngsú bùtóng.

China is very big: different places have different customs.

5. 风味 **fēngwèi** special flavor

这是 广东 风味菜。

Zhè shì Guǎngdōng fēngwèicài.

This is a typical Cantonese dish.

Helpful tips: The second stroke ends with a hook.											**4 strokes**
风	丿	凡	风	风							

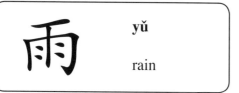

雨　　yǔ

　　rain

Radical: 雨 # 172 "rain"

Compounds, sentences, and meanings

1. 雨 **yǔ** rain

   天气 预报 说 今天 有 雨。

   Tiānqì yùbào shuō jīntiān yǒu yǔ.

   Rain is forecast today.

2. 阵雨 **zhènyǔ** showers

   今天 下午 有 阵雨。

   Jīntiān xiàwǔ yǒu zhènyǔ.

   There'll be showers this afternoon.

3. 下雨 **xiàyǔ** rain

   天气 预报 说 今天 下雨。

   Tiānqì yùbào shuō jīntiān xiàyǔ.

   Rain is forecast today.

4. 雨季 **yǔjì** rainy season

   五, 六月 是 上海 的雨季。

   Wǔ, Liùyuè shì Shànghǎi de yǔjì.

   The time around May and June is the rainy season in Shanghai.

5. 雨伞 **yǔsǎn** umbrella

   我 忘了 带 雨伞。

   Wǒ wàngle dài yǔsǎn.

   I forgot to bring my umbrella.

Helpful tips: The dots come down firmly to the right.　　　　**8 strokes**

雨	一	一	雨	雨	雨	雨	雨	雨			

雪

xuě

snow

Radical: 雨 # 172 "rain"

Compounds, sentences, and meanings

1. 雪 **xuě** snow

   在 北区　冬天　　常常　　下雪。

   Zài běiqū dōngtiān chángcháng xiàxuě.

   In Northern areas during winter it often snows.

2. 雪花 **xuěhuā** snowflake

   每 个 雪花　都 不 一样。

   Měi ge xuěhuā dōu bù yíyàng.

   Every snowflake is not the same.

3. 雪球 **xuěqiú** snowball

   小　孩子 喜欢　投 雪球。

   Xiǎo háizi xǐhuan tóu xuěqiú.

   Children enjoy throwing snowballs.

4. 雪白 **xuěbái** snow-white

   她 雪白 的　服装　真　漂亮。

   Tā xuěbái de fúzhuāng zhēn piàoliang.

   Her snow-white dress is very pretty.

5. 雪亮 **xuěliàng** bright and sparkling

   那个　金环 太　漂亮　了，非常　雪亮。

   Nà ge jīnhuán tài piàoliang le, fēicháng xuěliàng.

   That gold ring is really pretty, it's very sparkly.

Helpful tips: The fourth stroke is the vertical stroke at the top.										**11 strokes**
雪	一	广	币	帀	帀	需	雪	雷	雪	雪

Lesson 14: Review Activities

A. Pronunciation and *Pinyin* Practice

Please supply the appropriate description of the weather for each of the following illustrations. Write the description in Chinese characters. Then write the phrase in *pinyin*.

_____   _____   _____   _____

_____   _____   _____   _____

B. Reading Comprehension

Please read the following description of the weather for five continuous days. Notice that the starting day (今天) is at the center of the chart. Then demonstrate understanding by illustrating the weather as described for each of the days.

星期三	星期四	星期五（今天）	星期六	星期天

今天的天气不太好。我们都希望星期五有很好的天气，可是今天下雨了。天气不太冷但是下雨的时候我们不可能做运动。明天听说天气比较好。天气不下雨，天气也不热。可是，星期天会很热。天气非常非常热的时候我不喜欢去外边。昨天天气也下雨了。但是昨天我不关心什么天气，我要看书。星期三天气不错，不下雨也不热。我看球赛很好玩儿。

C. Questions and Responses

Please answer the following questions based on your personal opinion and information. Then create a question in response that connects to the original question. This should result in a sequence of related questions and answers as might occur in a conversation.

1. 你喜不喜欢今天的天气?

   (回答) _____

   (问题) _____

2. 下雪的时候, 你喜欢做什么?

   (回答) _____

   (问题) _____

3. 明天你要做什么?

   (回答) _____

   (问题) _____

4. 这个星期天, 如果天气很好, 你做什么?

   (回答) _____

   (问题) _____

5. 明年春天你要去什么地方?

   (回答) _____

   (问题) _____

Section 3 Review (Lessons 11–14)

A. Verb Object Matching

Please match an object to each of the following verbs. Then, in the space provided, write a complete sentence demonstrating context for the verb-object relationship.

1. 上 _____ 2. 下 _____ 3. 看 _____ 4. 吃 _____

5. 学习 _____ 6. 练习 _____ 7. 要 _____ 8. 喜欢 _____

1. _____

2. _____

3. _____

4. _____

5. _____

6. _____

7. _____

8. _____

B. Describing an Image

Please describe the illustration below. Pay attention to as much of the context in the illustration as possible; also remember to indicate what happened before this scene and what may happen after this scene. A strong demonstration of understanding would indicate the different characters and relationships between events and activities.

_____

_____

_____

_____

_____

_____

C. Describing a Day

Please utilize the space provided to fully describe the topic below. This free writing exercise should demonstrate the range of expression possible about a known topic. Attempt to explore the topic with vocabulary and construction that show both an ability to speak on it with depth and the awareness of the cultural concerns that surround the topic.

今天星期五，是下雨天。你喜欢做什么，你要做什么？ 下雨的时候好不好，觉得高不高兴？

_____

_____

_____

_____

_____

_____

_____

D. Reflective Questions

Use these questions to both check the expressiveness of the previous section and to confirm your understanding of the previous topic. For additional practice, say and then respond to these questions aloud.

你喜欢星期五吗？

星期五你常常做什么？

星期五你有没有课？

下雨的时候你高不高兴？

下雨的时候，你喜欢去散步还是留在家里？

你喜欢什么天气？

什么季节有那样的天气？

对你来说，天气能不能影响人的感觉？

如果天气让我们感觉特别坏，我们就应该做什么？

你希望住在什么地方，为什么？

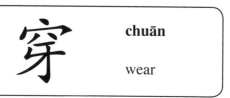

穿

chuān

wear

Radical: 穴 # 110 "cave"

Compounds, sentences, and meanings

1. 穿 **chuān** wear

   穿得 这么 少, 不 冷 吗?

   Chuānde zhème shǎo, bù lěng ma?

   Aren't you cold with so little on?

2. 穿不住 **chuānbuzhù** cannot go on wearing

   天 热了, 毛衣 穿不住 了。

   Tiān rè le, máoyī chuānbuzhù le.

   It's too warm to wear woolen sweaters now.

3. 穿过 **chuān'guò** go across or through

   我们 从 操场 穿 过 去 吧。

   Wǒmen cóng cāochǎng chuān'guò qù ba.

   Let's cut across the sports field.

4. 穿越 **chuānyuè** pass through

   这 条 铁路 穿越 国境。

   Zhe tiáo tiělù chuānyuè guójǐng.

   This railroad goes across the border.

5. 穿着 **chuānzhuó** apparel, dress

   他 不 讲究 穿着。

   Tā bù jiǎngjiu chuānzhuó.

   He is not particular about what he wears.

Helpful tips: The last stroke sweeps down from right to left.										**9 strokes**
穿	丶	⺊	穴	宀	穴	空	空	穷	穿		

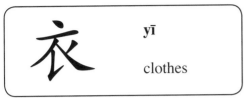

衣 yī

clothes

Radical: 衣 # 132 "clothes"

Compounds, sentences, and meanings

1. 衣 **yī** clothing

   老百姓 最 关心 的 是 衣食住行。

   Lǎobǎixìng zuì guānxīn de shì yī-shí-zhù-xíng.

   Ordinary people are mainly concerned with clothing, food, shelter and transportation—the basic necessities of life.

2. 毛衣 **máoyī** woolen sweater

   今天 比较 冷, 要 穿 毛衣。

   Jīntiān bǐjiào lěng, yào chuān máoyī.

   Today is quite cold, you need to wear a sweater.

3. 衣服 **yīfu** clothes

   外边 冷, 多 穿 些衣服。

   Wàibiān lěng, duō chuān xiē yīfu.

   It's cold outside. Put on more clothes.

4. 衣料 **yīliào** material for clothing

   这 种 衣料适合 做 裙子。

   Zhè zhǒng yīliào shìhé zuò qúnzi.

   This type of material is suitable for making skirts.

5. 衣架 **yījià** coat hanger

   这里 有 没有 衣架?

   Zhèlǐ yǒu méiyǒu yījià?

   Are there any clothes hangers here?

Helpful tips: The last stroke tapers off.											**6 strokes**
衣	丶	二	广	产	产	衣					

服　**fú**

clothes; service

Radical: 月 # 103 "moon/flesh"

Compounds, sentences, and meanings

1. 服 **fú** be convinced

   你 说得 有道理, 我服了。

   Nǐ shuōde yǒu dàoli, wǒ fú le.

   What you've said makes sense. I'm convinced.

2. 服从 **fúcóng** be subordinated to

   少数 服从 多数。

   Shǎoshù fúcóng duōshù.

   The minority should give way to the majority.

3. 服软 **fúruǎn** yield to persuasion

   他 服软 不服硬。

   Tā fúruǎn bù fúyìng.

   He yields to persuasion but not to coercion.

4. 服务 **fúwù** give service to

   这个 饭店 的服务 非常 好。

   Zhè ge fàndiàn de fúwù fēicháng hǎo.

   The service at the hotel is very good.

5. 服装店 **fúzhuāngdiàn** boutique

   这家 服装店 的衣服很 时髦。

   Zhè jiā fúzhuāngdiàn de yīfu hěn shímáo.

   The clothes in this boutique are very fashionable.

Helpful tips: The fifth stroke ends with a hook.											**8 strokes**
服	刀	月	月	月	月	肌	朋	服			

裤　**kù**

pants, trousers

褲

Radical: 衤 # 113 "clothing"

Compounds, sentences, and meanings

1. 裤子 **kùzi** pants

   上班 的 时候 人 要 穿 裤子。

   Shàngbān de shíhou rén yào chuān kùzi.

   At work people want to wear pants.

2. 短裤 **duǎnkù** shorts

   天气 很热 的 时候 人 喜欢 穿

   Tiānqì hěn rè de shíhou rén xǐhuan chuān

   短裤。

   duǎnkù.

   When the weather is hot people enjoy wearing shorts.

3. 牛仔裤 **niúzǎikù** blue jeans, cowboy jeans

   牛仔裤 是 美国 特别的衣服。

   Niúzǎikù shì Měiguó tèbié de yīfu.

   Blue jeans are America's special clothes.

Helpful tips: Each horizontal stroke is evenly spaced.											**12 strokes**
裤	丶	﹁	礻	礻	礻	礻	裢	裢	裤	裤	裤

裙　　qún

skirt

Radical: 衤 # 113 "clothing"

Compounds, sentences, and meanings

1. 裙子 **qúnzi** skirt

   裙子 是一 种　女性化 的衣服。

   Qúnzi shì yì zhǒng nǔxìnghuà de yīfu.

   Skirts are a type of feminine clothing.

2. 围裙 **wéiqún** apron

   做 饭的 时候，厨师　穿　围裙。

   Zuò fàn de shíhou, chúshī chuān wéiqún.

   When cooking, a chef wears an apron.

Helpful tips: The last stroke goes from left to right.											**12 strokes**

裙　丶　亍　衤　衤　衤　衤　裙　裙　裙　裙　裙

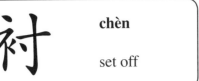

衬　chèn

set off

襯

Radical: 衤 # 113 "clothing"

Compounds, sentences, and meanings

1. 衬 chèn place something underneath

   你 说 红色 衬 不 衬 黑色?

   Nǐ shuō hóngsè chèn bu chèn hēisè?

   Do you think red and black go well together?

2. 衬裙 chènqún petticoat

   这 种 裙子要 穿 衬裙。

   Zhè zhǒng qúnzi yào chuān chènqún.

   This type of skirt needs a petticoat.

3. 衬衫 chènshān shirt

   这 是 女装 衬衫。

   Zhè shì nǚzhuāng chènshān.

   This is a blouse.

4. 衬托 chèntuō set off

   红花 要 有绿叶 衬托。

   Hónghuā yào yǒu lǜyè chèntuō.

   Red flowers should be set off by green leaves.

5. 衬衣 chènyī shirt

   这 是 女装 衬衣。

   Zhè shì nǚzhuāng chènyī.

   This is a blouse.

Helpful tips: Note the component 衤. It has two dots on the right side.　　　　**8 strokes**

衬	丶	冫	衤	衤	衤	衤	衬	衬			

装 zhuāng

clothing, dress, outfit

裝

Radical: 衣 # 132 "clothes"

Compounds, sentences, and meanings

1. 服装 **fúzhuāng** dress, costume

面试 的 时候 服装 很 重要。

Miànshì de shíhou fúzhuāng hěn zhòngyào.

When in an interview, one's dress is very important.

2. 装备 **zhuāngbèi** equipment

厨房 有 很 多 装备。

Chúfáng yǒu hěn duō zhuāngbèi.

A kitchen has a good deal of equipment.

3. 洋装 **yángzhuāng** dress, gown

她 穿 一件 红色的 洋装。

Tā chuān yíjiàn hóngse de yángzhuāng.

She is wearing a red dress.

4. 西装 **xīzhuāng** suit

西装 是 欧洲 商人 特色的衣服。

Xīzhuāng shì Ōuzhōu shāngrén tèsè de yīfu.

Suits are European businesspeople's special clothes.

5. 装饰 **zhuāngshì** decoration

你 房间 的 装饰 很 好看。

Nǐ fángjiān de zhuāngshì hěn hǎokàn.

The decoration of your room is very nice.

6. 装配 **zhuāngpèi** to assemble

孩子 生日 以前 父母 装配 自行车

Háizi shēngrì yǐqián fùmǔ zhuāngpèi zìxíngchē

要 给 孩子。

yào gěi háizi.

Before a child's birthday, the parents assemble a bicycle to give to their child.

Helpful tips: The top and bottom of the character should be balanced. **12 strokes**

鞋　xié

shoe

Radical: 革 # 179 "leather"

Compounds, sentences, and meanings

1. 鞋 **xié** shoe

   请 稍 等, 我把鞋 穿上。

   Qǐng shāo děng, wǒ bǎ xié chuānshang.

   Please wait while I put my shoes on.

2. 鞋带 **xiédài** shoelace

   请 稍 等, 我把 鞋带 绑好。

   Qǐng shāo děng, wǒ bǎ xiédài bǎnghǎo.

   Please wait while I tie my shoelaces.

3. 鞋匠 **xiéjiang** cobbler

   附近 有 没有 鞋匠?

   Fùjìn yǒu méiyǒu xiéjiang?

   Is there a cobbler nearby?

4. 鞋油 **xiéyóu** shoe polish

   哪里 能 买到 鞋油?

   Nǎlǐ néng mǎidào xiéyóu?

   Where can I get some shoe polish?

5. 皮鞋 **píxié** leather shoes

   皮鞋 穿起来 没有 布鞋 舒服。

   Píxié chuānqǐlái méiyǒu bùxié shūfu.

   Leather shoes are not as comfortable as shoes made of cloth.

Helpful tips: The second and bottom horizontal strokes of 圭 are longer.											15 strokes

鞋

二₁ 艹₂ 艹₃ 苦₄ 苦₅ 苦₆ 茸₇ 茸₈ 革₉ 革₁₀ 革₁₁ 鞋₁₂

鞋₁₃ 鞋₁₄ 鞋₁₅

件

jiàn

[measure word]; document

Radical: 亻 # 19 "upright person"

Compounds, sentences, and meanings

1. 件 **jiàn** measure word

   这 件衣服 很 好看。

   Zhè jiàn yīfu hěn hǎokàn.

   This garment is very pretty.

2. 软件 **ruǎnjiàn** software

   这是 盗版 软件, 我 不要。

   Zhè shì dàobǎn ruǎnjiàn, wǒ bú yào.

   This is pirated software, I don't want it.

3. 配件 **pèijiàn** fittings

   我们 需要买 管子 配件。

   Wǒmen xūyào mǎi guǎnzi pèijiàn.

   We need to buy plumbing fittings.

4. 零件 **língjiàn** part

   新 的 零件 太贵了, 买 二手 的吧。

   Xīn de língjiàn tài guì le, mǎi èrshǒu de ba.

   New parts are too expensive, what if we buy secondhand ones?

5. 文件 **wénjiàn** document

   请 把 文件 放好, 别 丢失了。

   Qǐng bǎ wénjiàn fànghǎo, bié diūshī le.

   Please put the document in a safe place, don't lose it.

Helpful tips: The second horizontal stroke is longer. **6 strokes**

件	丿	亻	仁	仨	乍	件					

双

shuāng

pair

雙

Radical: 又 #24 "again"

Compounds, sentences, and meanings

1. 双 **shuāng** pair

我 今天 买了 一 双 运动鞋。

Wǒ jīntiān mǎile yì shuāng yùndòngxié.

I bought a pair of sports shoes today.

2. 双胞胎 **shuāngbāotāi** twins

他们 是 双胞胎。

Tāmen shì shuāngbāotāi.

They are twins.

3. 双层 **shuāngcéng** double-deck

卧室里 有一 张 双层床。

Wòshì lǐ yǒu yì zhāng shuāngcéngchuáng.

There's a bunkbed in the room.

4. 双重 **shuāngchóng** dual, double

我 是 双重 国籍人。

Wǒ shì shuāngchóng guójí rén.

I have dual nationality.

5. 双人床 **shuāngrénchuáng** double bed

我 要 双人床。

Wǒ yào shuāngrénchuáng.

I would like a double bed.

Helpful tips: The first 又 ends firmly like a dot, but the second 又 tapers off.													**4 strokes**
双	𡿨	又	㕚	双									

A. Pronunciation and *Pinyin* Practice

Please give the *pinyin* transcription for each of the following characters. Then illustrate the article of clothing that is being described.

裤子	裙子	两件衬衫	一双鞋子	衣服

B. Sentence Completion and Translation

Please complete each of the following sentences by adding one of the following verbs into each sentence as appropriate. Then, translate the resulting sentence into English. Please note that the verbs can be utilized more than once (as there are more sentences than verbs).

穿   看   喜欢   要

1. 今天你_____很好看的衣服。

_____

2. 我_____你的鞋子；请问你什么时候买的？

_____

3. 他们的衬衫都一样, 请_____！很有意思！

_____

4. 明天, 你_____穿裙子还是裤子?

_____

5. 什么时候女人要_____洋装?

_____

C. Illustrative Discussion

Please write a short discussion of the following topic. In order to facilitate the discussion use the space provided to create a small illustration of the clothing that will be described.

每天人上班, 很多人穿特别的衣服, 请介绍你工作的时候穿的衣服。

钱

qián

money

錢

Radical: 钅 # 122 "metal"

Compounds, sentences, and meanings

1. 钱 **qián** money

   你一个月的工资 多少 钱?

   Nǐ yí ge yuè de gōngzī duōshao qián?

   What's your monthly wage?

2. 钱包 **qiánbāo** wallet, purse

   他的 钱包 被贼 抢了。

   Tāde qiánbāo bèi zéi qiǎng le.

   His wallet was snatched by a thief.

3. 有钱 **yǒuqián** wealthy

   她父母 很 有钱。

   Tā fùmǔ hěn yǒuqián.

   Her parents are very wealthy.

4. 零钱 **língqián** small change

   我 要 换 点 零钱。

   Wǒ yào huàn diǎn língqián.

   I want to get some small change.

5. 压岁钱 **yāsuìqián** money given to children during the Lunar New Year

   中国 小孩 过年 都 可以拿到

   Zhōngguó xiǎohái guònián dōu kěyǐ nádào

   很多 压岁钱。

   hěnduō yāsuìqián.

   Chinese children get quite a bit of gift money during the Lunar New Year.

Helpful tips: The last stroke appears at the top right corner.								**10 strokes**
钱								

元

yuán

first; Chinese dollar

Radical: 二 # 10 "two" or 儿 # 21 "son"

Compounds, sentences, and meanings

1. 元 **yuán** dollar

   买 一 辆 小 汽车 要 八 万 元。

   Mǎi yí liàng xiǎo qìchē yào bā wàn yuán.

   It costs ¥80,000 to buy a small car.

2. 美元 **Měiyuán** American dollars

   一百 美元 兑换 九百 人民币。

   Yìbǎi Měiyuán duìhuàn jiǔbǎi Rénmínbì.

   US$100 exchanges for ¥900.

3. 元旦 **Yuándàn** New Year's Day

   一月 一号 是 元旦, 放假 一天。

   Yīyuè-yīhào shì Yuándàn, fàngjià yì tiān.

   January 1st, being New Year's Day, is a holiday.

4. 公元 **Gōngyuán** A.D., the Christian era

   公元 一九一二 年 民 国 建立。

   Gōngyuán yījiǔyī'èr nián Mín'guó jiànlì.

   In 1912 the Republic was established.

5. 公元前 **Gōngyuánqián** B.C. (before the Christian era)

   公元前 二二一 年 秦始皇

   Gōngyuánqián èr'èryī'nián Qínshǐhuáng

   统一 中国。

   tǒngyī Zhōngguó.

   In 221 B.C. the Qin Emperor unified China.

Helpful tips: The lower horizontal stroke is longer.										**4 strokes**
元	一	二	丆	元						

块　kuài

[measure word]

塊

Radical: 土 # 40 "earth"

Compounds, sentences, and meanings

1. 块 **kuài** piece

   她 吃了 两 块 面包。

   Tā chīle liǎng kuài miànbāo.

   She ate two pieces of bread.

2. 鱼块 **yúkuài** fish pieces

   我 要了 一个 糖醋 鱼块。

   Wǒ yàole yí ge tángcù yúkuài.

   I've ordered a plate of sweet and sour fish.

4. 一块儿 **yíkuàir** together

   你 有 兴趣 跟 我们 一块儿 去 吗?

   Nǐ yǒu xìngqù gēn wǒmen yíkuàir qù ma?

   Would you be interested in coming along with us?

3. 一块钱 **yí kuài qián** a dollar (literally, a piece of money)

   她一个 月 的 工资 五百 块 钱。

   Tā yí ge yuè de gōngzī wǔbǎi kuài qián.

   Her monthly wage is 500 dollars.

5. 方块字 **fāngkuàizì** square characters

   汉字 是 方块字, 很 难记。

   Hànzì shì fāngkuàizì, hěn nán jì.

   Chinese characters are square-shaped characters, so they are hard to remember.

Helpful tips: The last stroke tapers off.　　　　　　　　　　**7 strokes**

块　二　十　土　圫　圠　块

角 jiǎo

horn, angle, corner

Radical: 角 # 169 "horn"

Compounds, sentences, and meanings

1. 角 **jiǎo** a tenth of a 元, ten cents

   十 角 是 一 元 人民币。

   Shí jiǎo shì yì yuán rénmínbi.

   Ten jiao is one yuan RMB.

2. 直角 **zhíjiǎo** right angle

   有 直角 的 三角形 很 有意思。

   Yǒu zhíjiǎo de sānjiǎoxíng hěn yǒu yìsi.

   Triangles that have a right angle are very interesting.

3. 角度 **jiǎodù** viewpoint, perspective

   每 个 人 的 角度 不 一样。

   Měi ge rén de jiǎodù bù yíyàng.

   Every person's perspective is different.

4. 牛角 **niújiǎo** ox-horn

   家人 常常 谈问题 钻牛 角尖。

   Jiārén chángcháng tán wèntí zuānniú jiǎojiān.

   Often family members split hairs when discussing problems.

Helpful tips: The fourth stroke ends in a hook; end the last stroke firmly. **7 strokes**

角	⺈¹	⺈²	⺈³	角⁴	角⁵	角⁶	角⁷					

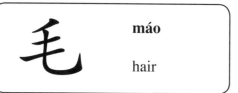

máo

hair

Radical: 毛 # 97 "hair"

Compounds, sentences, and meanings

1. 毛 **máo** hair

   这 猫 长得 一身 好 毛。

   Zhè māo zhǎngde yì shēn hǎo máo.

   This cat has a fine coat of fur.

2. 毛衣 **máoyī** woolen sweater

   今天 比较 冷,要 穿 毛衣。

   Jīntiān bǐjiào lěng, yào chuān máoyī.

   Today is quite cold, you need to wear a sweater.

3. 毛笔 **máobǐ** writing brush

   我 会 用 毛笔 写字。

   Wǒ huì yòng máobǐ xiězì.

   I can write with a brush.

4. 毛病 **máobìng** problem

   复印机 有 点 毛病。

   Fùyìnjī yǒu diǎn máobìng.

   There's something wrong with the photocopier.

5. 一毛(钱) **yì máo (qián)** ten cents

   报纸 一块 五毛 (钱) 一份。

   Bàozhǐ yíkuài-wǔmáo (qián) yí fèn.

   The newspaper is $1.50 a copy.

Helpful tips: Note the difference between 毛 and 手.											**4 strokes**
毛	丿	二	三	毛							

分

fēn

divide

Radical: 八 # 17 "eight" or 刀 # 30 "knife"

Compounds, sentences, and meanings

1. 分 fēn divide

   这 药 分 三 次 吃。

   Zhè yào fēn sān cì chī.

   This medicine is to be taken in three separate doses.

2. 分钟 fēnzhōng minute

   我 五 分钟 就 回来。

   Wǒ wǔ fēnzhōng jiù huílai.

   I'll be back in five minutes.

3. 分别 fēnbié difference

   有 什么 分别?

   Yǒu shénme fēnbié?

   What's the difference?

4. 分辨 fēnbiàn distinguish

   很 难 分辨 谁 是 谁 非。

   Hěn nán fēnbiàn shéi shì shéi fēi.

   It's hard to tell who is right and who is wrong.

5. 百分之三十 bǎifēnzhīsānshí 30%

   房租 涨了 百分之三十。

   Fángzū zhǎngle bǎifēnzhīsānshí.

   Rent has gone up 30 percent.

Helpful tips: Leave a gap between the top two strokes.				**4 strokes**

分 ノ 八 今 分

Traditional Form

价

jià

price

價

Radical: 亻 # 19 "upright person"

Compounds, sentences, and meanings

1. 价 jià price

可以 减价 吗?

Kěyǐ jiǎnjià ma?

Can you reduce the price?

2. 价钱 jiàqián price

这 个 价钱 是 最 便宜 的了。

Zhè ge jiàqián shì zuì piányi de le.

This is the cheapest price.

3. 价值 jiàzhí value

这些 资料 对 我们 很 有 价值。

Zhèxiē zīliào duì wǒmen hěn yǒu jiàzhí.

This data is of great value to us.

4. 讲价 jiǎngjià bargain

在 中国 买 东西 要 讲价。

Zài Zhōngguó mǎi dōngxi yào jiǎngjià.

You have to bargain when you shop in China.

5. 涨价 zhǎngjià rise in price

昨天 汽油 涨价 了。

Zuótiān qìyóu zhǎngjià le.

Yesterday the price of gasoline went up.

Helpful tips: The left vertical stroke of 介 sweeps to the left.　　　　**6 strokes**

价	丿	亻	仒	价	价	价					

便 **biàn/pián**

convenient; cheap

Radical: 亻 # 19 "upright person"

Compounds, sentences, and meanings

1. 便 **biàn** then

   这 几 天 不 是 刮风， 便 是 下雨。

   Zhè jǐ tiān bú shì guāfēng, biàn shì xiàyǔ.

   During the last few days, if it was not windy, then it was raining.

2. 方便 **fāngbiàn** convenient

   什么 时候 方便， 什么 时候 来。

   Shénme shíhou fāngbiàn, shénme shíhou lái.

   Drop in whenever it's convenient.

3. 便利 **biànlì** convenient

   这里 交通 便利。

   Zhèlǐ jiāotōng biànlì.

   Transport is convenient here.

4. 便条 **biàntiáo** short note

   你给 他 写个 便条 吧。

   Nǐ gěi tā xiě ge biàntiáo ba.

   Why don't you write him a note?

5. 便宜 **piányi** cheap

   这里 的 东西 价钱 很 便宜。

   Zhèlǐ de dōngxi jiàqián hěn piányi.

   The things here are really inexpensive.

Helpful tips: The eighth stroke starts under the horizontal stroke.								**9 strokes**		
便	丿	亻	仁	仨	佰	佰	便	便		

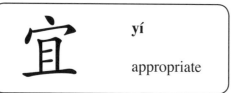

宜　yí　appropriate

Radical: 宀 # 34 "roof"

Compounds, sentences, and meanings

1. 宜 **yí** appropriate

   老幼 咸宜。

   Lǎoyòu xiányí.

   Suitable for both young and old.

2. 不宜 **bùyí** not fitting

   对 孩子不宜 要求 过 高。

   Duì háizi bùyí yāoqiú guò gāo.

   You shouldn't ask too much of a child.

3. 宜人 **yírén** pleasant

   这里 气候宜人。

   Zhèlǐ qìhòu yírén.

   The weather's pleasant here.

4. 便宜 **piányi** inexpensive

   这里的 东西 价钱 很 便宜。

   Zhèlǐ de dōngxi jiàqián hěn piányi.

   The things here are really inexpensive.

5. 适宜 **shìyí** appropriate

   游泳 对 老年人 很 适宜。

   Yóuyǒng duì lǎoniánrén hěn shìyí.

   Swimming is good for old people.

Helpful tips: The last horizontal stroke is longer.　　**8 strokes**

贵   guì

expensive

貴

Radical: 贝 # 92 "seashell"

Compounds, sentences, and meanings

1. 贵 **guì** expensive

这 本 书 很 好, 也 不 贵。

Zhè běn shū hěn hǎo, yě bú guì.

This book is good and is not expensive.

2. 贵姓 **guìxìng** your name (honorific)

您 贵姓?

Nín guìxìng?

What's your surname, please?

3. 贵国 **guìguó** your country (honorific)

贵国 是 哪国?

Guìguó shì nǎguó?

What nationality (polite form) are you?

Helpful tips: The last stroke finishes firmly.											**9 strokes**
贵	`	一	口	中	虫	虫	贵	贵	贵		

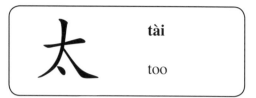

太   **tài**

too

Radical: 大 # 43 "big"

Compounds, sentences, and meanings

1. 太 **tài** too

   太 贵了,可以 便宜点儿 吗?

   Tài guì le, kěyǐ piányidiǎnr ma?

   It's too expensive! Can you make it cheaper?

2. 太阳 **tàiyáng** the sun

   你看, 太阳 出来了。

   Nǐ kàn, tàiyáng chūlai le.

   Look, the sun is out.

3. 太空 **tàikōng** outer space

   美国 发明 太空梭。

   Měiguó fāmíng tàikōngsuō.

   The Americans invented the space shuttle.

4. 太平洋 **Tàipíngyáng** the Pacific Ocean

   中国 在 太平洋 西边。

   Zhōngguó zài Tàipíngyáng xībian.

   China is situated at the west of the Pacific Ocean.

5. 太极拳 **tàijíquán** tai chi

   我 会 打太极拳,可是 打得不 好。

   Wǒ huì dǎ tàijíquán, kěshì dǎde bù hǎo.

   I can do tai chi, but not very well.

Helpful tips: The last stroke ends firmly.   **4 strokes**

太　一　ナ　大　太

A. Character and Pronunciation Practice

Please write the following money amounts in Chinese characters. Then write in *pinyin* how the amount would be expressed in speaking. Note that there can be a difference between expressing written and spoken money amounts.

Amount	Characters	*Pinyin*
$2.50		
$1.99		
$10.10		
$45.05		
$100.00		
$450.75		
$205.21		
67¢		
25¢		
$51.50		

B. Price Descriptions

Please construct a brief sentence that introduces a price for an item of clothing. Each sentence should agree with the descriptive phrase about the price given for each sentence. While different items of clothing can have different prices, each sentence should be clear in both the item of clothing and the price being described.

1. (很贵) _____

_____

2. (很便宜) _____

_____

3.（太便宜）_____

_____

4.（不贵）_____

_____

5.（太贵）_____

_____

C. Money Comparison

Money represents the people and politics of the culture that designed it. Study the following versions of paper money. On the left is a ¥100 (RMB) note from the People's Republic of China. On the right is a $1 bill from the United States of America. Take note of the different images, languages, and other features of the two bills. Then, in the space provided, please create 3 comparative statements between the two banknotes.

中国人民币   美国美元

1. _____

2. _____

3. _____

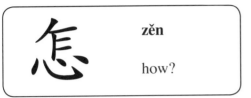

怎 **zěn**

how?

Radical: 心 # 76 "heart"

Compounds, sentences, and meanings

1. 怎 **zěn** why

   你 怎 不 早 说 呀?

   Nǐ zěn bù zǎo shuō ya?

   Why didn't you say so earlier?

2. 怎么 **zěnme** how

   这 个 词儿 英语 怎么 说?

   Zhè ge cír Yīngyǔ zěnme shuō?

   How do you say this word in English?

3. 怎样 **zěnyàng** how, what

   这 件 事 你 怎样 解释?

   Zhè jiàn shì nǐ zěnyàng jiěshì?

   How do you explain this matter?

4. 怎么样 **zěnmeyàng** what's it like?

   最近 怎么样, 忙 吗?

   Zuìjìn zěnmeyàng, máng ma?

   How have things been recently, busy?

Helpful tips: The top horizontal stroke is longer.　　　　　　**9 strokes**

怎	丿	仁	仁	乍	乍	乍	怎	怎	怎			

样　yàng

appearance

様

Radical: 木 # 81 "tree"

Compounds, sentences, and meanings

1. 样 **yàng** appearance

几年 没 见面，他还是那个样。

Jǐ nián méi jiànmiàn, tā hái shì nà ge yàng.

It's years since I last saw him, but he still looks the same.

2. 怎么样 **zěnmeyàng** what's it like?

最近 怎么样， 忙 吗?

Zuìjìn zěnmeyàng, máng ma?

How have things been recently, busy?

3. 样子 **yàngzi** appearance

这 件大衣的 样子 很 好看。

Zhè jiàn dàyī de yàngzi hěn hǎokàn.

This coat is well cut.

4. 一样 **yíyàng** the same

他们 兄弟 相貌 一样。

Tāmen xiōngdì xiàngmào yíyàng.

The brothers are alike in appearance.

5. 花样 **huāyàng** variety

这家 服装店 花样 很多。

Zhè jiā fúzhuāngdiàn huāyàng hěnduō.

There is a great variety of styles in this boutique shop.

Helpful tips: The last stroke of 木 should be written firmly.　　　**10 strokes**

样	一	十	才	木	术	村	栏	栏	栏	样		

想 **xiǎng**

think

Radical: 心 # 76 "heart"

Compounds, sentences, and meanings

1. 想 **xiǎng** think

   你 想得 很 周到。

   Nǐ xiǎngde hěn zhōudào.

   You have thought of everything.

2. 想到 **xiǎngdào** think of

   我们 没 想到 你会来。

   Wǒmen méi xiǎngdào nǐ huì lái.

   We didn't expect you to come.

3. 想法 **xiǎngfa** idea, opinion

   把你的 想法 给大家 说说。

   Bǎ nǐde xiǎngfa gěi dàjiā shuōshuo.

   Tell us what you have in mind.

4. 想念 **xiǎngniàn** remember with longing

   我们 都很 想念 你。

   Wǒmen dōu hěn xiǎngniàn nǐ.

   We all miss you very much.

5. 想象力 **xiǎngxiànglì** imagination

   这 孩子 很 有 想象力。

   Zhè háizi hěn yǒu xiǎngxiànglì.

   This child is full of imagination.

Helpful tips: The horizontal hook in 心 curves to the left.											**13 strokes**
想	一₁	十₂	才₃	木₄	札₅	相₆	相₇	相₈	相₉	相₁₀	想₁₁ 想₁₂
想₁₃											

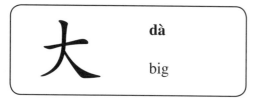

CHARACTER 175

大 **dà**

big

Radical: 大 # 43 "big"

Compounds, sentences, and meanings

1. 大 **dà** big

   把 收音机 开 大一点。

   Bǎ shōuyīnjī kāi dàyìdiǎn.

   Turn the volume of the radio up a bit.

2. 大声 **dàshēng** loudly

   请 别 大声 说话。

   Qǐng bié dàshēng shuōhuà.

   Please don't speak so loudly.

3. 大家 **dàjiā** everybody

   请 大家 坐好。

   Qǐng dàjiā zuòhǎo.

   Please be seated, everyone.

4. 大小 **dàxiǎo** size (literally, big small)

   这 双 鞋 大小 正 合适。

   Zhè shuāng xié dàxiǎo zhèng héshì.

   These shoes fit me perfectly.

5. 大概 **dàgài** in general

   我 只 知道 个 大概。

   Wǒ zhǐ zhīdao ge dàgài.

   I have only a general idea.

Helpful tips: The last stroke tapers off.   **3 strokes**

大	一	大	大								

214

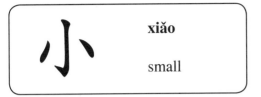

小   **xiǎo**

small

Radical: 小 # 49 "small"

Compounds, sentences, and meanings

1. 小 **xiǎo** little

   我 比 你 小。

   Wǒ bǐ nǐ xiǎo.

   I'm younger than you.

2. 小时 **xiǎoshí** hour

   我 每天 工作 八个 小时。

   Wǒ měitiān gōngzuò bā ge xiǎoshí.

   I work eight hours every day.

3. 小时候 **xiǎoshíhou** in one's childhood

   这 是 她 小时候 的 照片。

   Zhè shì tā xiǎoshíhou de zhàopiàn.

   These are her childhood photos.

4. 小吃 **xiǎochī** snacks

   北京 的 小吃 很 出名。

   Běijīng de xiǎochī hěn chūmíng.

   Beijing is famous for its snacks.

5. 小心 **xiǎoxīn** be careful (literally, little heart)

   过 马路 要 小心。

   Guò mǎlù yào xiǎoxīn.

   Be careful when crossing the road.

| Helpful tips: The middle stroke ends with a hook. | | | | | | | | | | **3 strokes** |

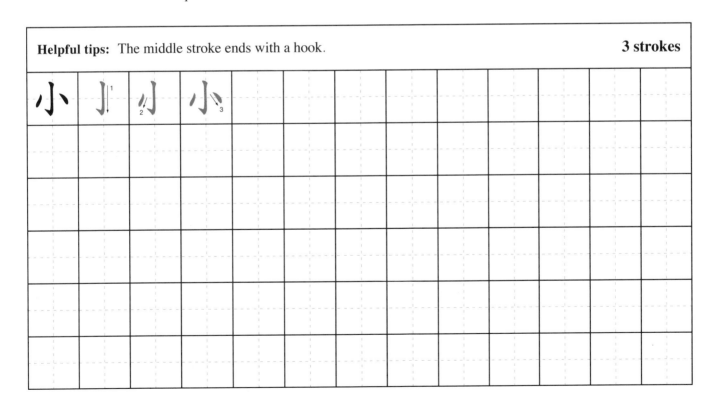

漂

piāo/piǎo/piào

adrift/bleach/beautiful

Radical: 氵 # 32 "3 drops of water"

Compounds, sentences, and meanings

1. 漂 **piāo** float

   树叶 在 水上 漂着。

   Shùyè zài shuǐshang piāozhe.

   Leaves were floating on the water.

2. 漂游 **piāoyóu** lead a wandering life

   他 喜欢 四处 漂游。

   Tā xǐhuan sìchù piāoyóu.

   He likes to wander from place to place.

3. 漂白粉 **piǎobáifěn** bleaching powder

   有 没有 漂白粉?

   Yǒu méiyǒu piǎobáifěn?

   Do you have bleaching powder?

4. 漂亮 **piàoliang** pretty

   女孩子 都 喜欢 穿 漂亮 的衣服。

   Nǚháizi dōu xǐhuan chuān piàoliang de yīfu.

   Girls like to wear pretty dresses.

5. 漂亮话 **piàolianghuà** fancy talk

   说 漂亮话 没用, 干出来 才算。

   Shuō piàolianghuà méi yòng, gànchūlái cái suàn.

   Actions speak louder than words.

Helpful tips: The eighth stroke is a short vertical without a bend. **14 strokes**

漂	氵1	氵2	氵3	沪4	沪5	沪6	沪7	沪8	沪9	漂10	漂11	漂12
漂13	漂14											

亮 　liàng

bright

Radical: 亠 # 6 "top of 六"

Compounds, sentences, and meanings

1. 亮 **liàng** bright
那个 灯泡 很 亮。
Nà ge dēngpào hěn liàng.
That lightbulb is very bright.

2. 亮晶晶 **liàngjīngjīng** glittering
今晚 可以 看到 亮晶晶 的 星星。
Jīnwǎn kěyǐ kàndào liàngjīngjīng de xīngxīng.
You can see the stars shining tonight.

3. 亮堂 **liàngtang** light, bright
这 屋子 又 宽敞 又 亮堂。
Zhè wūzi yòu kuānchang yòu liàngtang.
The room is spacious and bright.

4. 明亮 **míngliàng** bright, shining
我 喜欢 赵 薇 那 双 明亮 的
Wǒ xǐhuan Zhào Wēi nà shuāng míngliàng de
眼睛。
yǎnjing.
I like Zhao Wei's bright eyes.

5. 月亮 **yuèliang** the moon
中秋节 的 月亮 最 圆。
Zhōngqiūjié de yuèliang zuì yuán.
The moon is at its fullest at Mid-autumn Festival.

Helpful tips: The last stroke is a horizontal-bend ending with a hook.　　**9 strokes**

217

错

cuò

wrong

错

Radical: 钅 # 122 "metal"

Compounds, sentences, and meanings

1. 错 **cuò** wrong

   他 弄错 了。

   Tā nòngcuò le.

   He has got it wrong.

2. 错误 **cuòwù** mistake

   这 是 一个 严重 的 错误。

   Zhè shì yí ge yánzhòng de cuòwù.

   This is a serious mistake.

3. 不错 **búcuò** not bad, pretty good

   这 个 电影 不错。

   Zhè ge diànyǐng búcuò.

   This movie is quite good.

4. 错过 **cuòguò** miss, let slip

   错过 这 趟 汽车 就要 等 一个 小时。

   Cuòguò zhè tàng qìchē jiù yào děng yí ge xiǎoshí.

   If we miss this bus, we have to wait an hour (for the next one).

5. 错别字 **cuòbiézì** wrongly written or mispronounced characters

   我 经常 会 写 错别字。

   Wǒ jīngcháng huì xiě cuòbiézì.

   I often write characters wrongly.

Helpful tips: The fifth stroke is a vertical lift to the right.　　　　**13 strokes**

错	⺧	⻓	⻓	⻓	钅	钅	钜	钳	锘	错	错	错
错												

同 **tóng**

equivalent, identical

Radical: # 16 "border"

Compounds, sentences, and meanings

1. 同意 **tóngyì** to agree

   如果 你的 意见 有 道理, 人们 大概 会
   Rúguǒ nǐ de yìjiàn yǒu dàolǐ, rénmen dàgài huì
   同意。
   tóngyì.

   If an opinion has merit, people will likely agree with it.

2. 同学 **tóngxué** classmate

   同班 的 同学 上 一样 的 课。
   Tóngbān de tóngxué shàng yíyàng de kè.

   Classmates in the same group go to the same classes.

3. 同一 **tóngyī** identical, same

   我们 的 衬衫 是 同一 种。
   Wǒmen de chènshān shì tóngyī zhǒng.

   Our shirts are of the same type.

4. 同辈 **tóngbèi** same generation

   同辈 的 人 大概 会 做 一样 的 事。
   Tóngbèi de rén dàgài huì zuò yíyàng de shì.

   People of the same generation probably are doing the same things.

5. 同情 **tóngqíng** sympathize, empathize

   大家 都 能 同情 朋友们 的 情况。
   Dàjiā dōu néng tóngqíng péngyoumen de qíngkuàng.

   People can empathize with friends.

6. 同时 **tóngshí** at the same time

   同时 我 也 看 那个 电视 节目。
   Tóngshí wǒ yě kàn nà ge diànshì jiémù.

   At the same time I was also watching that television program.

| **Helpful tips:** The internal components are written last. | | | | | | | | | | | **6 strokes** |

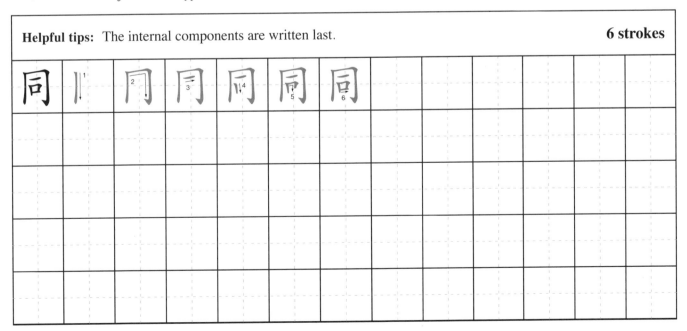

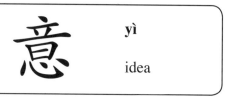

意   yì

idea

Radical: 心 # 76 "heart"

Compounds, sentences, and meanings

1. 意 **yì** trace, hint

   今天 的 天气 颇 有 秋意。

   Jīntiān de tiānqì pō yǒu qiū yì.

   Today's weather has a hint of autumn.

2. 意见 **yìjiàn** idea, opinion

   我们的 意见一致。

   Wǒmende yìjiàn yízhì.

   We have identical views.

3. 意思 **yìsi** meaning

   我 不 明白 你的意思。

   Wǒ bù míngbai nǐde yìsi.

   I don't understand what you mean.

4. 没意思 **méi yìsi** boring, uninteresting

   这 本 书 没意思。

   Zhè běn shū méi yìsi.

   This book is boring.

5. 拿主意 **ná zhǔyi** make a decision

   究竟 去不去, 你拿 主意 吧。

   Jiūjìng qù buqù, nǐ ná zhǔyi ba.

   Please decide whether to go or not.

Helpful tips: The second horizontal stroke is longer.   **13 strokes**

意	丶	二	亠	立	立	产	音	音	音	音	意	意
意												

A. Pronunciation and *Pinyin* Practice

Please write the following questions in pinyin. Then practice saying them aloud. For additional practice, respond to the questions aloud.

1. 春天的花很漂亮吗?

_____

2. 这件毛衣很好看, 你同不同意?

_____

3. 你的工作怎么样?

_____

B. Descriptive Sentences

Please illustrate an example of each item in the boxes provided. Then, based on each illustration, respond to each question.

衣服

1. 这些衣服怎么样, 好不好看?

_____

天气

2. 今天的天气, 怎么样?

_____

朋友

3. 你的朋友怎么了?

_____

C. Short Description

Please consider the following question and respond in a short discussion written in Chinese characters. A strong discussion will include some understanding of opinion and desire along with different activities.

有一天你没有别的事情, 你想做什么?

_____

_____

_____

_____

_____

_____

_____

这 zhè

this

這

Radical: 辶 # 38 "movement"

Compounds, sentences, and meanings

1. 这 **zhè** this

   这 消息 我 知道 了。

   Zhè xiāoxi wǒ zhīdao le.

   I've already heard that news.

2. 这个 **zhè ge** this one

   我 就 买 这个。

   Wǒ jiù mǎi zhè ge.

   I'll buy this one.

3. 这儿 **zhèr** here

   这儿 不准 停车。

   Zhèr bùzhǔn tíngchē.

   Parking is prohibited here.

4. 这些 **zhèxiē** these

   这些 日子 我们 特别 忙。

   Zhèxiē rìzi wǒmen tèbié máng.

   We've been really busy lately.

5. 这样 **zhèyàng** this way

   我 觉得 这样 做 会 快一点儿。

   Wǒ juéde zhèyàng zuò huì kuàiyìdiǎnr.

   I think this way is faster.

Helpful tips: The fourth stroke finishes firmly.							**7 strokes**				
这	丶	二	方	文	文	这	这				

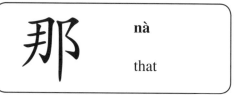

那 **nà**

that

Radical: 阝 # 28 "right earlobe"

Compounds, sentences, and meanings

1. 那 **nà** that

   那是 谁?

   Nà shì shéi/shuí?

   Who is that?

2. 那个 **nà ge** that one

   那 个孩子 很可爱。

   Nà ge háizi hěn kě'ài.

   That child is cute.

3. 那么 **nàme** in that way

   别 走得那么 快, 好不好?

   Bié zǒude nàme kuài, hǎobuhǎo?

   Don't walk so fast, okay?

4. 那边 **nàbian** over there

   请把 东西 放在 那边。

   Qǐng bǎ dōngxi fàng zài nàbian.

   Please put those things over there.

5. 从那儿起 **cóng nàr qǐ** since then

   从那儿起, 他就 用心   念书 了。

   Cóng nàr qǐ, tā jiù yòngxīn niànshū le.

   He's been studying hard since then.

Helpful tips: The fifth stroke looks like the number 3.						**6 strokes**
那	刁	彐	彐	刟	那	那

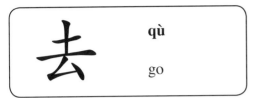

CHARACTER 184

去   qù

go

Radical: 厶 # 23 "private" or 土 # 40 "earth"

Compounds, sentences, and meanings

1. 去 **qù** go

   假期你到哪儿去玩儿?

   Jiàqī nǐ dào nǎr qù wánr?

   Where are you going during the holidays?

2. 去处 **qùchù** place to go

   这是一个 风景 优美 的去处。

   Zhè shì yí ge fēngjǐng yōuměi de qùchù.

   This is a scenic place to visit.

3. 去世 **qùshì** (of adults) die

   我 父亲 三 年 前 去世了。

   Wǒ fùqin sān nián qián qùshì le.

   My father passed away three years ago.

4. 去年 **qùnián** last year

   我 是 去年 开始学 跳舞 的。

   Wǒ shì qùnián kāishǐ xué tiàowǔ de.

   I started learning to dance last year.

5. 拿去 **náqù** take away

   谁 把我的 字典 拿去了?

   Shéi bǎ wǒde zìdiǎn náqù le?

   Who's taken my dictionary?

Helpful tips: The second horizontal stroke is longer.											**5 strokes**
去	一	士	土	去	去						

225

到 **dào**

arrive

Radical: 刂 # 15 "upright knife"

Compounds, sentences, and meanings

1. 到 **dào** arrive

   火车 到站 了。

   Huǒchē dàozhàn le.

   The train has arrived at the station.

2. 到处 **dàochù** everywhere, anywhere

   烟头 不要 到处 乱 扔。

   Yāntóu búyào dàochù luàn rēng.

   Don't drop cigarette butts all over the place.

3. 到底 **dàodǐ** finally

   你到底 是 什么 意思?

   Nǐ dàodǐ shì shénme yìsi?

   What on earth do you mean?

4. 到家 **dàojiā** be excellent

   这几个 汉字 写得 很 到家。

   Zhè jǐ ge Hànzì xiěde hěn dàojiā.

   These Chinese characters are remarkably well written.

5. 到期 **dàoqī** become due

   这 本 书 已经 到期了。

   Zhè běn shì yǐjīng dàoqī le.

   This book is due for return.

| Helpful tips: The sixth stroke goes upwards. | | | | | | | | **8 strokes** |

到

| 二 1 | 云 2 | 云 3 | 云 4 | 至 5 | 至 6 | 到 7 | 到 8 | | | | | |

校   jiào/xiào

check; school

Radical: 木 # 81 "tree"

Compounds, sentences, and meanings

1. 校 **jiào** check, proofread

先 校 错字, 然后 校 标点 符号。

Xiān jiào cuòzì, ránhou jiào biāodiǎn fúhào.

First proofread for typos, then correct the punctuation.

2. 校对 **jiàoduì** check, proofread

校对 汉字 时, 要 注意 笔顺。

Jiàoduì Hànzì shí, yào zhùyì bǐshùn.

When proofreading Chinese characters, pay attention to the stroke order.

3. 学校 **xuéxiào** school

这 个 学校 有 一百 年 的 历史。

Zhè ge xuéxiào yǒu yìbǎi nián de lìshǐ.

This school has a 100-year history.

4. 校园 **xiàoyuán** campus

校园 进行 绿化 已经 一 年 了。

Xiàoyuán jìnxíng lùhuà yǐjīng yì nián le.

The greening of our campus has been underway for a year.

5. 母校 **mǔxiào** alma mater

悉尼大学 是 我的 母校。

Xīní Dàxué shì wǒde mǔxiào.

Sydney University is my alma mater.

Helpful tips: The top and bottom of the right half of the character should be balanced and of equal size.									10 strokes

校 一 十 才 木 术 杉 杉 杉 校

CHARACTER 187

院　　yuàn

courtyard

Radical: 阝 # 27 "left earlobe"

Compounds, sentences, and meanings

1. 院 **yuàn** courtyard

   院里 种了 几棵 果树。
   Yuànli zhòngle jǐ kē guǒshù.
   There are some fruit trees in the courtyard.

2. 院子 **yuànzi** courtyard

   我家 有 个 院子，孩子们 可以 在 那儿
   Wǒ jiā yǒu ge yuànzi, háizimen kěyǐ zài nàr
   玩儿。
   wánr.
   My house has a yard for the children to play in.

3. 医院 **yīyuàn** hospital

   医院　对面 是 公园。
   Yīyuàn duìmian shì gōngyuán.
   Opposite the hospital is a park.

4. 住院 **zhùyuàn** stay in hospital

   他 住了 两个 星期 的 院。
   Tā zhùle liǎng ge xīngqī de yuàn.
   He was hospitalized for two weeks.

5. 电影院 **diànyǐngyuàn** cinema

   这是 新开 的　电影院。
   Zhè shì xīnkāi de diànyǐngyuàn.
   This is a new cinema.

Helpful tips: The final stroke ends with a hook.											**9 strokes**
院	了	阝	阝	阝	院	院	院	院	院		

228

商

shāng

commerce

Radical: 亠 # 6 "top of 六"

Compounds, sentences, and meanings

1. 商 **shāng** commerce

中国 正在 发展 工商 企业。

Zhōngguó zhèngzài fāzhǎn gōngshāng qǐyè.

China is developing its industrial and commercial enterprises.

2. 商人 **shāngrén** merchant

现在 中国 商人 的地位 提高了。

Xiànzài Zhōngguó shāngrén de dìwèi tígāo le.

Nowadays the status of merchants in China is higher.

3. 商店 **shāngdiàn** shop

商店 几点 开门?

Shāngdiàn jǐ diǎn kāimén?

What time does the shop open?

4. 商业 **shāngyè** commerce

上海 是一个 商业 城市。

Shànghǎi shì yí ge shāngyè chéngshì.

Shanghai is a commercial city.

5. 商量 **shāngliang** discuss

我 有事儿要 跟 你 商量。

Wǒ yǒu shìr yào gēn nǐ shāngliang.

I have something to discuss with you.

Helpful tips: The sixth stroke ends with a hook.										**11 strokes**
商	丶	二	亠	立	产	商	商	商	商	商

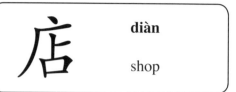

店

diàn

shop

Radical: 广 # 36 "broad"

Compounds, sentences, and meanings

1. 店 **diàn** shop

   他 开了一个 什么 店?

   Tā kāile yí ge shénme diàn?

   What shop did he run?

2. 书店 **shūdiàn** bookshop

   书店 里有 很多 人。

   Shūdiàn li yǒu hěnduō rén.

   There are lots of people in the bookshop.

3. 文具店 **wénjùdiàn** stationery shop

   附近 有 没有 文具店?

   Fùjìn yǒu méiyǒu wénjùdiàn?

   Is there a stationery shop nearby?

4. 服装店 **fúzhuāngdiàn** boutique

   这家 服装店 的衣服很 特别。

   Zhè jiā fúzhuāngdiàn de yīfu hěn tèbié.

   The clothes in this boutique are quite special.

5. 店员 **diànyuán** shop assistant

   店员 的服务态度 很 热情。

   Diànyuán de fúwù tàidu hěn rèqíng.

   The shop assistants are very friendly.

Helpful tips: 占 can be confused with 古.								**8 strokes**			
店	`	二	广	广	庐	庐	店	店			

花

huā

flower

Radical: 艹 # 42 "grass"

Compounds, sentences, and meanings

1. 花 **huā** flower

   春天 来了，百 花 开了。

   Chūntiān lái le, bǎi huā kāi le.

   Spring is here, the flowers are blossoming.

2. 花白 **huābái** gray

   他的头发 花白，看起来有 六十岁。

   Tāde tóufa huābái, kànqǐlai yǒu liùshí suì.

   His hair is gray, he looks 60.

3. 花生 **huāshēng** peanuts

   我 喜欢 吃 花生米。

   Wǒ xǐhuan chī huāshēngmǐ.

   I like to eat peanuts.

4. 花钱 **huāqián** spend (money)

   在 中国 旅行 花不了 很多 钱。

   Zài Zhōngguó lǚxíng huābuliǎo hěnduō qián.

   It doesn't cost very much to travel in China.

5. 花样 **huāyàng** variety

   这家 时装店 的衣服 花样 繁多。

   Zhè jiā shízhuāngdiàn de yīfu huāyàng fánduō.

   This boutique has a great variety of clothes.

Helpful tips: The final stroke ends with a hook.										**7 strokes**
花	一	十	艹	艿	芘	花	花			

CHARACTER 191

公	**gōng**
	public

Radical: 八 # 17 "eight"

Compounds, sentences, and meanings

1. 公 **gōng** official business

   我 今天 因 公 外出。

   Wǒ jīntiān yīn gōng wàichū.

   Today I'm going out on official business.

2. 公共 **gōnggòng** public

   公共 场所 不准 抽烟。

   Gōnggòng chǎngsuǒ bùzhǔn chōuyān.

   No smoking in public places.

3. 公里 **gōnglǐ** kilometer

   我 家 离 学校 一 公里。

   Wǒ jiā lí xuéxiào yì gōnglǐ.

   My house is one kilometer from the school.

4. 公斤 **gōngjīn** kilogram

   买 一 公斤 桔子。

   Mǎi yì gōngjīn júzi.

   Give me [buy] a kilogram of oranges.

5. 公升 **gōngshēng** liter

   买 四十 公升 汽油。

   Mǎi sìshí gōngshēng qìyóu.

   Give me [buy] 40 liters of gasoline.

Helpful tips: Leave a gap between the first two strokes.   **4 strokes**

公	丿¹	八²	公³	公⁴									

232

园

yuán

garden; park

園

Radical: 囗 # 51 "4-sided frame"

Compounds, sentences, and meanings

1. 园 **yuán** garden

我 家 园子 种了 几棵 果树。

Wǒ jiā yuánzi zhòngle jǐ kē guǒshù.

There are a few fruit trees in my garden.

2. 公园 **gōngyuán** park

假日里 很多 人 到 公园 去玩儿。

Jiàrìli, hěnduō rén dào gōngyuán qù wánr.

On holidays, many people go to the park to enjoy themselves.

3. 花园 **huāyuán** (flower) garden

我 家 前面 有 一个 小 花园。

Wǒ jiā qiánmiàn yǒu yí ge xiǎo huāyuán.

There's a small garden in front of our house.

4. 苹果园 **píngguǒyuán** apple orchard

这里一带 都 是 苹果园。

Zhèlǐ yídài dōu shì píngguǒyuán.

There are apple orchards around here.

5. 动物园 **dòngwùyuán** zoo

北京 动物园 有 大熊猫。

Běijīng dòngwùyuán yǒu dàxióngmāo.

There are pandas in Beijing Zoo.

Helpful tips: The sealing stroke is written last.   **7 strokes**

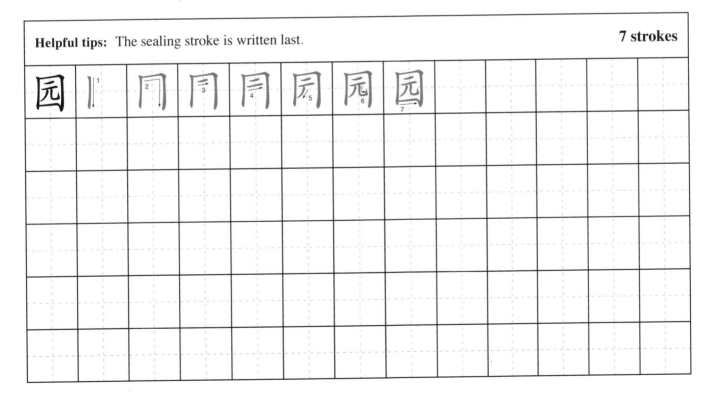

Lesson 18: Review Activities

A. Vocabulary Identification and *Pinyin*

Please match the following vocabulary with an appropriate illustration. Then, under each illustration, write the vocabulary term utilizing *pinyin*.

A. 学校

D. 花园

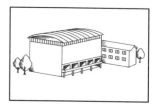

1. _____

B. 大学

3. _____

E. 医院

5. _____

C. 商店

F. 公园

2. _____

4. _____

6. _____

B. Descriptive Sentences

Using arrows, please add to the map an indication of movement between the locations. Then create sentences that express the movement diagrammed on the map. Pay careful attention to correct sentence construction between locations and movement.

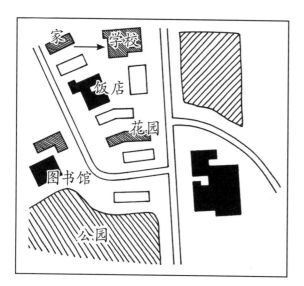

1. _____

_____

2. _____

_____

3. _____

_____

4. _____

234

C. Comparative Discussion

Please create a comparison between two locations. First, illustrate an example for each of the two locations. Then provide 4 or 5 adjectives for each location. Finally, create a two-paragraph discussion that clearly expresses a comparison between the locations.

花园	（这里）：	电影院	（那里）：

_____

_____

_____

_____

_____

_____

_____

_____

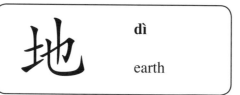

地   **dì**

earth

Radical: 土 # 40 "earth"

Compounds, sentences, and meanings

1. 地 **dì** fields

   农民 在地里干活儿。

   Nóngmín zài dìli gànhuór.

   The peasants are working in the fields.

2. 地方 **dìfang** place, space

   这 个 地方 不错。

   Zhè ge dìfang búcuò.

   This is quite a nice place.

3. 地图 **dìtú** map

   你 有 没有 中国 地图?

   Nǐ yǒu méiyǒu Zhōngguó dìtú?

   Do you have a map of China?

4. 地下 **dìxià** on the ground

   你的毛衣 掉 在 地下了。

   Nǐde máoyī diào zài dìxià le.

   Your sweater fell on the ground.

5. 地道 **dìdao** authentic, typical

   他的 广州话 说得 真 地道。

   Tāde Guǎngzhōuhuà shuōde zhēn dìdao.

   He speaks Cantonese like a native.

Helpful tips: The last stroke ends with a hook.											**6 strokes**
地	一₁	十₂	土₃	圳₄	地₅	地₆					

方　fāng

direction

Radical: 方 # 74 "direction"

Compounds, sentences, and meanings

1. 方 **fāng** method

   他 母亲 教导 有 方。

   Tā mǔqin jiàodǎo yǒu fāng.

   His mother taught him the right way to do it.

2. 方便 **fāngbiàn** convenient

   什么 时候 方便， 什么 时候 来。

   Shénme shíhou fāngbiàn, shénme shíhou lái.

   Drop in whenever it's convenient.

3. 方向 **fāngxiàng** direction

   他 往 学校 的 方向 走了。

   Tā wǎng xuéxiào de fāngxiàng zǒu le.

   He went in the direction of the school.

4. 方法 **fāngfǎ** method

   这 个 学习 方法 很 好。

   Zhè ge xuéxí fāngfǎ hěn hǎo.

   This is a good study method.

5. 方面 **fāngmiàn** aspect

   应该 考虑各 方面 的 意见。

   Yīnggāi kǎolǜ gè fāngmiàn de yìjiàn.

   One should consider opinions from different quarters.

Helpful tips: The last stroke bends.						**4 strokes**

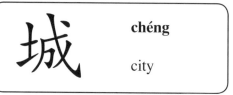

城   **chéng**

city

Radical: 土 # 40 "earth"

Compounds, sentences, and meanings

1. 城 **chéng** city

   城里 的 商店 比较 高档。
   Chéngli de shāngdiàn bǐjiào gāodǎng.
   The shops in the city sell better quality goods.

2. 城乡 **chéngxiāng** town and country

   在 中国， 城乡 的 差别 很 大。
   Zài Zhōngguó, chéngxiāng de chābié hěn dà.
   There is quite a large difference between urban and rural areas in China.

3. 城市 **chéngshì** city

   上海 是 中国 最大的 城市。
   Shànghǎi shì Zhōngguó zuìdàde chéngshì.
   Shanghai is the largest city in China.

4. 进城 **jìnchéng** go to the city

   我 坐 地铁 进城。
   Wǒ zuò dìtiě jìnchéng.
   I take the subway to get to the city.

5. 长城 **Chángchéng** Great Wall of China

   我 终于 登上了 长城。
   Wǒ zhōngyú dēngshangle Chángchéng.
   I finally climbed the Great Wall of China.

Helpful tips: The third stroke slants upward.   **9 strokes**

城	一	十	土	坛	圹	城	城	城			

市   shì

city, market

Radical: 亠 # 6 "top of 六"

Compounds, sentences, and meanings

1. 城市 **chéngshì** city

世界 上 有 几个 有名 的 城市, 例如
Shìjiè shàng yǒu jǐ ge yǒumíng de chéngshì, lìrú

上海。
Shànghǎi.

There are many famous cities in the world, for example Shanghai.

2. 市场 **shìchǎng** market

在 小 城市 里老人 天天 去 市场
Zài xiǎo chéngshì lǐ lǎorén tiāntiān qù shìchǎng

买 食品。
mǎi shípǐn.

In small cities, every day elderly people go to the market to buy food.

3. 市区 **shìqū** municipal area

北京 的 市区 非常 非常 大。
Běijīng de shìqū fēicháng fēicháng dà.

Beijing's municipal area is very large.

4. 市民 **shìmín** city residents, city folk

市民 住在 城市 里。
Shìmín zhùzài chéngshì lǐ.

City folk live inside of a city.

5. 市价 **shìjià** market price, "going" price

这样 的 手表 市价要 一千 多 美元。
Zhèyàng de shǒubiǎo shìjià yào yìqiān duō Měiyuán.

This sort of watch has a going price of more than one thousand U.S. dollars.

Helpful tips: The vertical stroke does not cross the second stroke.										**5 strokes**
市	㇒	亠	市	市	市					

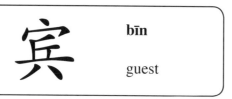

bīn

guest

Radical: 宀 # 34 "roof"

Compounds, sentences, and meanings

1. 宾馆 **bīnguǎn** hotel, guesthouse

   旅游 的 时候旅客 住在 宾馆。

   Lǚyóu de shíhou lǚkè zhùzài bīnguǎn.

   When traveling, travelers stay in hotels.

2. 宾客 **bīnkè** guest, visitor

   欢迎 宾客来 我们 的 家。

   Huānyíng bīnkè lái wǒmen de jiā.

   Guest, welcome to our home.

3. 贵宾 **guìbīn** honored guest

   你的爷爷是 一个 贵宾。

   Nǐ de yéye shì yí ge guìbīn.

   Your grandfather is an honored guest.

Helpful tips: The eighth stroke is the longest stroke.									**10 strokes**	
宾	丶	丷	宀	它	宀	宫	宫	宾	宾	宾

馆　　**guǎn**

　　dwelling

館

Radical: 饣 # 59 "food"

Compounds, sentences, and meanings

1. 馆 **guǎn** accommodation for guests

   宾馆 是高级的 旅馆。

   Bīnguǎn shì gāojí de lǚguǎn.

   A guesthouse is a high-class hotel.

2. 博物馆 **bówùguǎn** museum

   这 个 博物馆 值得一去。

   Zhè ge bówùguǎn zhíde yí qù.

   This museum is well worth visiting.

3. 领事馆 **lǐngshìguǎn** consulate

   我 要 去 领事馆 办 签证。

   Wǒ yào qù lǐngshìguǎn bàn qiānzhèng.

   I need to go to the consulate to get my visa.

4. 大使馆 **dàshǐguǎn** embassy

   请问, 美国 大使馆 在哪儿?

   Qǐngwèn, Měiguó Dàshǐguǎn zài nǎr?

   Excuse me, can you tell me where the American Embassy is?

5. 图书馆 **túshūguǎn** library

   北京 图书馆 的 藏书 很多。

   Běijīng Túshūguǎn de cángshū hěnduō.

   Beijing Library has a large collection of books.

Helpful tips: Note the difference between 官 and 宫.											11 strokes
馆	ノ¹	⺈²	饣³	饣⁴	饣⁵	馆⁶	馆⁷	馆⁸	馆⁹	馆¹⁰ 馆¹¹	

银   yín

silver

銀

Radical: 金 # 122 "metal"

Compounds, sentences, and meanings

1. 银 **yín** silver

   金 银 财宝
   Jīn, yín, cái, bǎo
   Gold, silver, treasures, and jewels

2. 银行 **yínháng** bank

   银行 离邮局 不 远。
   Yínháng lí yóujú bù yuǎn.
   The bank is not far from the post office.

3. 银色 **yínsè** silver color

   我 喜欢 银色。
   Wǒ xǐhuan yínsè.
   I like the color silver.

4. 银牌 **yínpái** silver medal

   她在 2000 年 奥运会 赢过 女子
   Tā zài 2000 nián Àoyùnhuì yíngguo nǚzi

   一百米 银牌。
   yìbǎimǐ yínpái.
   She won the silver medal at the 2000 Olympics for the women's 100 meters.

5. 银杏 **yínxìng** gingko tree

   秋天 来了, 银杏 的叶子 变黄了。
   Qiūtiān láile, yínxìng de yèzi biànhuángle.
   Autumn is here, the leaves on the gingko tree have turned yellow.

Helpful tips: The tenth stroke sweeps left, pointing at but not joining the ninth stroke.   **11 strokes**

银	⺧	⺧	钅	钅	钅	钌	钌	钼	银	银	银	

xíng/háng

travel/line, row

Radical: 彳 # 54 "double person"

Compounds, sentences, and meanings

1. 行 **xíng** capable, competent

   你 看 他 干 这 个 工作 行 吗?

   Nǐ kàn tā gàn zhè ge gōngzuò xíng ma?

   Do you think he is up to it?

2. 行李 **xíngli** luggage

   这 是 我 的 手提 行李。

   Zhè shì wǒde shǒutí xíngli.

   This is my hand luggage.

3. 行业 **hángyè** profession

   他 是 干 什么 行业 的?

   Tā shì gàn shénme hángyè de?

   What work does he do?

4. 银行 **yínháng** bank

   中国 银行 兑换 外币。

   Zhōngguó Yínháng duìhuàn wàibì.

   The Bank of China exchanges foreign currency.

5. 行驶 **xíngshǐ** travel (of a vehicle, ship etc.)

   在 中国 车辆 靠 右 行驶。

   Zài Zhōngguó chēliàng kào yòu xíngshǐ.

   In China, vehicles travel on the right side of the road.

Helpful tips: The fifth stroke is longer than the one above it.

6 strokes

行	彳	彳	彳	行	行						

CHARACTER 201

每   **měi**

every

Radical: 母 # 108 "mother"

Compounds, sentences, and meanings

1. 每 **měi** every, each

   每 到 北京, 我 总 要 去 逛 一下
   Měi dào Běijīng, wǒ zǒng yào qù guàng yíxià
   长城。
   Chángchéng.
   Every time I am in Beijing, I have to visit the Great Wall.

2. 每每 **měiměi** often

   他们 常 在一起, 每每 一谈 就 是
   Tāmen cháng zài yìqǐ, měiměi yì tán jiù shì
   半天。
   bàntiān.
   They often got together, and when they did, they'd talk for hours.

3. 每天 **měitiān** every day

   我 母亲 每天 都 去 散步。
   Wǒ mǔqin měitiān dōu qù sànbù.
   My mother goes for a walk every day.

4. 每年 **měinián** every year

   我 每年 都 去 旅行。
   Wǒ měinián dōu qù lǚxíng.
   I go for a trip every year.

5. 每个星期 **měi ge xīngqī** every week

   她 每个星期 都 请客。
   Tā měi ge xīngqī dōu qǐngkè.
   She entertains guests every week.

Helpful tips: 每 can be confused with 母.   **7 strokes**

每											

都 **dōu/dū**

all; city

Radical: 阝 # 28 "right earlobe"

Compounds, sentences, and meanings

1. 都 **dōu** all

 大家 都 到 了 吗?

 Dàjiā dōu dào le ma?

 Is everybody here?

2. 都市 **dūshì** city

 上海 是一个大 都市。

 Shànghǎi shì yí ge dà dūshì.

 Shanghai is a big city.

3. 首都 **shǒudū** capital city

 北京 是 中国 的 首都。

 Běijīng shì Zhōngguó de shǒudū.

 Beijing is the capital of China.

Helpful tips: The first stroke of 阝 looks like the figure 3.									**10 strokes**

都 　 二₁ 　 扗₂ 　 圥₃ 　 耂₄ 　 者₅ 　 者₆ 　 者₇ 　 者₈ 　 都₉ 　 都₁₀

A. Pronunciation and *Pinyin* Practice

Please transcribe the following sentences into *pinyin*, then practice saying them. The name for each city is given in Chinese characters; use the illustration and the sentence to understand the name in English.

纽约   伦敦   洛杉矶

这个城市是美国最大的城市。   这个城市是英国的首都。   很多有名人住在这个城市。

_____   _____   _____

_____   _____   _____

B. Completion and Translation

Please complete each sentence with an appropriate noun. Then translate the resulting sentence into English.

1. 每个_____都喜欢练习写汉字。

_____

2. 我朋友的每件_____都非常好看。

_____

3. 每个_____都有邮局。

_____

4. 每个_____都卖有意思的书。

_____

C. Descriptive Sentences

Consider the places listed below. Then write a sentence for each, expressing your opinion as to whether a city or town should have this location or not. A strong demonstration of understanding will also indicate the reason for that feature being part of a city. An example sentence is given below.

每个城市应该有邮局。

1.（银行）_____

_____

2.（学校）_____

_____

3.（公安局）_____

_____

4.（宾馆）_____

_____

5.（服装店）_____

_____

A. Items and Prices

Please create an illustration for each of the following items. Then provide a price for each. For extra practice, ask and answer questions about the items, prices, and other important descriptions.

东西：	衣服	毛衣	饭店	宾馆
画：				
多少钱：				

B. Reading Comprehension

Label the map's items in Chinese based on the information in the following passage. Then answer the following questions in English.

我的老家是一个很小的美国城市。我认为我的老家是城市，但是有人说我的老家不是城市是村庄。对我来说，城市一定要有学校，公安局，邮局，银行，等等，才能叫城市。我的老家有这些地方。我的老家也有很小的宾馆。虽然没有很多旅客可是还有这一家宾馆。再说很多的城市有很大的花园。我的老家在城市中心有很大的花园，很美丽！我觉得我的老家很漂亮，可以说是一个很美丽的小城市。

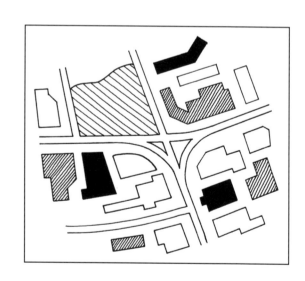

1. What place is the speaker talking about?

_____

2. What types of places does a city need?

_____

3. Does this small city have those places?

_____

4. What does the speaker feel a large city needs?

_____

5. Does this small city have one and where is it?

_____

6. Do you feel that this place is a small city or not?

_____

C. Location Comparison

Please discuss the following topic. Note this discussion is comparing the conditions in two different locations. A strong demonstration of understanding will cover a variety of topics but relates to a consistent theme or thesis. Proper use of connecting and descriptive construction is important for greater clarity.

有人说住在美国很贵, 住在中国很便宜。请介绍绍你的意见, 你同不同意? 想一想生活的特点: 饭, 衣服, 东西, 等等。

_____

_____

_____

_____

_____

_____

_____

_____

D. Reflective Questions

Use these questions to both check the expressiveness of the previous section and to confirm your understanding of the previous topic. For additional practice, say and then respond to these questions aloud.

一元美元多少人民币？

在美国一张邮票多少钱？在中国多少钱？

在美国一升石油几块钱？在中国一升多少？

在美国你要买新的衣服，你可以去什么商店？

在中国你要去一样的商店吗？

美国的衣服大概从哪儿来的？

中国的衣服从哪儿来的？

对你来说，最重要是物价还是收入？

有人说很贵的东西才是很好的东西，你同意吗？

如果许多东西从中国来美国的，在美国为什么这些东西很贵可是在中国很便宜？

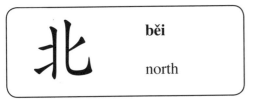

北 **běi**

north

Radical: | # 3 "vertical stroke"

Compounds, sentences, and meanings

1. 北 **běi** north

   你 从 这儿 往 北 走。

   Nǐ cóng zhèr wǎng běi zǒu.

   Go north from here.

2. 北方 **běifāng** northern

   这 个 饭馆儿 做 的 是 北方菜。

   Zhè ge fànguǎnr zuò de shì běifāngcài.

   This restaurant serves northern Chinese cuisine.

3. 东北 **dōngběi** northeast

   大连市 在 中国 东北。

   Dàliánshì zài Zhōngguó dōngběi.

   The city of Dalian is in northeast China.

4. 北京 **Běijīng** Beijing

   二零零八年 奥运会 在 北京 举办。

   Èrlínglíngbā'nián Àoyùnhuì zài Běijīng jǔbàn.

   The 2008 Olympic Games was hosted by Beijing.

5. 北美洲 **Běiměizhōu** North America

   北美洲 包括 美国 和 加拿大。

   Běiměizhōu bāokuò Měiguó hé Jiā'nádà.

   North America includes the U.S. and Canada.

Helpful tips: The last stroke is a vertical-bend hook.　　　　**5 strokes**

北	丿	丬	丬	北	北						

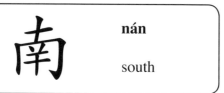

nán

south

Radical: 十 # 11 "ten"

Compounds, sentences, and meanings

1. 南 **nán** south

   你 从 这儿 往 南 走。

   Nǐ cóng zhèr wǎng nán zǒu.

   Go south from here.

2. 南边 **nánbian** south side

   学校 南边 有 一个 公园。

   Xuéxiào nánbian yǒu yí ge gōngyuán.

   There is a park on the southern side of the school.

3. 南部 **nánbù** southern part

   广州 在 广东 省 南部。

   Guǎngzhōu zài Guǎngdōng shěng nánbù.

   Canton is in the south of Guangdong province.

4. 南方 **nánfāng** south of a country

   他 说话 带 南方 腔调。

   Tā shuōhuà dài nánfāng qiāngdiào.

   He speaks with a southern accent.

5. 南半球 **nánbànqiú** Southern Hemisphere

   澳大利亚 在 南半球。

   Àodàlìyà zài Nánbànqiú.

   Australia is in the Southern Hemisphere.

| **Helpful tips:** Note the difference between 羊 and 半 in the bottom half of the character. | | | | | | | | **9 strokes** |

南	一	十	冄	南	南	南	南	南	南

东　dōng

east

東

Radical: 一　# 2 "horizontal stroke"

Compounds, sentences, and meanings

1. 东 dōng east

    我 住 在 城 东。

    Wǒ zhù zài chéng dōng.

    I live in the eastern part of the city.

2. 东边 dōngbian east

    太阳 从 东边 升起来。

    Tàiyáng cóng dōngbian shēngqilai.

    The sun rises in the east.

3. 东南亚 Dōngnányà Southeast Asia

    东南亚 有 很多 华人。

    Dōngnányà yǒu hěnduō Huárén.

    There are many Chinese in Southeast Asia.

4. 东西 dōngxi thing (literally, east west)

    她 买 东西 去了。

    Tā mǎi dōngxi qù le.

    She's out shopping.

5. 房东 fángdōng landlord

    他 是 我的 房东。

    Tā shì wǒde fángdōng.

    He is my landlord.

Helpful tips: The second stroke is a downward-left bend.　　　　**5 strokes**

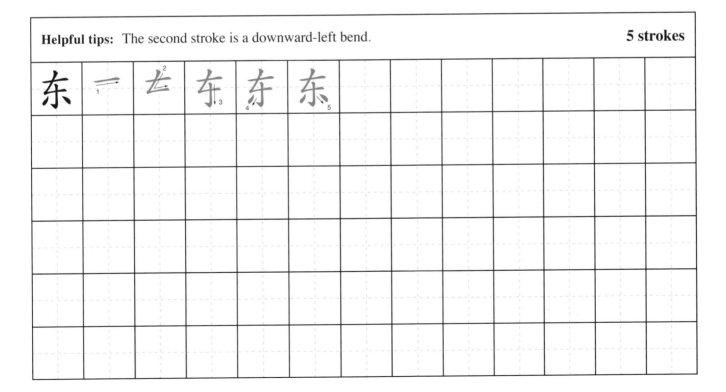

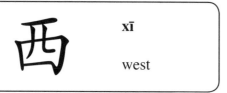

西 xī

west

Radical: 西 # 139 "west"

Compounds, sentences, and meanings

1. 西 **xī** west

   夕阳 西下。

   Xīyáng xī xià.

   The sun sets in the west.

2. 西方 **Xīfāng** the West

   澳大利亚是西方 国家。

   Àodàlìyà shì Xīfāng guójiā.

   Australia is a Western country.

3. 西餐 **Xīcān** Western food

   你 喜欢 吃　中餐　还是 西餐?

   Nǐ xǐhuan chī Zhōngcān háishi Xīcān?

   Do you prefer Chinese or Western food?

4. 西药 **Xīyào** Western medicine

   在　中国　哪里可以 买到 西药?

   Zài Zhōngguó nǎli kěyǐ mǎidào Xīyào?

   Where can one buy Western medicine in China?

5. 西式 **Xīshì** Western style

   西式 快餐 在 北京 很 流行。

   Xīshì kuàicān zài Běijīng hěn liúxíng.

   Western-style fast food is very popular in Beijing.

Helpful tips: The inside right stroke bends.												**6 strokes**
西	一	一	冂	丙	西	西						

前

qián

in front of, ahead

Radical: 八 # 17 "eight"

Compounds, sentences, and meanings

1. 前 **qián** forward, ahead

   我们 应该 往 前看。

   Wǒmen yīnggāi wǎng qián kàn.

   We should look ahead.

2. 前面 **qiánmian** in front of, ahead

   前面 有 座位。

   Qiánmian yǒu zuòwèi.

   There are seats in the front.

3. 前边 **qiánbian** in front of, ahead

   前边 有 座位 吗?

   Qiánbian yǒu zuòwèi ma?

   Are there seats in the front?

4. 前天 **qiántiān** day before yesterday

   前天 他来过 这里。

   Qiántiān tā láiguo zhèlǐ.

   He came here the day before yesterday.

5. 前途 **qiántú** future prospect

   你的 工作 很 有 前途。

   Nǐde gōngzuò hěn yǒu qiántú.

   Your work has great potential.

Helpful tips: The final stroke ends with a hook.										**9 strokes**

前 | 丶 | 丷 | 丷 | 首 | 首 | 首 | 首 | 前 | 前 | | |

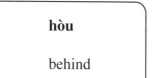

CHARACTER 208

Traditional Form

后 **hòu**
behind

後

Radical: 丿 # 4 "downward-left-stroke" or 口 # 50 "mouth"

Compounds, sentences, and meanings

1. 后 **hòu** back

   屋后 种着 很多 花儿。

   Wūhòu zhǒngzhe hěnduō huār.

   There are flowers growing at the back of the house.

2. 后面 **hòumian** at the back, behind

   后面 还有 座位。

   Hòumian hái yǒu zuòwèi.

   There are still some seats at the back.

3. 后天 **hòutiān** day after tomorrow

   后天 你 有 没有 空儿?

   Hòutiān nǐ yǒu méiyǒu kòngr?

   Are you free the day after tomorrow?

4. 后果 **hòuguǒ** consequence

   后果 不堪 设想。

   Hòuguǒ bùkān shèxiǎng.

   The consequences would be too ghastly to contemplate.

5. 以后 **yǐhòu** afterwards

   以后 你 会 有 机会去 的。

   Yǐhòu nǐ huì yǒu jīhuì qù de.

   You will have a chance to go later.

Helpful tips: The first two strokes are written separately.											**6 strokes**
后	一₁	厂₂	斤₃	斤₄	后₅	后₆					

左　zuǒ

left

Radical: 工 # 39 "work"

Compounds, sentences, and meanings

1. 左 zuǒ left

   在　前面　红绿灯　左　拐弯。

   Zài qiánmian hónglùdēng zuǒ guǎiwān.

   Turn left at the lights.

2. 左边 zuǒbian the left

   房子　左边　有一棵大树。

   Fángzi zuǒbian yǒu yì kē dà shù.

   There's a big tree on the left side of the house.

3. 左手 zuǒshǒu left hand

   他　能　用　左手写字。

   Tā néng yòng zuǒshǒu xiězì.

   He writes with his left hand.

4. 左撇子 zuǒpiězi left-handed person

   他　是个　左撇子。

   Tā shì ge zuǒpiězi.

   He's left-handed.

5. 左右 zuǒyòu about (used after a numeral)

   他　说　八点　左右　到这儿来。

   Tā shuō bādiǎn zuǒyòu dào zhèr lái.

   He said he'll be here around 8:00.

Helpful tips: Don't mistake 左 for 在. Note the difference between them.												**5 strokes**
左	一	𠂇	左	左	左							

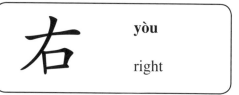

右

yòu

right

Radical: 口 # 50 "mouth"

Compounds, sentences, and meanings

1. 右 **yòu** right

   在 中国 车辆 靠 右 走。

   Zài Zhōngguó chēliàng kào yòu zǒu.

   In China, traffic keeps to the right.

2. 右边 **yòubian** the right

   房子 右边 有一棵 大 树。

   Fángzi yòubian yǒu yì kē dà shù.

   There's a big tree on the right side of the house.

3. 右手 **yòushǒu** right hand

   大部分 人 用 右手 写字。

   Dàbùfen rén yòng yòushǒu xiězì.

   Most people write with their right hand.

4. 右侧 **yòucè** right-hand side

   房子 右侧 种了 很多 花儿。

   Fángzi yòucè zhòngle hěnduō huār.

   There are flowers planted on the right-hand side of the house.

5. 左思右想 **zuǒsī-yòuxiǎng** think over from different angles (literally, think left and right)

   她 躺 在 床上 左思右想， 一夜

   Tā tǎng zài chuángshang zuǒsī-yòuxiǎng, yí yè

   也没 睡好。

   yě méi shuìhǎo.

   She lay awake all night, thinking about it over and over again.

Helpful tips: Note the difference between 右 and 石.											**5 strokes**
右	一	大	大	右	右						

内　**nèi**

internal, inside

Radical: | # 3 "vertical stroke"

Compounds, sentences, and meanings

1. 内部 **nèibù** internal

国家　重视 内部 事务。

Guójiā zhòngshì nèibù shìwù.

A country considers seriously internal affairs.

2. 内容 **nèiróng** content

这 个课的 内容 很 丰富。

Zhè ge kè de nèiróng hěn fēngfù.

The content of this class is very rich and developed.

3. 内科 **nèikē** internal medicine

医院 有 很 多 分部, 内科 是 一部。

Yīyuàn yǒu hěn duō fēnbù; nèikē shì yí bù.

Hospitals have many divisions; internal medicine is one division.

3. 内衣 **nèiyī** underwear

百货 公司 卖 多 牌子的内衣。

Bǎihuò gōngsi mài duō páizi de nèiyī.

Department stores sell many brands of underwear.

5. 内政 **nèizhèng** domestic politics

内政 的 政客 不 管理 国外 联系。

Nèizhèng de zhèngkè bù guǎnlǐ guówài liánxì.

Politicians focusing on internal politics do not oversee foreign relations.

Helpful tips: The second stroke ends in a hook.									**4 strokes**
内									

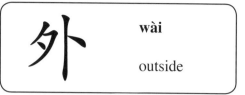

外　**wài**

outside

Radical: 卜 # 14 "divination"

Compounds, sentences, and meanings

1. 外 **wài** outside

这 是 意料 外 的 事。

Zhè shì yìliào wài de shì.

That's outside my expectation.

2. 外面 **wàimian** outside

今天 我们 要 在 外面 吃饭。

Jīntiān wǒmen yào zài wàimian chīfàn.

We are dining out today.

3. 外表 **wàibiǎo** outward appearance

不要 从 外表 看人。

Búyào cóng wàibiǎo kàn rén.

Don't judge people by their outward appearances.

4. 外国人 **wàiguórén** foreigner

你 有 没有 外国人 居留证?

Nǐ yǒu méiyǒu wàiguórén jūliúzhèng?

Do you have a residence permit for foreigners?

5. 外人 **wàirén** stranger, outsider

别客气, 我 又 不是 外人。

Bié kèqi, wǒ yòu búshì wàirén.

Don't stand on ceremony, I'm no stranger.

Helpful tips: End the last stroke firmly.											**5 strokes**
外	⺈	夕	夕	外	外						

旁 **páng**

next to

Radical: 方 # 74 "direction"

Compounds, sentences, and meanings

1. 旁 **páng** other

   旁 的 还要 什么?

   Páng de hái yào shénme?

   Do you want anything else?

2. 旁边 **pángbiān** next to

   坐 在 我 旁边 吧。

   Zuò zài wǒ pángbiān ba.

   Why don't you sit next to me.

3. 旁听 **pángtīng** be a visitor in a school class

   我 明天 旁听 你的课可以吗?

   Wǒ míngtiān pángtīng nǐde kè kěyǐ ma?

   May I sit in on your lecture tomorrow?

4. 两旁 **liǎngpáng** both sides

   马路 两旁 种了 很多 树。

   Mǎlù liǎngpáng zhòngle hěnduō shù.

   There are lots of trees planted on both sides of the road.

5. 旁观者 **pángguānzhě** onlooker

   旁观者 清视。

   Pángguānzhě qīngshì.

   The spectator sees most clearly.

Helpful tips: The last stroke ends with a hook.　　　　**10 strokes**

旁	丶	二	亠	立	产	竒	帝	产	旁	旁		

边 **biān**

side

邊

Radical: 辶 # 38 "movement"

Compounds, sentences, and meanings

1. 边 **biān** side

   马路 两 边 种了 很多 树。

   Mǎlù liǎng biān zhòngle hěnduō shù.

   There are lots of trees planted on both sides of the road.

2. 边 ... 边 **biān ... biān** as ... as

   他 边 唱歌 边 跳舞。

   Tā biān chànggē biān tiàowǔ.

   He sings as he dances.

3. 上边 **shàngbian** above

   大桥 上边 走 汽车。

   Dàqiáo shàngbian zǒu qìchē.

   The upper deck of the bridge is for cars.

4. 外边 **wàibian** outside

   请 到 外边 抽烟。

   Qǐng dào wàibian chōuyān.

   Please go outside to smoke.

5. 海边 **hǎibiān** seaside

   夏天 很多 人 到 海边 游泳。

   Xiàtiān hěnduō rén dào hǎibiān yóuyǒng.

   In summer, many people go to the seaside to swim.

Helpful tips: 辶 is written in 3 strokes.												**5 strokes**
边	刁	力	力	边	边							

A. Vocabulary and *Pinyin* Practice

Please identify the *pinyin* transcription for each of the following characters. Then write an opposite character for each character given. Finally, provide the *pinyin* transcription for the new character.

	pinyin		*pinyin*		*pinyin*		*pinyin*		*pinyin*
北		东		前		左		内	

B. Location Description

Please label the illustration using the vocabulary items provided. Then, for each of the directional terms given, create a sentence that expresses an appropriate description of the location in the illustration.

地方：

饭店

商店

公园

宾馆

学校

1.（左边）＿＿＿＿＿＿＿＿＿＿＿＿＿＿＿＿＿＿＿＿＿＿＿＿＿＿

2.（右边）＿＿＿＿＿＿＿＿＿＿＿＿＿＿＿＿＿＿＿＿＿＿＿＿＿＿

3.（旁边）＿＿＿＿＿＿＿＿＿＿＿＿＿＿＿＿＿＿＿＿＿＿＿＿＿＿

4.（南边）＿＿＿＿＿＿＿＿＿＿＿＿＿＿＿＿＿＿＿＿＿＿＿＿＿＿

5.（后边）＿＿＿＿＿＿＿＿＿＿＿＿＿＿＿＿＿＿＿＿＿＿＿＿＿＿

C. Short Description

Consider your present location and prepare to describe that location completely. Then for each of the directional phrases provided below, create an appropriate descriptive sentence.

1. （里边）_____

2. （外边）_____

3. （左边）_____

4. （右边）_____

5. （旁边）_____

6. （东边）_____

7. （北边）_____

8. （上边）_____

9. （下边）_____

10. （前边）_____

时　shí
　　time

Radical: 日 # 90 "sun"

Compounds, sentences, and meanings

1. 时 **shí** time

   大夫 说 要 按时 吃药。

   Dàifu shuō yào ànshí chīyào.

   The doctor said to take the medicine at the right time.

2. 时间 **shíjiān** time

   没有 时间 了, 我们 得 走了。

   Méiyǒu shíjiān le, wǒmen děi zǒu le.

   There's no time, we must be going.

3. 时候 **shíhou** time

   现在 什么 时候 了?

   Xiànzài shénme shíhou le?

   What's the time now?

4. 时机 **shíjī** opportunity

   他 在 等待 时机。

   Tā zài děngdài shíjī.

   He is waiting for an opportunity.

5. 时髦 **shímáo** fashionable

   她 喜欢 穿 时髦 的 服装。

   Tā xǐhuan chuān shímáo de fúzhuāng.

   She likes to wear fashionable clothes.

Helpful tips: The sixth stroke ends with a hook.											7 strokes
时	丨	刂	日	日	日一	时	时				

265

候

hòu

time; wait

Radical: 亻 # 19 "upright person"

Compounds, sentences, and meanings

1. 候 **hòu** wait

   请 稍 候一会儿。

   Qǐng shāo hòu yíhuìr.

   Please wait a moment.

2. 时候 **shíhou** time

   现在 什么 时候 了?

   Xiànzài shénme shíhou le?

   What's the time now?

3. 有时候 **yǒu shíhou** sometimes

   我 有 时候 去 看 电影。

   Wǒ yǒu shíhou qù kàn diànyǐng.

   Sometimes I go to see a movie.

4. 气候 **qìhòu** climate

   他不 适应 这里的气候。

   Tā bú shìyìng zhèlǐ de qìhòu.

   He's not used to the climate here.

5. 问候 **wènhòu** give regards to

   请 代 我 问候 你父母。

   Qǐng dài wǒ wènhòu nǐ fùmǔ.

   Please send my regards to your parents.

Helpful tips: Remember to write the third stroke.									**10 strokes**
候	丿¹	亻²	亻³	亻⁴	㑉⁵	侯⁶	侯⁷	侯⁸	侯⁹ 候¹⁰

钟　zhōng　clock

鐘

Radical: 钅 # 122 "metal"

Compounds, sentences, and meanings

1. 钟 **zhōng** clock

   送 礼物 千万 不要 送 钟。

   Sòng lǐwù qiānwàn búyào sòng zhōng.

   When buying a gift, be sure that it is not a clock.

   [Note that the homonym of **sòng zhōng** *is* **sòngzhōng** *"attend upon a dying person."]*

2. 点钟 **diǎnzhōng** o'clock

   他 上午 十 点钟 来。

   Tā shàngwǔ shí diǎnzhōng lái.

   He's coming here at 10 A.M.

3. 一刻钟 **yí kèzhōng** 15 minutes, a quarter of an hour

   我 等了 一 刻钟。

   Wǒ děngle yí kèzhōng.

   I waited for a quarter of an hour.

4. 钟头 **zhōngtóu** hour

   我 看了 三个 钟头 电视。

   Wǒ kànle sān ge zhōngtóu diànshì.

   I've spent three hours watching television.

5. 钟情 **zhōngqíng** be deeply in love

   他们 两个 一见 钟情。

   Tāmen liǎng ge yí jiàn zhōngqíng.

   They fell in love at first sight.

Helpful tips: The fifth stroke is a vertical tick.											**9 strokes**
钟	丿	仨	牟	钅	金	钟	钥	钥	钟		

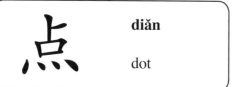

点   **diǎn**

dot

點

Radical: 灬 **# 71** "fire"

Compounds, sentences, and meanings

1. 点 **diǎn** a little
   他 今天 好 点 了。
   Tā jīntiān hǎo diǎn le.
   He's a bit better today.

2. 五点零七分 **wǔ diǎn líng qī fēn** 5:07.
   现在 五 点 零 七 分。
   Xiànzài wǔ diǎn líng qī fēn.
   It's now seven minutes past five.

3. 晚点 **wǎndiǎn** behind schedule
   飞机 晚点 了。
   Fēijī wǎndiǎn le.
   The plane is late.

4. 点菜 **diǎncài** choose dishes from a menu
   可以 点菜 了。
   Kěyǐ diǎncài le.
   We're ready to order now.

5. 点头 **diǎntóu** nod one's head
   他已经 点头 了。
   Tā yǐjīng diǎntóu le.
   He's already okayed it.

Helpful tips: Note the order of the dots from left to right.   **9 strokes**

点											

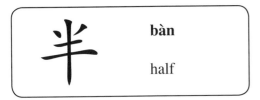

半　　bàn

half

Radical: 八 # 17 "eight" or 十 # 11 "ten"

Compounds, sentences, and meanings

1. 半 **bàn** half

   从 这里 去要 半（个）小时。

   Cóng zhèlǐ qù yào bàn (ge) xiǎoshí.

   It'll take half an hour from here.

2. 一半 **yíbàn** half

   这 箱 桔子 有 一半 坏了。

   Zhè xiāng júzi yǒu yíbàn huàile.

   Half of this box of oranges is rotten.

3. 一倍半 **yíbèibàn** 150%

   这里的 房价 十 年 内 增加了 一倍半。

   Zhèlǐ de fángjià shí nián nèi zēngjiāle yíbèibàn.

   Property values have increased one and a half times over the last ten years.

4. 半天 **bàntiān** a long time (literally, half the day)

   我们 谈了 半天 也 没 结果。

   Wǒmen tánle bàntiān yě méi jiéguǒ.

   We discussed the matter for a long time but did not come to any conclusion.

5. 半新不旧 **bànxīn-bújiù** showing signs of wear (literally, no longer new)

   他 穿着 一 身 半新不旧 的衣服。

   Tā chuānzhe yì shēn bànxīn-bújiù de yīfu.

   The clothes he was wearing, though not shabby, were far from new.

Helpful tips: The bottom horizontal stroke is longer.									**5 strokes**
半									

久 **jiǔ**

a long time

Radical: ﾉ # 4 "downward-left stroke"

Compounds, sentences, and meanings

1. 久 **jiǔ** for a long time

   我们 久不 见面 了。

   Wǒmen jiǔ bú jiànmiàn le.

   We haven't seen each other for a long time.

2. 多久 **duō jiǔ** how long?

   你来了多 久?

   Nǐ láile duō jiǔ?

   How long have you been here?

3. 久等 **jiǔděng** wait for a long time

   对不起 让 你 久等 了。

   Duìbuqǐ, ràng nǐ jiǔděng le.

   Sorry to have kept you waiting.

4. 久留 **jiǔliú** stay a long time

   我 有 要事 在 身, 不能 久留。

   Wǒ yǒu yàoshì zài shēn, bùnéng jiǔliú.

   I can't stay long because I have some important business to attend to.

5. 不久 **bùjiǔ** not long after

   回家 不久 就下 大雨了。

   Huíjiā bùjiǔ jiù xià dàyǔ le.

   Not long after I came home, it rained.

Helpful tips: The last stroke tapers off.											3 strokes
久	ノ	夕	久								

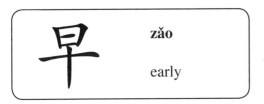

早　**zǎo**

early

Radical: 日 # 90 "sun"

Compounds, sentences, and meanings

1. 早 **zǎo** early

   我 早 知道 了。

   Wǒ zǎo zhīdao le.

   I knew that long ago.

2. 早饭 **zǎofàn** breakfast

   我 早饭 吃 点儿 水果。

   Wǒ zǎofàn chī diǎnr shuǐguǒ.

   I eat fruit for my breakfast.

3. 早上 **zǎoshang** morning

   早上 好!

   Zǎoshang hǎo!

   Good morning!

4. 早晨 **zǎochén** early morning

   早晨 空气 清新。

   Zǎochén kōngqì qīngxīn.

   The air is fresh early in the morning.

5. 早日 **zǎorì** at an early date

   祝 你 早日 恢复 健康。

   Zhù nǐ zǎorì huīfú jiànkāng.

   I hope you'll get well soon.

Helpful tips: The bottom horizontal stroke is longer.											**6 strokes**
早	丿	冂	日	旦	旦	早					

晚   **wǎn**

late, evening

Radical: 日 # 90 "sun"

Compounds, sentences, and meanings

1. 晚 **wǎn** late

现在 去 还 不 晚。

Xiànzài qù hái bù wǎn.

It's still not too late to go.

2. 晚上 **wǎnshang** evening

今天 晚上 我 请客。

Jīntiān wǎnshang wǒ qǐngkè.

I'm buying dinner tonight.

3. 晚饭 **wǎnfàn** evening meal

今天 晚饭 很 丰盛。

Jīntiān wǎnfàn hěn fēngshèng.

Tonight's dinner is sumptuous.

4. 晚班 **wǎnbān** evening shift

这个 工作 需要 上 晚班。

Zhè ge gōngzuò xūyào shàng wǎnbān.

This job involves working night shifts.

5. 晚点 **wǎndiǎn** behind schedule (train/bus/plane/ferry)

飞机 晚点 了。

Fēijī wǎndiǎn le.

The plane is late.

Helpful tips: The final stroke is a vertical-bend-hook.										**11 strokes**
晚	l	ll	刖	日	日'	旷	旷	晚	晗	晚	晚

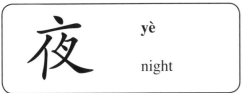

夜　**yè**　night

Radical: 亠 # 6 "top of 六"

Compounds, sentences, and meanings

1. 夜 **yè** night

   三 天 三 夜　讲不完。

   Sān tiān sān yè jiǎngbuwán.

   It's a long story. (Literally, three days and three nights wouldn't be enough time to finish it.)

2. 夜间 **yèjiān** night time

   　上海　很 多　工 地　都　进行

   Shànghǎi hěnduō gōngdì dōu jìngxíng

   夜间　施工。

   yèjiān shīgōng.

   In Shanghai, work on lots of building sites goes on all night.

3. 夜景 **yèjǐng** night scene

   　香港　 的 夜景 很　有名。

   Xiānggǎng de yèjǐng hěn yǒumíng.

   Hong Kong's night scene is very famous.

4. 夜生活 **yèshēnghuó** night life

   这里的　夜生活　很 丰富。

   Zhèlǐ de yèshēnghuó hěn fēngfù.

   The night life here is vibrant.

5. 夜总会 **yèzǒnghuì** night club

   我们　　常常　 去 夜总会　跳舞。

   Wǒmen chángcháng qù yèzǒnghuì tiàowǔ.

   We often go to night clubs to dance.

Helpful tips: The bottom component is placed under the horizontal stroke.　　　**8 strokes**

夜	亠	亠	亣	疒	疒	夜	夜				

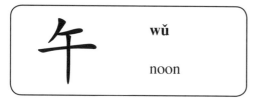

午 **wǔ**

noon

Radical: ノ # 4 "downward-left stroke"

Compounds, sentences, and meanings

1. 午 **wǔ** noon

午 前 就是 中午 一点 之前。

Wǔ qián jiùshì zhōngwǔ yìdiǎn zhīqián.

Noontime is before 1:00 P.M.

2. 中午 **zhōngwǔ** noon

我 跟 他 约好 中午 见面。

Wǒ gēn tā yuēhǎo zhōngwǔ jiànmiàn.

I've arranged to meet with him at noon.

3. 午饭 **wǔfàn** lunch

今天 午饭 吃 什么?

Jīntiān wǔfàn chī shénme?

What's for lunch today?

4. 午睡 **wǔshuì** afternoon nap

中国人 有 午睡 的 习惯。

Zhōngguórén yǒu wǔshuì de xíguàn.

Chinese people have a habit of taking an afternoon nap.

5. 午间 **wǔjiān** afternoon (adjective)

现在 播送 的 是 午间 新闻。

Xiànzài bōsòng de shì wǔjiān xīnwén.

We are now broadcasting the afternoon news.

Helpful tips: The bottom horizontal stroke is longer.												**4 strokes**
午	ノ	ﾉ	一	午								

周 zhōu

week

週

Radical: 冂 # 16 "border"

Compounds, sentences, and meanings

1. 周 **zhōu** week

上周 我 有事儿, 没 去 跳舞。

Shàngzhōu wǒ yǒu shìr, méi qù tiàowǔ.

Last week I was busy, so I didn't go dancing.

2. 周日 **zhōurì** Sunday

周日 晚上 我 都 没 空儿。

Zhōurì wǎnshang wǒ dōu méi kòngr.

I'm always busy on Sunday nights.

3. 周年 **zhōunián** anniversary

今天 是 我 结婚 二十五 周年 纪念。

Jīntiān shì wǒ jiéhūn èrshíwǔ zhōunián jìniàn.

Today is my 25th wedding anniversary.

4. 周身 **zhōushēn** all over the body

今天 我 觉得 周身 疼痛。

Jīntiān wǒ juéde zhōushēn téngtòng.

Today, my whole body aches.

5. 周围 **zhōuwéi** around

这里 周围 环境 都 很 美。

Zhèlǐ zhōuwéi huánjìng dōu hěn měi.

The surroundings here are beautiful.

Helpful tips: The second stroke ends with a hook.								**8 strokes**			
周	丿	冂	冃	用	周	周	周	周			

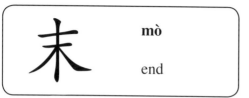

CHARACTER 226

末　　**mò**

end

Radical: 木 # 81 "tree"

Compounds, sentences, and meanings

1. 末 **mò** end

   今天 是 学期 最末 一天。

   Jīntiān shì xuéqī zuì mò yì tiān.

   Today is the last day of the semester.

2. 周末 **zhōumò** weekend

   周末 我 一般 都 出去玩儿。

   Zhōumò wǒ yìbān dōu chūqu wánr.

   I generally go out during the weekends.

3. 末期 **mòqī** last phase

   我 是第二次世界 大战 末期 出生 的。

   Wǒ shì dì'er cì shìjiè dàzhàn mòqī chūshēng de.

   I was born during the last stage of the Second World War.

4. 末班车 **mòbānchē** last train/bus

   末班车 午夜 十二点 一刻 开。

   Mòbānchē wǔyè shí'èrdiǎn yíkè kāi.

   The last bus leaves at 12:15 A.M.

5. 末日 **mòrì** doomsday

   核子 战争 将 导致 世界 末日。

   Hézi zhànzhēng jiāng dǎozhì shìjiè mòrì.

   Nuclear wars will result in the end of the world.

Helpful tips: The second stroke is shorter.									**5 strokes**
末									

A. Character and Pronunciation Practice

Please write the following times in accurate Chinese constructions. Then write those characters in *pinyin*. Please indicate appropriately the time of day for those times that specify that information.

Time	Characters	*Pinyin*
10:00		
5:30		
2:05		
7:15		
8:45 P.M.		
9:10 A.M.		
3:50 P.M.		
11:00 A.M.		

B. Descriptive Sentences

Please create a sentence that describes concurrent activities using a 的时候 construction for each of the activities given. Create a prepositional phrase utilizing that activity and add the activity, thought, or event that occurs at the same time. An example is given below.

我看汉语书的时候，我也练习说汉语。

1.（看电视）_____

2.（跟家人吃饭）_____

3.（想我的老家）_____

4.（写汉字）_____

5.（跟朋友们一起玩儿）_____

C. Short Description

Please describe a weekend day and the events that take place in it. Divide your description into three sections, one section for each of the major segments of the day, and provide a few activities for each of part of the day. A strong description will relate and connect the activities while still being clear about the progression and time of each activity.

（早上）_____

_____

_____

_____

_____

（下午）_____

_____

_____

_____

_____

（晚上）_____

_____

_____

_____

_____

CHARACTER 227

現 xiàn

appear

現

Radical: 王 # 79 "king"

Compounds, sentences, and meanings

1. 现 **xiàn** appear

   他 脸上 现出了 笑容。

   Tā liǎnshang xiànchūle xiàoróng.

   A smile appears on his face.

2. 现在 **xiànzài** now

   现在 几点了?

   Xiànzài jǐ diǎn le?

   What's the time now?

3. 现金 **xiànjīn** cash (literally, ready money)

   你可以 给 现金 吗?

   Nǐ kěyǐ gěi xiànjīn ma?

   Can you pay cash?

4. 现成 **xiànchéng** ready-made

   定做 衣服太贵了, 买 现成 的吧。

   Dìngzuò yīfu tài guì le, mǎi xiànchéng de ba.

   It's too expensive to buy tailor-made clothes, let's buy ready-made ones.

5. 表现 **biǎoxiàn** behavior

   他 今天 的 表现 很 好。

   Tā jīntiān de biǎoxiàn hěn hǎo.

   He's behaving very well today.

Helpful tips: The final stroke is a vertical-bend hook.　　　　**8 strokes**

现	一	二	王	王	邘	珇	现	现			
	1	2	3	4	5	6	7	8			

Traditional Form

来 lái

come

來

Radical: 一 **# 2** "horizontal stroke"

Compounds, sentences, and meanings

1. 来 **lái** come

   来 客人 了。

   Lái kèrén le.

   The guests are here.

2. 来不及 **láibují** there's not enough time

   今天 我们 来不及 去 看 他了。

   Jīntiān wǒmen láibují qù kàn tā le.

   There's no time for us to go and see him today.

3. 来回 **láihuí** a return journey

   来回 有 多 远？

   Láihuí yǒu duō yuǎn?

   How far is it there and back?

4. 来往 **láiwǎng** come and go

   街上 来往 的人 很多。

   Jiēshang láiwǎng de rén hěnduō.

   There are many people coming and going on the streets.

5. 从来 **cónglái** all along, never

   我 从来 没有 见过 他。

   Wǒ cónglái méiyǒu jiànguo tā.

   I've never seen him before.

Helpful tips: The bottom horizontal stroke is longer than the one above.　　　　**7 strokes**

来	一	二	二	亚	平	来	来				

CHARACTER 229

买

mǎi

buy

買

Radical: 一 # 5 "horizontal-hook"

Compounds, sentences, and meanings

1. 买 **mǎi** buy
   我 买了〈汉英 词典〉。
   Wǒ mǎile Hànyīng Cídiǎn.
   I've bought the Chinese-English Dictionary.

2. 买得起 **mǎideqǐ** can afford
   两百 元 不太贵, 我 买得起。
   Liǎngbǎi yuán bú tài guì, wǒ mǎideqǐ.
   ¥200 is not too much to pay, I can afford it.

3. 买不起 **mǎibuqǐ** can't afford
   五百 元 太贵了, 我 买不起。
   Wǔbǎi yuán tài guì le, wǒ mǎibuqǐ.
   ¥500 is too much, I can't afford it.

4. 买卖 **mǎimài** business (literally, buying and selling)
   我 父亲 是 做 买卖 的。
   Wǒ fùqin shì zuò mǎimài de.
   My father is a businessman.

5. 买不到 **mǎibudào** out of stock
   这 种 皮包 现在 买不到 了。
   Zhè zhǒng píbāo xiànzài mǎibudào le.
   You can't buy this kind of briefcase now.

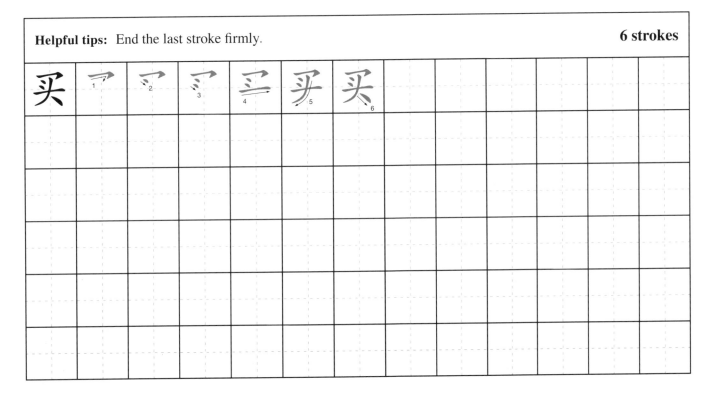

Helpful tips: End the last stroke firmly.

6 strokes

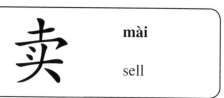

Radical: 十 # 11 "ten"

Compounds, sentences, and meanings

1. 卖 **mài** sell

   这 台 电视机 怎么 卖? / 这 台 电视机
   Zhè tái diànshìjī zěnme mài? / Zhè tái diànshìjī
   卖 多少 钱?
   mài duōshao qián?
   How much is this TV set?

2. 卖座 **màizuò** draw large audiences (literally, seat seller)

   那部 电影 可 卖座 啦。
   Nà bù diànyǐng kě màizuò la.
   That movie drew audiences.

3. 卖力 **màilì** exert all one's strength

   她 做事 很 卖力。
   Tā zuòshì hěn màilì.
   She puts in her best when she works.

4. 卖弄 **màinòng** show off one's cleverness

   他 喜欢 卖弄 小 聪明。
   Tā xǐhuan màinòng xiǎo cōngmíng.
   He likes to show off his smartness.

5. 买卖 **mǎimài** business

   我 父亲 是 做 买卖 的。
   Wǒ fùqin shì zuò mǎimài de.
   My father is a businessman.

Helpful tips: End the last stroke firmly.   **8 strokes**

卖	二	十	击	击	击	壶	卖	卖			

用 yòng

use

Radical: 用 # 128 "use"

Compounds, sentences, and meanings

1. 用 **yòng** use
   你 会 不 会 用 电脑?
   Nǐ huì bú huì yòng diànnǎo?
   Can you use a computer?

2. 用处 **yòngchù** use
   抱怨 有 什么 用处?
   Bàoyuàn yǒu shénme yòngchù?
   What's the use of complaining?

3. 用功 **yònggōng** hardworking
   学生 都 很 用功。
   Xuésheng dōu hěn yònggōng.
   The students are very hardworking.

4. 用力 **yònglì** exert oneself physically
   他 用力 把 门 推开。
   Tā yònglì bǎ mén tuīkāi.
   He gave the door a hard push to open it.

5. 用心 **yòngxīn** attentively
   学生 都 用心 听讲。
   Xuésheng dōu yòngxīn tīngjiǎng.
   The students listen attentively to the lecture.

Helpful tips: The first stroke tapers off; the second stroke ends with a hook.										5 strokes
用	丿	刀	月	月	用					

能

néng

possible

Radical: 厶 # 23 "private"

Compounds, sentences, and meanings

1. 能 **néng** be capable of

   我 能 用 左手 写字。

   Wǒ néng yòng zuǒshǒu xiězì.

   I write with my left hand.

2. 能够 **nénggòu** be capable of

   她 能够 说 三 种 外国语。

   Tā nénggòu shuō sān zhǒng wàiguóyǔ.

   She can speak three foreign languages.

3. 能干 **nénggàn** capable

   她 是 个 很 能干 的 人。

   Tā shì ge hěn nénggàn de rén.

   She's a very capable person.

4. 能力 **nénglì** ability

   她的 分析 能力 很 强。

   Tāde fēnxi nénglì hěn qiáng.

   She has strong analytical skills.

5. 能源 **néngyuán** energy

   世界 正在 面临 能源 危机。

   Shìjiè zhèngzài miànlín néngyuán wēijī.

   The world is facing an energy crisis.

Helpful tips: The seventh and ninth strokes sweep to the left.   **10 strokes**

能	厶¹	厶²	刍³	刍⁴	育⁵	育⁶	育⁷	能⁸	能⁹	能¹⁰		

听 tīng listen

聽

Radical: 口 # 50 "mouth"

Compounds, sentences, and meanings

1. 听 **tīng** listen

   请 听 一下 电话。

   Qǐng tīng yíxià diànhuà.

   Please answer the phone.

2. 听不懂 **tīngbudǒng** not understand (by listening)

   我 听不懂 你说 什么。

   Wǒ tīngbudǒng nǐ shuō shénme.

   I don't understand what you said.

3. 听得懂 **tīngdedǒng** understand (by listening)

   我 听得懂 法语。

   Wǒ tīngdedǒng Fǎyǔ.

   I can understand French.

4. 听见 **tīngjiàn** hear

   我 听见 有人 敲门。

   Wǒ tīngjiàn yǒu rén qiāomén.

   I heard a knock at the door.

5. 听说 **tīngshuō** be told

   听说 她到 上海 工作 去了。

   Tīngshuō tā dào Shànghǎi gōngzuò qù le.

   I hear that she went to work in Shanghai.

Helpful tips: The left side of 斤 is made up of two strokes.											**7 strokes**
听	丨	口	口	口	听	听	听				

喝

hē

drink

Radical: 口 # 50 "mouth"

Compounds, sentences, and meanings

1. 喝 **hē** drink

   你喝 什么 饮料?

   Nǐ hē shénme yǐnliào?

   What would you like to drink?

2. 喝墨水 **hē mòshuǐ** drink ink (meaning: go to school)

   他 没 喝过 几 年 墨水。

   Tā méi hēguo jǐ nián mòshuǐ.

   He's had only a few years of school.

3. 喝茶 **hēchá** drink tea

   中国人 有 喝茶的 习惯。

   Zhōngguórén yǒu hēchá de xíguàn.

   Chinese people drink a lot of tea.

4. 喝醉 **hēzuì** drunk

   昨晚 他喝醉了。

   Zuówǎn tā hēzuì le.

   He was drunk last night.

5. 好喝 **hǎohē** tasty (drink)

   你觉得 中国 的啤酒 好喝 吗?

   Nǐ juéde Zhōngguó de píjiǔ hǎohē ma?

   Do you like Chinese beer?

Helpful tips: The ninth stroke ends with a hook.											**12 strokes**
喝	丨	口	口	口	吗	吗	吗	喝	喝	喝	喝

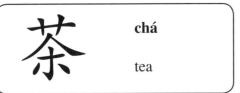

茶　chá

tea

Radical: 艹 # 42 "grass"

Compounds, sentences, and meanings

1. 茶 **chá** tea

   我们 喝点儿 茶 吧。

   Wǒmen hē diǎnr chá ba.

   Let's have some tea.

2. 茶褐色 **cháhèsè** dark brown

   我 觉得茶褐色 那件 也 不错。

   Wǒ juéde cháhèsè nà jiàn yě búcuò.

   I think the dark brown one looks quite nice.

3. 茶壶 **cháhú** teapot

   我 喜欢 这个 小 茶壶。

   Wǒ xǐhuan zhè ge xiǎo cháhú.

   I like this little teapot.

4. 茶碗 **cháwǎn** tea-bowl (without handles)

   这 是 茶碗，那 是 茶杯。

   Zhè shì cháwǎn, nà shì chábēi.

   This is a tea-bowl, that is a teacup.

5. 茶叶 **cháyè** tea leaves, tea

   龙井 是 名贵 的茶叶。

   Lóngjǐng shì míngguì de cháyè.

   Longjing tea is famous and precious.

Helpful tips: The last two strokes do not meet in the center.								**9 strokes**			
茶	一	艹	艹	艻	苂	苓	茶	茶	茶			

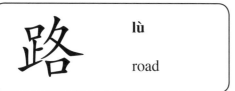

路　lù

road

Radical: 足 # 164 "foot"

Compounds, sentences, and meanings

1. 路 lù route

   312路　公共汽车　去 大学。

   Sānyāo'èrlù gōnggòngqìchē qù dàxué.

   Route 312 goes to the university.

2. 路标 lùbiāo road sign

   前面　有 路标。

   Qiánmiàn yǒu lùbiāo.

   There are road signs ahead.

3. 路上 lùshang en route

   路上 不要 耽搁。

   Lùshang búyào dān'ge.

   Don't waste any time on the way.

4. 路口 lùkǒu intersection

   在 路口 左 拐弯。

   Zài lùkǒu zuǒ guǎiwān.

   Turn left at the intersection.

5. 路线 lùxiàn route, itinerary

   请 你　说说　旅行 路线。

   Qǐng nǐ shuōshuo lǚxíng lùxiàn.

   Please tell me about the itinerary of the tour.

Helpful tips: The seventh stroke slants upwards slightly.												**13 strokes**
路												
路												

bào

report

報

Radical: 扌 # 48 "hand"

Compounds, sentences, and meanings

1. 报 **bào** report

   请假 要 报 上级 批准。

   Qǐngjià yào bào shàngjí pīzhǔn.

   You need your boss's approval to take leave.

2. 报酬 **bàochou** reward, pay

   这个 工作 很累, 报酬 不多。

   Zhè ge gōngzuò hěn lèi, bàochou bùduō.

   This job is hard, and it pays very little.

3. 报告 **bàogào** report

   现在 报告 新闻。

   Xiànzài bàogào xīnwén.

   Here is the news.

4. 报关 **bàoguān** declare something at customs

   你有 什么 东西 要 报关 吗?

   Nǐ yǒu shénme dōngxi yào bàoguān ma?

   Have you got anything to declare?

5. 报名 **bàomíng** sign up

   我 报名 参加了 百米 赛跑。

   Wǒ bàomíng cānjiāle bǎi mǐ sàipǎo.

   I've signed up for the 100 meter dash.

Helpful tips: The fourth stroke is a horizontal-bend-hook. **7 strokes**

报 ｜ 一 ｜ 扌 ｜ 扌 ｜ 扌 ｜ 护 ｜ 报 ｜ 报

zhāng

[measure word]

Traditional Form

張

Radical: 弓 # 63 "bow"

Compounds, sentences, and meanings

1. 张 **zhāng** measure word

   这 间 房 有 两 张 床。

   Zhè jiān fáng yǒu liǎng zhāng chuáng.

   There are two beds in this room.

2. 张开 **zhāngkāi** open

   张开 嘴。

   Zhāngkāi zuǐ.

   Open your mouth.

3. 紧张 **jǐnzhāng** nervous

   慢慢 讲，别 紧张。

   Mànmàn jiǎng, bié jǐnzhāng.

   Speak slowly, don't be nervous.

4. 张罗 **zhāngluó** get busy

   要 带的 东西 早点儿 收拾 好，不要

   Yào dài de dōngxi zǎodiǎnr shōushí hǎo, búyào

   临时 张罗。

   línshí zhāngluó.

   Get your things ready in advance so as to avoid a last-minute rush.

5. 张扬 **zhāngyáng** make widely known

   这 事 还 没 定下来，先 别 张扬出去。

   Zhè shì hái méi dìngxiàlai, xiān bié zhāngyángchūqu.

   The final decision hasn't been made yet, so don't spread this around.

Helpful tips: Both downward strokes to the left and the right on 长 are diagonals.　　　**7 strokes**

张	⁷	²	弓	弓⁴	弘⁵	张⁶	张⁷				

Lesson 22: Review Activities

A. Pronunciation and *Pinyin* Practice

Please wirte the *pinyin* for each of the following Chinese characters. Then practice differentiating between similar sounds and tones clearly and accurately.

师 _____ 十 _____ 谢 _____ 写 _____

电 _____ 店 _____ 数 _____ 书 _____

市 _____ 识 _____ 学 _____ 雪 _____

买 _____ 卖 _____ 是 _____ 史 _____

友 _____ 有 _____ 左 _____ 做 _____

工 _____ 公 _____ 南 _____ 男 _____

B. Sentence Completion and Translation

Please complete each of the following sentences with one of the phrases provided. Then translate the resulting sentence into English.

有名   有用   有意思   有问题   有道理

1. 你的意见很好, 真的_____。

_____

2. 我的母亲说这个冰箱很好, 冰箱很_____。

_____

3. 老师说: "这个文章明白吗? 学生们, 你们有没_____?

_____

291

4. 如果很多人都知道你的名字，我们就可能说你很＿＿＿＿＿＿＿＿。

＿＿＿＿＿＿＿＿＿＿＿＿＿＿＿＿＿＿＿＿＿＿＿＿＿＿＿＿

5. 学生常常觉得学习汉语很＿＿＿＿＿＿＿＿。

＿＿＿＿＿＿＿＿＿＿＿＿＿＿＿＿＿＿＿＿＿＿＿＿＿＿＿＿

C. Comparative Description

Consider the following topic and compose a personal reaction or opinion in response to it. A strong description will demonstrate an understanding of conditional and relative expressions.

请问：你喜欢买东西还是卖东西？

＿＿＿＿＿＿＿＿＿＿＿＿＿＿＿＿＿＿＿＿＿＿＿＿＿＿＿＿＿＿＿＿

＿＿＿＿＿＿＿＿＿＿＿＿＿＿＿＿＿＿＿＿＿＿＿＿＿＿＿＿＿＿＿＿

＿＿＿＿＿＿＿＿＿＿＿＿＿＿＿＿＿＿＿＿＿＿＿＿＿＿＿＿＿＿＿＿

＿＿＿＿＿＿＿＿＿＿＿＿＿＿＿＿＿＿＿＿＿＿＿＿＿＿＿＿＿＿＿＿

＿＿＿＿＿＿＿＿＿＿＿＿＿＿＿＿＿＿＿＿＿＿＿＿＿＿＿＿＿＿＿＿

＿＿＿＿＿＿＿＿＿＿＿＿＿＿＿＿＿＿＿＿＿＿＿＿＿＿＿＿＿＿＿＿

＿＿＿＿＿＿＿＿＿＿＿＿＿＿＿＿＿＿＿＿＿＿＿＿＿＿＿＿＿＿＿＿

＿＿＿＿＿＿＿＿＿＿＿＿＿＿＿＿＿＿＿＿＿＿＿＿＿＿＿＿＿＿＿＿

＿＿＿＿＿＿＿＿＿＿＿＿＿＿＿＿＿＿＿＿＿＿＿＿＿＿＿＿＿＿＿＿

＿＿＿＿＿＿＿＿＿＿＿＿＿＿＿＿＿＿＿＿＿＿＿＿＿＿＿＿＿＿＿＿

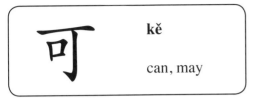

可 kě

can, may

Radical: 一 # 2 "horizontal stroke" or 口 # 50 "mouth"

Compounds, sentences, and meanings

1. 可 **kě** (used for emphasis)

   可 别 忘 了。

   Kě bié wàng le.

   Mind you don't forget it.

2. 可是 **kěshì** but

   我的 房间 比较 小，可是 很 舒适。

   Wǒde fángjiān bǐjiào xiǎo, kěshì hěn shūshì.

   My room is a bit small, but it's very comfortable.

3. 可爱 **kě'ài** lovable, lovely

   多么 可爱的孩子!

   Duōme kě'ài de háizi!

   What a cute child!

4. 可以 **kěyǐ** can, may

   这 间 屋子可以住 两 个人。

   Zhè jiān wūzi kěyǐ zhù liǎng ge rén.

   This room can accommodate two people.

5. 可能 **kěnéng** possible

   很 可能 他已经 到 家了。

   Hěn kěnéng tā yǐjīng dào jiā le.

   He's most likely to be home by now.

Helpful tips: The final stroke ends with a hook.									5 strokes
可	一	丁	丁	口	可				

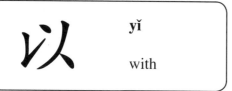

以 yǐ

with

Radical: 人 # 18 "person"

Compounds, sentences, and meanings

1. 以 **yǐ** with, by means of

   我们 不 应该 以 貌 取 人。

   Wǒmen bù yīnggāi yǐ mào qǔ rén.

   We should not judge people solely by their appearance.

2. 以便 **yǐbiàn** in order to

   做好 准备，以便 明天 一早 动身。

   Zuòhǎo zhǔnbèi, yǐbiàn míngtiān yì zǎo dòngshēn.

   Get ready so that we can start early tomorrow.

3. 以后 **yǐhòu** afterwards

   以后 你 会 有 机会 去 的。

   Yǐhòu nǐ huì yǒu jīhuì qù de.

   You will have a chance to go later.

4. 以前 **yǐqián** prior to, former

   她 是 我 以前 的 同事。

   Tā shì wǒ yǐqián de tóngshì.

   She's a former colleague of mine.

5. 以为 **yǐwéi** consider

   他 以为 那样 做 比较 好。

   Tā yǐwéi nàyàng zuò bǐjiào hǎo.

   He thinks it's better to do it that way.

Helpful tips: Both dots finish firmly.　　　　　　　　　　　**4 strokes**

以	以	以	以	以							

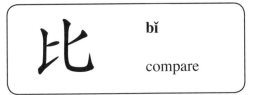

比 **bǐ**

compare

Radical: 比 # 86 "compare"

Compounds, sentences, and meanings

1. 比 **bǐ** compare to

   我 比 我 哥哥 小 两 岁。

   Wǒ bǐ wǒ gēge xiǎo liǎng suì.

   I'm 2 years younger than my brother.

2. 比较 **bǐjiào** comparatively

   最近 我 比较 忙。

   Zuìjìn wǒ bǐjiào máng.

   I've been busy of late.

3. 比赛 **bǐsài** competition

   今晚 有 一个 足球比赛, 你看 吗?

   Jīnwǎn yǒu yí ge zúqiú bǐsài, nǐ kàn ma?

   Are you going to watch the soccer match tonight?

4. 比方 **bǐfāng** analogy

   可以 给 我 打个 比方 吗?

   Kěyǐ gěi wǒ dǎ ge bǐfāng ma?

   Can you give me an example?

5. 比不上 **bǐbushàng** not as good as

   我的 汉语 比不上 他。

   Wǒde Hànyǔ bǐbushàng tā.

   My Chinese is not as good as his.

Helpful tips: The first stroke is a vertical lift.											**4 strokes**
比	比	比	比	比							

CHARACTER 242

但　dàn

but, yet

Radical: 亻 # 19 "person"

Compounds, sentences, and meanings

1. 但 **dàn** but

   他 早 已 年 过 六十, 但 毫 不 见 老。

   Tā zǎo yǐ nián guò liùshí, dàn háo bú jiàn lǎo.

   Although he is well over sixty, he doesn't look at all old.

2. 但凡 **dànfán** in every case

   但凡 认识 她 的 人, 没有 一 个 不 说

   Dànfán rénshi tā de rén, méiyǒu yí ge bù shuō

   她好。

   tā hǎo.

   Everyone who meets her says she is nice.

3. 但是 **dànshì** but

   他 很 聪明, 但是 不 喜欢 学习。

   Tā hěn cōngmíng, dànshì bù xǐhuan xuéxí.

   Although he is clever, he doesn't like studying.

4. 但愿 **dànyuàn** if only

   但愿 天气 赶快 下雨。

   Dànyuàn tiānqì gǎnkuài xiàyǔ.

   If only it would rain soon.

5. 不但 **búdàn** not only

   这里 的 东西 不但 好吃, 而且 便宜。

   Zhèlǐ de dōngxi búdàn hǎochī, érqiě piányi.

   The food here is not only delicious, it's also inexpensive.

Helpful tips: The final stroke is longer than the ones above.										**7 strokes**
但	丿	亻	仁	但	但	但	但			

CHARACTER 243

而   **ér**

and, but

Radical: 一 # 2 "horizontal stroke"

Compounds, sentences, and meanings

1. 而且 **érqiě** and, but, yet

他 喜欢 学习 汉语, 而且他的弟弟也
Tā xǐhuan xuéxí Hànyǔ, érqiě tā de dìdi yě

喜欢。
xǐhuan.

He enjoys studying Chinese language, and his
younger brother also enjoys it.

2. 而已 **éryǐ** that is all

这 是一个 小 问题, 而已。
Zhè shì yí ge xiǎo wèntí, éryǐ.

This is a small problem, and that's it.

3. 而后 **érhòu** after that, then

现在 我们 走路走路, 而后 我们 喝
Xiànzài wǒmen zǒulù zǒulù, érhòu wǒmen hē

一点 茶。
yìdiǎn chá.

Now we are taking a walk, after that we'll have
some tea.

Helpful tips: Each vertical stroke should be evenly spaced.													**6 strokes**
而	一	丆	广	而	而	而							

297

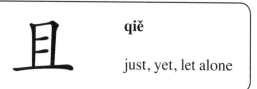

CHARACTER 244

且

qiě

just, yet, let alone

Radical: | # 3 "vertical stroke"

Compounds, sentences, and meanings

1. 且 **qiě** also, and

   这 辆 汽车既贵 且 快。

   Zhè liàng qìchē jì guì qiě kuaì.

   This car is both expensive and fast.

2. 而且 **érqiě** and, but, yet

   那件 衬衫 很 便宜, 而且 有 一点

   Nà jiàn chènshān hěn piányi, érqiě yǒu yìdiǎn

   难看。

   nánkàn.

   That shirt is cheap, but it's a little ugly.

3. 且慢 **qiěmàn** wait a moment

   且慢, 我们 还 有 一些问题。

   Qiěmàn, wǒmen hái yǒu yìxiē wèntí.

   Wait a moment, we still have a few questions.

4. 尚且 **shàngqiě** even

   世界 经济 关联 很复杂, 经济 教授

   Shìjiè jīngjì guānlián hěn fùzǎ, jīngjì jiàoshòu

   尚且 不 了解, 何况 我们 老 百姓!

   shàngqiě bù liǎojiě, hékuàng wǒmen lǎo bǎixìng!

   The relationships in international economics are complex, even economics professors don't understand them, let alone average people!

Helpful tips: The final stroke is the longest.												**5 strokes**
且	丨	冂	目	目	且							

298

就 jiù

right away

Radical: 亠 # 6 "top of 六"

Compounds, sentences, and meanings

1. 就 **jiù** as early as

   今天 我 七 点钟 就来了。

   Jīntiān wǒ qī diǎnzhōng jiù lái le.

   I was here as early as 7 o'clock today.

2. 就是 **jiùshì** exactly

   就 是 嘛, 我 也 是 这么 想 的。

   Jiù shì ma, wǒ yě shì zhème xiǎng de.

   Precisely, that's just what I had in mind.

3. 就手 **jiùshǒu** while you are at it

   就手 把 门 关上。

   Jiùshǒu bǎ mén guānshàng.

   Close the door behind you.

4. 就要 **jiùyào** be going to

   火车 就要 开了。

   Huǒchē jiùyào kāi le.

   The train is about to leave.

5. 就算 **jiùsuàn** even if

   就算 你 等了 半 个 钟头，也 不

   Jiùsuàn nǐ děngle bàn ge zhōngtóu, yě bù

   应该 发 这么 大 的 脾气 吧。

   yīnggāi fā zhème dà de píqi ba.

   Granted that you have waited for half an hour, still there is no reason to blow your top.

Helpful tips: The eleventh stroke ends with a hook.											**12 strokes**
就	丶	二	亠	亠	古	京	京	京	就	就	就

Traditional Form

还   **hái/huán**

still, return

還

Radical: 辶 # 38 "movement"

Compounds, sentences, and meanings

1. 还 **hái** still
   他 还 在 睡觉。
   Tā hái zài shuìjiào.
   He's still sleeping.

2. 还有 **hái yǒu** still more
   我 有 一个 姐姐, 还 有 一个 妹妹。
   Wǒ yǒu yí ge jiějie, hái yǒu yí ge mèimei.
   I have an older sister and a younger sister.

3. 还是 **háishi** or
   他 是 日本人 还是 韩国人?
   Tā shì Rìběnrén háishi Hánguórén?
   Is he Japanese or Korean?

4. 还 **huán** return
   下个 月 我 就 还 你 钱。
   Xià ge yuè wǒ jiù huán nǐ qián.
   I'll repay the money next month.

5. 还价 **huánjià** counteroffer, bid
   如果 你 不 想 买 就 别 还价。
   Rúguǒ nǐ bù xiǎng mǎi jiù bié huánjià.
   Don't bid if you don't intend to buy.

Helpful tips: Write the middle component before 辶.											7 strokes
还	一	丆	不	不	不	还	还				

所

suǒ

[measure word]; dwelling

Radical: 户 # 77 "household" or 斤 # 101 "ax"

Compounds, sentences, and meanings

1. 所 **suǒ** measure word (for building)

    这 所 学校 的 历史 悠久。

    Zhé suǒ xuéxiào de lìshǐ yōujiǔ.

    This school has a long history.

2. 所以 **suǒyǐ** therefore

    因为 天 太 冷, 所以 我 不 去 了。

    Yīnwèi tiān tài lěng, suǒyǐ wǒ bú qù le.

    I'm not going because it's too cold.

3. 所有 **suǒyǒu** all

    把 所有 的 劲儿 都 使出来。

    Bǎ suǒyǒude jìnr dōu shǐchūlai.

    Exert all your strength.

4. 诊所 **zhěnsuǒ** clinic, surgery

    这里 有 一个 中医 诊所。

    Zhélǐ yǒu yí ge Zhōngyī zhěnsuǒ.

    There's a clinic for Chinese medicine here.

5. 医务所 **yīwùsuǒ** clinic

    请问, 医务所 在哪儿?

    Qǐngwèn, yīwùsuǒ zài nǎr?

    Excuse me, where is the clinic?

Helpful tips: The first and fifth strokes sweep down sharply.								8 strokes

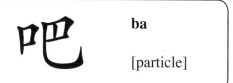

吧   **ba**

[particle]

Radical: 口 # 50 "mouth"

Compounds, sentences, and meanings

1. 吧 **ba** suggestion [particle]

   我们 走 吧。

   Wǒmen zǒu ba.

   Let's go.

2. 就 ... 吧 **jiù ... ba** consent or approval

   明天 就 明天 吧。

   Míngtiān jiù míngtiān ba.

   All right, let's make it tomorrow.

3. 会 ... 吧 **huì ... ba** confirmation

   他 会 来 吧?

   Tā huì lái ba?

   He'll come, won't he?

4. 好像是 ... 吧 **hǎoxiàng shì ... ba** doubt or uncertainty

   他 好像 是 这么 说 的 吧。

   Tā hǎoxiàng shì zhème shuō de ba.

   It seems that's what he said.

5. ... 吧, ... 吧, **...ba, ... ba,** marking a pause

   去 吧, 不好; 不去 吧, 也 不好。

   Qù ba, bùhǎo; búqù ba, yě bùhǎo.

   If I go, it's no good; if I don't, it's no good either.

Helpful tips: The final stroke finishes with a hook.   **7 strokes**

吧	丨	口	口	口	口	口	吧				

呢　ne
[particle]

Radical: 口 # 50 "mouth"

Compounds, sentences, and meanings

1. 呢 **ne** particle (rhetorical question)

   我 怎么 能 不记得呢?

   Wǒ zěnme néng bú jìde ne?

   How could I forget this?

2. 呢 **ne** particle (declarative sentence)

   远 的 很 呢。

   Yuǎn de hěn ne.

   It's a long way.

3. 呢 **ne** particle (to mark continuous action)

   他 还 在 睡觉 呢。

   Tā hái zài shuìjiào ne.

   He's still asleep.

4. 呢 **ne** particle (to ask a return question)

   我 叫 大伟, 你呢?

   Wǒ jiào Dàwěi, nǐ ne?

   My name is David, what's yours?

5. 呢 **ne** particle (to mark a pause)

   不 下雨 呢, 就去; 下雨 呢, 就不 去。

   Bú xiàyǔ ne, jiù qù; xiàyǔ ne, jiù bú qù.

   If it doesn't rain, we'll go; if it rains, we won't go.

Helpful tips: The seventh stroke sweeps from right to left.　　　　**8 strokes**

呢	⼁¹	⼝²	⼝³	⼝⁴	⼝⁵	呎⁶	呢⁷	呢⁸			

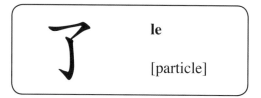

Radical: ⌐ # 5 "horizontal bend"

Compounds, sentences, and meanings

1. 了 **le** (new situation)

现在 几点 了?
Xiànzài jǐ diǎn le?
What's the time now?

2. 了 **le** (new situation)

下雨 了。
Xiàyǔ le.
It's starting to rain.

3. 了 **le** (completed action)

我 学了 一百二十 个 汉字。
Wǒ xuéle yìbǎi-èrshí ge Hànzì.
I've learned 120 Chinese characters.

Helpful tips: The last stroke ends with a hook.　　**2 strokes**

了　⇀　了

Lesson 23: Review Activities

A. Pronunciation and *Pinyin* Practice

Please transcribe the following questions into *pinyin*. For additional practice, say and then respond to these questions aloud.

1. 你的同学要学习英文但是你要学习中文吗?

_____

2. 今天的天气很美丽, 我们都去花园吧!

_____

3. 你住在你的国家的北部还是南部?

_____

B. Sentence Completion and Translation

Please complete each of the following sentences with one of the terms provided. Then translate the resulting sentence into English.

可是   可以   可能   比   吧

1. 在饭店你可以吃饭, _____你不可以做饭!

_____

2. 美国的英语_____英国的英语好听, 你同意吗?

_____

3. 我们_____在什么地方踢足球?

_____

4. 我们两个人一起上课, 好_____!

_____

5. 对不起，我不会开车所以现在我不＿＿＿＿＿＿＿开车。

_____

C. Describing Consequence

Consider the following situation. Then, based on each conjunction provided, create a statement that introduces a consequence of that situation. A strong description shows good awareness of the relationship formed by each of the following conjunctions.

今天你有一个很大的汉语考试，但是你没有你自己的汉语词典。

（所以）_____

_____

（于是）_____

_____

（而且）_____

_____

（以后）_____

_____

（可是）_____

_____

Section 5 Review (Lessons 20–23)

A. Vocabulary and *Pinyin* Review

Please transcribe the following vocabulary terms into *pinyin*. Then translate each term into effective, clear English.

	Pinyin	English
但是		
可是		
而且		
就是		
所以		
还是		
以前		
以后		
然后		
而已		

B. Short Description

Consider the illustration provided. Drawing on both the location and the activity shown in the illustration create a sentence based on each preposition given.

1.（这里）_____

_____

2.（前边）_____

_____

3. (后边) _____

_____

4. (现在) _____

_____

5. (以前) _____

_____

6. (以后) _____

_____

C. Relationship Description

Consider the following topic. Then write a discussion that demonstrates an understanding of the relationship between location and activity. A strong response will also demonstrate proficiency describing conditional aspects of the situation, and communicating the order and influence of events.

人都有自己喜欢去的地方。你喜欢什么地方？什么时候你去过这个地方？你天天去还是很少去？在这个特色的地方你可以做什么？

_____

_____

_____

_____

_____

_____

_____

_____

D. Reflective Questions

Use these questions to both check the expressiveness of the previous section and to confirm your understanding of the previous topic. For additional practice, say and then respond to these questions aloud.

你喜欢的地方在哪里？

你去过还是没去过？

你怎么找到了这个地方？

离你的老家很远吗？如果不远，你每个星期去吗？

你去过几次？

对别的人来说，这个地方有没有意思？

在那儿你要做什么？为什么？

这种的活动，在别的地方你也喜欢做吗？

如果你第二次来这个地方可是你不喜欢了，你觉得怎么样？

对你来说，什么改变了：人还是地方？

Alphabetical Index

The number on the right of each column refers to the character number, followed by the compound/sentence number.

B

bā	八	8.1
bāchéng	八成	8.2
bāzhé	八折	8.3
bà	爸	48.1
bàba	爸爸	48.2
ba	吧	248.1
... ba, ...ba,	... 吧, ... 吧	248.5
bǎi	百	12.1
bǎifēndiǎn	百分点	12.5
bǎifēnzhībǎi	百分之百	12.2
bǎifēnzhīsánshí	百分之三十	166.5
bǎihuò	百货	12.3
bǎiwàn	百万	12.4
bàinián	拜年	146.5
bàn	半	219.1
bànqiú	半球	116.3
bàntiān	半天	219.4
bànxīn-bújiù	半新不旧	219.5
bào	报	237.1
bàochou	报酬	237.2
bàogào	报告	237.3
bàoguān	报关	237.4
bàomíng	报名	237.5
běi	北	203.1
běifāng	北方	203.2
Běijīng	北京	203.4
Běiměizhōu	北美洲	203.5
bǐ	比	241.1
bǐbushàng	比不上	241.5
bǐfāng	比方	241.4
bǐjiào	比较	241.2
bǐsài	比赛	241.3
biān	边	214.1
biān ... biān	边 ... 边	214.2

biàn	便	168.1
biànlì	便利	168.3
biàntiáo	便条	168.4
biǎoxiàn	表现	227.5
bīn	宾	197.0
bīnguan	宾馆	197.1
bīnkè	宾客	197.2
bówù guǎn	博物馆	198.2
bú/bù	不	18.1
búcuò	不错	18.2/179.3
bùduō-bùshǎo	不多不少	18.4
bù hǎo yìsi	不好意思	18.3
bùjiǔ	不久	18.5/220.5
bùshǎo	不少	40.2
búshì	不是	19.3
bùyí	不宜	169.2

C

chá	茶	235.1
chá hèsè	茶褐色	235.2
chá hú	茶壶	235.3
chá wǎn	茶碗	235.4
cháyè	茶叶	235.5
Chángchéng	长城	195.5
chèn	衬	156.1
chènqún	衬裙	156.2
chènshān	衬衫	156.3
chèntuō	衬托	156.4
chènyī	衬衣	156.5
chéng	城	195.1
chéngshì	城市	195.3/196.1
chéngxiāng	城乡	195.2
chī	吃	108.1
chībuxià	吃不下	108.4
chīdexià	吃得下	108.3

chīfàn	吃饭	108.2
chīkǔ	吃苦	108.5
chuān	穿	151.1
chuānbuzhù	穿不住	151.2
chuān'guò	穿过	151.3
chuānyuè	穿越	151.4
chuānzhuó	穿着	151.5
chūn	春	129.1
chūnfēng	春风	129.4
chūnjié	春节	129.3
chūntiān	春天	129.2
chūnyào	春药	129.5
cóng nàr qǐ	从那儿起	183.5
cónglái	从来	228.5/211.5
cuò	错	179.1
cuòbiézì	错别字	179.2
cuòguò	错过	179.4
cuòwù	错误	179.3

D

dà	大	175.1
dàgài	大概	175.5
dàgē	大哥	50.3
dàjiā	大家	175.3
dàkǎo	大考	121.4
dàshēng	大声	175.2
dàshǐguǎn	大使馆	198.4
dàxiǎo	大小	175.4
dàxiě	大写	100.3
dàxióngmāo	大熊猫	91.4
dàxuésheng	大学生	84.4
dǎ	打	115.1
dǎ diànhuà	打电话	115.2
dǎsǎo	打扫	115.3
dǎtīng	打听	115.4
dǎzì	打字	115.5
dàn	但	242.1
dànfán	但凡	242.2
dànshì	但是	242.3

dànyuàn	但愿	242.4
dào	到	185.1
dàochù	到处	185.5
dàodǐ	到底	185.3
dàojiā	到家	185.4
dàoqī	到期	141.5/185.5
dào	道	97.1
dàoli	道理	97.3
dàolù	道路	97.2
dàoqiàn	道歉	97.4
dàoyì	道义	97.5
de	的	20.1
Déguó	德国	61.3
dì	地	193.1
dìdao	地道	193.5
dìfang	地方	193.2
dìtú	地图	193.3
dìxià	地下	193.4
dì	弟	52.1
dìdi	弟弟	52.2
dìxí	弟媳	52.4
dìxiōng	弟兄	52.3
dìyī	第一	1.5
diǎn	点	218.1
diǎncài	点菜	218.4
diǎntóu	点头	218.5
diǎnzhōng	点钟	217.2
diàn	电	112.1
diànhu	电话	112.5
diànnǎo	电脑	112.4
diànshì	电视	112.3/113.1
diànyǐng	电影	112.2
diànyǐngyuàn	电影院	187.5
diàn	店	189.1
diànyuán	店员	189.5
dōng	东	205.1
dōngběi	东北	203.3
dōngbian	东边	205.2
Dōngnányà	东南亚	205.3
dōngxi	东西	205.4

dōng	冬	132.1
dōnggū	冬菇	132.4
dōngjì	冬季	132.3
dōngtiān	冬天	132.2
dōngzhuāng	冬装	132.5
dòngwùyuán	动物园	192.5
dōu/dū	都	202.1
dūshì	都市	202.2
dúyī-wú'èr	独一无二	2.5
duǎnkù	短裤	154.2
duì	对	69.1
duìbuqǐ	对不起	69.3
duìmiàn	对面	69.2
duìshǒu	对手	69.4
duìyú	对于	69.5
duō	多	39.1
duōbàn	多半	39.3
duō jiǔ	多久	220.2
duōme	多么	25.4/39.5
duōshao	多少	39.2/40.4
duōshù	多数	39.4
duōxiè	多谢	71.3

E

ér	儿	58.1
érgē	儿歌	58.4
érnǚ	儿女	58.3
értóng	儿童	58.5
érzi	儿子	58.2
ér	而	243.0
érhòu	而后	243.3
érqiě	而且	243.1/244.2
éryǐ	而已	243.2
èr	二	2.1
èrděng	二等	2.4
èrgē	二哥	2.2/50.4
èrjiě	二姐	51.4
Èryuè	二月	2.3

F

fàn	饭	112.1
fàncài	饭菜	112.2
fàndiàn	饭店	112.4
fànguǎnr	饭馆儿	112.3
fāng	方	194.1
fāngbiàn	方便	168.2/194.2
fāngfǎ	方法	194.4
fāngkuàizì	方块字	163.5
fāngmiàn	方面	194.5
fāngxiàng	方向	194.5
fángdōng	房东	205.5
fēn	分	166.1
fēnbiàn	分辨	166.4
fēnbié	分别	166.3
fēnzhōng	分钟	166.2
fēng	风	148.1
fēngkǒu	风口	148.2
fēngqù	风趣	148.3
fēngsú	风俗	148.4
fēngwèi	风味	148.5
fú	服	153.1
fúcóng	服从	153.2
fúruǎn	服软	153.3
fúwù	服务	153.4
fēnzhuāng	服装	157.1
fúzhuāngdiàn	服装店	153.5/189.4
fù	父	76.1
fùmǔ	父母	76.3/77.3
fùqin	父亲	76.2/78.3
fù	复	118.0
fùxí	复习	118.1
fùxin	复信	118.2
fùyin	复印	118.3
fùyuán	复原	118.5
fùzá	复杂	118.2
fùnǚ	妇女	88.5

G

gǎnxiè	感谢	71.4
gàn ma?	干吗？	26.4
gē	哥	50.1
gēge	哥哥	50.2
gērmen	哥儿们	17.5/50.5
gèbié	个别	37.5
gègè	个个	37.3
gèrén	个人	37.4
ge	个	37.1
gōng	工	80.1
gōngchǎng	工厂	80.5
gōngyè	工业	80.4
gōngzī	工资	80.3
gōngzuò	工作	80.2
gōng	公	191.1
gōnggòng	公共	191.2
gōngjīn	公斤	191.4
gōnglǐ	公里	191.3
gōngshēng	公升	191.4
gōngyuán	公园	192.2
Gōngyuán	公元	162.4
Gōngyuánqián	公元前	162.5
gǒu	狗	90.1
gǒupì	狗屁	90.5
gǒuxióng	狗熊	90.4
gūmā	姑妈	49.5
gùkè	顾客	72.5
guā	刮	147.1
guāliǎn	刮脸	147.3
guāliǎndāo	刮脸刀	147.4
guā mù xiāng kàn	刮目相看	147.5
guāpò	刮破	147.2
guǎn	馆	198.1
guì	贵	170.1
guìbīn	贵宾	197.3
guìguó	贵国	170.3
guìxìng	贵姓	170.2
guó	国	61.1
guójì	国际	61.5
guójiā	国家	61.2
guóqìng	国庆	61.4

H

hái	还	246.1
háishi	还是	19.4/246.3
hái yǒu	还有	246.2
hái	孩	86.1
háizi	孩子	87.2
háizihuà	孩子话	86.5
háiziqì	孩子气	86.4
hǎibian	海边	214.5
Hàn	汉	101.1
Hànxué	汉学	101.5
Hànyǔ	汉语	101.2
Hànzì	汉字	28.5/101.3
Hànzú	汉族	101.4
hángyè	行业	200.3
hǎo	好	31.1
hǎo ma?	好吗？	26.1
hǎobàn	好办	31.2
hǎochī	好吃	31.3
hǎochù	好处	31.4
hǎohē	好喝	234.5
hǎokàn	好看	31.5
hǎoxiàng shì ... ba	好像是...吧	248.4
hē	喝	234.1
hēchá	喝茶	234.3
hēzuì	喝醉	234.4
hē mòshuǐ	喝墨水	234.2
hé	和	44.1
héhǎo	和好	44.2
hémù	和睦	44.4
hépíng	和平	44.3
héqì	和气	44.5
héyǐng	合影	114.1
hěn	很	30.1
hěnduō	很多	30.4

hěn hǎo	很好	30.2
hěn huài	很坏	30.3
hěn jìn	很近	30.5
hòu	后	208.1
hòubà	后爸	48.3
hòuguǒ	后果	208.4
hòumā	后妈	49.3
hòumian	后面	208.2
hòutiān	后天	208.3
hòu	候	216.1
húshuō-bādào	胡说八道	8.4
huā	花	190.1
huābái	花白	190.2
huāqián	花钱	190.4
huāshēng	花生	190.3
huāyàng	花样	190.5
huāyuán	花园	192.3
huàtí	话题	43.5
huān	欢	67.1
huānjù	欢聚	67.3
huānlè	欢乐	67.4
huānxǐ	欢喜	67.2/106.4
huānyíng	欢迎	68.1
huán	还	246.4
huánjià	还价	246.5
huánqiú	还球	116.4
huì	会	98.1/98.2
huì ... ba	会 ... 吧	248.3
huìhuà	会话	98.4
huìyì	会议	98.5

J

jǐ	几	54.1
jǐ cì	几次	54.3
jǐfēn	几分	54.5
jǐ ge	几个	54.2
jǐshí	几时	54.4
jìfù	继父	76.5
jiā	家	34.1

jiāchángcài	家常菜	34.3
jiātíng	家庭	34.2
jiāwùshì	家务事	34.4
jiàqī	假期	141.3
jià	价	167.1
jiàqián	价钱	167.2
jiàzhí	价值	167.3
jiàn	见	33.1
jiànmiàn	见面	33.2
jiànshi	见识	33.3
jiànxiào	见笑	33.4
jiàn	件	159.1
jiǎngjià	讲价	167.4
jiǎo	角	164.3
jiào	叫	23.1
jiàohǎn	叫喊	23.4
jiàomén	叫门	23.3
jiàozuò	叫座	23.5
jiàozuò	叫做	23.2
jiào	校	186.1
jiàoduì	校对	186.2
jiě	姐	51.1
jiěfu	姐夫	51.5
jiějie	姐姐	51.2
jiěmèi	姐妹	53.5
jīn	今	143.1
jīnhòu	今后	143.5
jīnnián	今年	143.4
jīntiān	今天	143.2
jīnwǎn	今晚	143.3
jìnchéng	进城	195.4
jīngcháng	经常	214.2
jīngguò	经过	214.3
jiǔ	九	9.1
jiǔgōnggér	九宫格儿	9.4
jiǔjífēng	九级风	9.3
jiǔjiǔbiǎo	九九表	9.2
Jiǔyāoyāo	九一一	9.5
jiǔ	久	220.1
jiǔděng	久等	220.3

jiǔliú	久留	220.4
jiù	就	245.1
jiù ... ba	就 ... 吧	248.2
jiùshì	就是	245.2
jiùshǒu	就手	245.3
jiùsuàn	就算	245.5
jiùyào	就要	245.4

K

kàn	看	110.1
kàn diànyǐng	看电影	110.2
kànjiàn	看见	110.4
kànlái	看来	110.5
kànshū	看书	110.3
kǎo	考	121.0
kǎolù	考虑	121.2
kǎoshàng	考上	121.5
kǎoshì	考试	121.1
kǎoyàn	考验	121.3
kè	科	128.0
kèmù	科目	128.5
kèjì	科技	128.6
kèxué	科学	128.1
kèyàn	科研	128.2
kě	可	239.1
kě'ài	可爱	239.3
kěnéng	可能	239.5
kěshì	可是	239.2
kěyǐ	可以	239.4
kè	客	72.1
kèguān	客观	72.2
kèqi	客气	72.3
kètàohuà	客套话	72.4
kè	课	120.0
kèběn	课本	120.2
kèchéng	课程	120.4
kètáng	课堂	120.1
kèwén	课文	120.3
kǒu	口	36.1

kǒufú	口福	36.2
kǒuqì	口气	36.4
kǒuwèi	口味	36.3
kǒuyīn	口音	36.5
kùzì	裤子	154.1
kuài	块	163.1
kuài	快	138.1
kuàicān	快餐	138.2
kuàihuó	快活	138.3
kuàilè	快乐	138.4
kuàimàn	快慢	138.5

L

là de	辣的	20.2
lái	来	228.1
láibují	来不及	228.2
láihuí	来回	228.3
láiwǎng	来往	228.4
lǎo	老	60.1
lǎobǎixìng	老百姓	29.4
lǎodà	老大	60.2
lǎopéngyou	老朋友	21.5
lǎopo	老婆	60.3
lǎoshī	老师	82.2
lǎoshi	老实	60.5
lǎowài	老外	60.4
le	了	250.1–250.3
lěng	冷	136.1
lěngbīngbīng	冷冰冰	136.5
lěngjìng	冷静	136.2
lěngluò	冷落	136.4
lěngshuǐ	冷水	136.3
lǐ	里	59.1
lǐbian	里边	59.4
lǐtou	里头	59.5
lǐkē	理科	128.4
lì	历	125.0
lìcì	历次	125.5
lìdài	历代	125.6

lìnián	历年	125.3
lìshǐ	历史	125.1/126.1
lìshū	历书	125.4
liàn	练	162.1
liànwǔ	练武	162.5
liànxí	练习	162.2
liànxíběn	练习本	162.3
liànxítí	练习题	162.4
liáng	凉	137.1
liángbàn	凉拌	137.2
liángkuài	凉快	137.4
liángshuǎng	凉爽	137.3
liángxié	凉鞋	137.5
liǎng	两	38.1
liǎngbànr	两半儿	38.5
liǎng cì	两次	38.3
liǎng ge	两个	38.2/39.2
liǎngpáng	两旁	213.4
liǎng suì	两岁	38.4
liàng	亮	178.1
liàngjīngjīng	亮晶晶	178.2
liàngtang	亮堂	178.3
líng	零	11.1
língjiàn	零件	159.4
língqián	零钱	11.3/161.4
língsuì	零碎	11.4
língxià	零下	11.2
língyòngqián	零用钱	11.5
lǐngshìguǎn	领事馆	198.3
liù	六	6.1
Liùyī	六一	6.4
Liùyuè	六月	6.2
lù	路	236.1
lùbiāo	路标	236.2
lùkǒu	路口	236.4
lùshang	路上	236.3
lùxiàn	路线	236.5
lǜshī	律师	82.5
luànqībāzāo	乱七八糟	8.5

M

mā	妈	49.1
māma	妈妈	49.2
mǎ	马	93.1
mǎhu	马虎	93.3
Mǎlāsōng	马拉松	93.5
mǎlù	马路	93.2
mǎshàng	马上	93.4
ma	吗	26.1
mǎi	买	229.1
mǎibudào	买不到	229.5
mǎibuqǐ	买不起	229.3
mǎideqǐ	买得起	229.2
mǎimài	买卖	229.4/230.5
mài	卖	230.1
màilì	卖力	230.3
màinòng	卖弄	230.4
màizuò	卖座	230.2
màn	慢	74.1
mànjìngtóu	慢镜头	74.2
mànmàn	慢慢	74.3
màntēngtēng	慢腾腾	74.4
màntiáo-sīlǐ	慢条斯理	74.5
māo	猫	91.1
māotóuyīng	猫头鹰	91.5
máo	毛	165.1
máobǐ	毛笔	165.3
máobìng	毛病	165.4
máoyī	毛衣	165.2/152.2
me	么	25.0
méi	没	46.1
méi guānxi	没关系	46.3
méiwán-méiliǎo	没完没了	46.5
méi yìsi	没意思	46.4/181.4
méiyǒu	没有	46.2
měi	美	63.1
Měiguó	美国	63.5
měihǎo	美好	63.3
měihuà	美化	63.4

měilì	美丽	63.2
Měiyuán	美元	162.2
měi	每	201.1
měi ge xīngqī	每个星期	201.5
měiměi	每每	201.2
měinián	每年	201.4
měitiān	每天	201.3
mèi	妹	53.1
mèifu	妹夫	53.4
men	们	17.0
mǐfàn	米饭	112.5
míng	名	27.1
míngpái	名牌	27.3
míngpiàn	名片	27.4
míngshèng	名胜	27.5
míngzi	名字	27.2
míng	明	144.1
míngbai	明白	144.3
míngliàng	明亮	178.4
míngtiān	明天	144.3
míngxiǎn	明显	144.5
míngzhī	明知	144.2
mò	末	226.1
mòbānchē	末班车	226.4
mòqī	末期	226.3
mòrì	末日	226.5
mǔ	母	77.1
mǔgǒu	母狗	90.3
mǔmāo	母猫	91.2
mǔqin	母亲	77.2/78.4
mǔxiào	母校	186.5
mǔyǔ	母语	77.4

N

nǎ	哪	57.1
nǎguórén	哪国人	57.5
nǎli	哪里	57.3/59.2
nǎr	哪儿	57.2
nǎxiē	哪些	57.4

nà	那	183.1
nà ge	那个	183.2
nàbian	那边	183.4
nàme	那么	25.2/183.3
nàqù	拿去	184.5
nàyìjiàn	拿意见	181.5
nán	男	89.1
nán cèsuǒ	男厕所	89.5
nán'gāoyīn	男高音	89.4
nánháir	男孩儿	86.2/89.2
nánpéngyou	男朋友	21.3/89.3
nánshìmen	男士们	17.4
nán	南	205.1
Nánbànqiú	南半球	205.5
nánbian	南边	205.2
nánbù	南部	205.3
nánfāng	南方	205.4
ne	呢	49.1-49.5
nèi	内	211.0
nèibù	内部	211.1
nèikē	内科	211.3
nèiróng	内容	211.2
nèiyī	内衣	211.4
nèizhèng	内政	211.5
néng	能	232.1
nénggàn	能干	232.3
nénggòu	能够	232.2
nénglì	能力	232.4
néngyuán	能源	232.5
nǐ	你	14.1
nǐ hǎo!	你好	14.2
nǐmen	你们	14.3/17.1
nǐmen hǎo!	你们好	14.4
nǐmende	你们的	14.5
nián	年	146.1
niánjì	年纪	146.3
niánqīng	年轻	146.4
niánsuì	年岁	55.3
niǎo	鸟	92.1
niǎowō	鸟窝	92.2

nín	您	66.1
nín hǎo!	您好！	66.2
nín zǎo!	您早！	66.3
niújiǎo	牛角	164.4
niúzǎikù	牛仔裤	154.3
nǚ	女	88.1
nǚ'ér	女儿	88.2
nǚháizi	女孩子	86.3
nǚqiángrén	女强人	88.3
nǚpéngyou	女朋友	21.4
nǚshēng	女生	88.4
nǚshìmen	女士们	17.3
nuǎn	暖	420.1
nuǎnhūhū	暖呼呼	420.2
nuǎnhuo	暖和	420.3
nuǎnqì	暖气	420.4

P

páng	旁	213.1
pángbiān	旁边	213.2
pángguānzhě	旁观者	213.4
pángtīng	旁听	213.3
pèijiàn	配件	159.3
péng	朋	21.1
péngyou	朋友	21.2
píxié	皮鞋	158.5
piányi	便宜	168.5/169.4
piāo	漂	177.1
piāoyóu	漂游	177.2
piǎobáifě	漂白粉	177.3
piàoliang	漂亮	177.4
piàolianghua	漂亮话	177.5
píngguǒyuán	苹果园	192.4

Q

qī	七	7.1
qīqībābā	七七八八	7.4
qīshàng-bāluò	七上八落	7.5

qī tiān	七天	7.2
Qīyuè	七月	7.3
qīzi	妻子	87.5
qī	期	141.1
qījiān	期间	141.2
qítā	其他 / 其它	15.3/94.4
qǐ	起	70.1
qǐchuáng	起床	70.2
qǐdòng	起动	70.3
qǐmǎ	起码	70.4
qì	气	73.1
qìhòu	气候	73.2/216.4
qìlì	气力	73.5
qìsè	气色	73.4
qìwèi	气味	73.3
qián	前	207.1
qiánbian	前边	207.3
qiánmian	前面	207.2
qiántiān	前天	207.4
qiántú	前途	207.5
qián	钱	161.1
qiánbāo	钱包	161.2
qiě	且	244.1
qiěmàn	且慢	244.3
qīn	亲	78.1
qīnqi	亲戚	78.5
qīnrén	亲人	78.2
qǐng	请	41.1/41.2
qǐngjiào	请教	41.5
qǐng jìnlai	请进来	41.4
qǐngwèn	请问	41.3
qiū	秋	132.1
qiūji	秋季	132.2
qiūsè	秋色	132.3
qiūshōu	秋收	132.4
qiūtiān	秋天	132.5
qiú	球	116.0
qiúsài	球赛	116.2
qiúyuán	球员	116.5
qù	去	184.1

shízì	识字	105.4
shízài	实在	56.5
shǐ	史	126.0
shǐcè	史册	126.2
shǐqián	史前	126.4
shǐshū	史书	126.3
shǐwúqiánlì	史无前例	126.5
shì	是	19.1
shìbushì	是不是	19.4
shìde	是的	19.2
shì	视	113.0
shìdiǎn	视点	113.3
shìérbújiàn	视而不见	113.4
shìlì	视力	113.2
shì	市	196.0
shìchǎng	市场	196.2
shìjià	市价	196.5
shìmín	市民	196.4
shìqū	市区	196.3
shìyí	适宜	150.5
shǒudū	首都	202.3
shǒuyào	首要	107.5
shū	书	111.1
shūbāo	书包	111.2
shūdiàn	书店	111.2/189.2
shūfǎ	书法	111.5
shūjià	书架	111.4
shūxiě	书写	100.5
shù	数	127.0
shùcí	数词	127.3
shùliàng	数量	127.5
shùxué	数学	127.2
shùzì	数字	127.4
shuāng	双	160.1
shuāngbāotāi	双胞胎	160.2
shuāngcéng	双层	160.3
shuāngchóng	双重	160.4
shuāngrénchuáng	双人床	160.5
shuí	谁	65.1
shuí zhīdao	谁知道	65.3

shuíde	谁的	65.2
shuō	说	99.1
shuōbudìng	说不定	99.4
shuōfú	说服	99.5
shuōhuà	说话	99.2
shuōhuǎng	说谎	99.3
sì	四	4.1
Sìchuān	四川	4.4
sìfāng	四方	4.2
sìjì	四季	4.3
sìtōng-bādá	四通八达	4.5
suì	岁	55.1
suìshù	岁数	55.2
suìyuè	岁月	55.4
suǒ	所	247.1
suǒyǐ	所以	247.2
suǒyǒu	所有	247.3

T

tā	他	15.1
tāmāde	他妈的	15.5
tāmen	他们	15.2
tārén	他人	15.4
tā	她	16.1
tāde	她的	16.2
tāmen	她们	16.3
tāmende	她们的	16.4
tā	它	94.1
tāde	它的	94.2
tāmen	它们	94.3
tài	太	171.1
tàijíquán	太极拳	171.5
tàikōng	太空	171.3
Tàipíngyáng	太平洋	171.4
tàiyáng	太阳	171.2
tí	题	43.1
tícái	题材	43.3
tímù	题目	43.4
tiān	天	133.1

tiāncái	天才	133.2
tiānqì	天气	133.3
tiānrán	天然	133.4
tiānzhēn	天真	133.5
tīng	听	233.1
tīngbudǒng	听不懂	233.2
tīngdedǒng	听得懂	233.3
tīngjiàn	听见	233.4
tīngshuō	听说	233.5
tóng	同	180.0
tóngbèi	同辈	180.4
tóngqíng	同情	180.5
tóngshí	同时	180.6
tóngxìng	同姓	29.5
tóngxué	同学	180.2
tóngyī	同一	180.3
tóngyì	同意	180.1
túdì	徒弟	52.5
túshūguǎn	图书馆	198.5

W

wài	外	212.1
wàibian	外边	214.4
wàibiǎo	外表	212.3
wàiguórén	外国人	212.4
wàimian	外面	212.2
wàirén	外人	212.5
wàiyǔ	外语	102.2
wàizǔmǔ	外祖母	77.5
wǎn	晚	222.1
wǎnbān	晚班	222.4
wǎndiǎn	晚点	222.5/218.3
wǎnfàn	晚饭	222.3
wǎnshang	晚上	222.2
wéiqún	围裙	155.2
wēnnuǎn	温暖	135.5
wén	文	103.1
wénhuà	文化	103.4
wénjiàn	文件	159.5

wénjùdiàn	文具店	189.3
wénkē	文科	128.3
wénxué	文学	103.5
wénzì	文字	103.3
wèn	问	42.1
wèndǎ	问答	42.2
wènhǎo	问好	42.4
wènhòu	问候	43.2/216.5
wèntí	问题	42.3
wǒ	我	13.1
wǒmen	我们	13.2
wǒmende	我们的	13.3
wǔ	五	5.1
wǔ diǎn líng qī fēn	五点零七分	218.2
wǔ ge yuè	五个月	5.3
wǔ tǐ tóu dì	五体投地	5.4
wǔyán-liùsè	五颜六色	5.5
Wǔyuè	五月	5.2
wǔ	午	224.1
wǔfàn	午饭	224.3
wǔjiān	午间	224.5
wǔshuì	午睡	224.4

X

xī	西	206.1
Xīcān	西餐	206.3
Xīfāng	西方	206.2
Xīshì	西式	206.5
Xīyào	西药	206.4
Xīzhuāng	西装	157.4
xí	习	119.1
xíguán	习惯	119.2
xíqì	习气	119.3
xírǎn	习染	119.4
xísú	习俗	119.5
xǐ	喜	106.1
xǐ'ài	喜爱	106.2
xǐhuan	喜欢	106.3
xǐshì	喜事	106.5

xià	下	124.1
xiàbān	下班	124.3
xià ge yuè	下个月	139.4
xiàmian	下面	124.2
xiàwǔ	下午	124.4
xià xīngqī	下星期	140.5
xiàyǔ	下雨	124.5/149.3
xià	夏	130.1
xiàlìngshí	夏令时	130.2
xiàlìngyíng	夏令营	130.4
xiàtiān	夏天	130.3
xiàzhuāng	夏装	130.5
xiàn	现	227.1
xiànchéng	现成	227.4
xiànjīn	现金	227.3
xiànzài	现在	227.2
xiǎng	想	174.1
xiǎngdào	想到	174.2
xiǎngfa	想法	174.3
xiǎngniàn	想念	174.4
xiǎngxiànglì	想象力	174.5
xiǎo	小	176.1
xiǎochī	小吃	176.4
xiǎogǒu	小狗	90.2
xiǎojie	小姐	51.3
xiǎomāo	小猫	91.3
xiǎomèi	小妹	53.3
xiǎoshí	小时	176.2
xiǎoshíhou	小时候	176.3
xiǎoxiě	小写	100.4
xiǎoxīn	小心	176.5
xiào	校	186.1
xiàoyuán	校园	186.4
xié	鞋	158.1
xiédài	鞋带	158.2
xiéjiang	鞋匠	158.3
xiéyóu	鞋油	158.4
xiě	写	100.1
xiězuò	写作	100.2
xiè	谢	71.1

xiètiān-xièdì	谢天谢地	71.5
xièxie	谢谢	71.2
xīng	星	140.1
xīngqī	星期	140.2
Xīngqīliù	星期六	6.3
Xīngqīsān	星期三	3.4
xíng	行	200.1
xíngli	行李	200.2
xíngshǐ	行驶	200.5
xìng	姓	29.1
xìngmíng	姓名	29.2
xìngshì	姓氏	29.3
xué	学	83.1
xuéfèi	学费	83.5
xuéqī	学期	141.4
xuésheng	学生	83.2
xuéshí	学识	105.5
xuéwèn	学问	42.5
xuéxí	学习	83.3
xuéxiào	学校	83.4/186.3
xuě	雪	150.1
xuěbái	雪白	150.4
xuěhuā	雪花	150.2
xuěliàng	雪亮	150.5
xuěqiú	雪球	150.3

Y

yāsuìqián	压岁钱	161.5
yàng	样	173.1
yàngzi	样子	173.3
yào	要	107.1
yàobù	要不	107.2
yàohǎo	要好	107.3
yàojǐn	要紧	107.4
yàome	要么	25.5
yángzhuāng	洋装	157.3
yě	也	47.1
... yěba, ... yěba	也罢 ... 也罢	47.4
yě ... yě	也 ... 也	47.2

yěhǎo	也好	47.5		yín	银	199.1
yěxǔ	也许	47.3		yínháng	银行	199.2/200.4
yè	夜	223.1		yínpái	银牌	199.4
yèjiān	夜间	223.2		yínsè	银色	199.3
yèjǐng	夜景	223.3		yínxìng	银杏	199.5
yèshēnghuó	夜生活	223.4		yīng	英	64.1
yèzǒnghuì	夜总会	223.5		Yīngguó	英国	64.3
yī/yí/yì	一	1.1		yīngjùn	英俊	64.2
yíbàn	一半	219.2		yīnglǐ	英里	64.5
yíbèibàn	一倍半	219.3		Yīngwén	英文	103.2
yí cì	一次	1.4		Yīngyǔ	英语	64.4
yí ge	一个	1.2		yíng	迎	68.0
yíhuìr	一会儿	98.3		yíngbīn	迎宾	68.3
yí kèzhōng	一刻钟	217.3		yíngjiē	迎接	68.4
yí kuài qián	一块钱	163.4		yíngxīn	迎新	68.2
yíkuàir	一块儿	163.3		yǐng	影	114.1
yíyàng	一样	173.4		yǐngmí	影迷	114.2
yì běn (shu)	一本（书）	1.3		yǐngxiǎng	影响	114.4
yì máo (qián)	一毛（钱）	165.5		yǐngyìn	影印	114.3
yìqǐ	一起	70.5		yòng	用	231.1
yī	衣	152.1		yòngchù	用处	231.2
yīfu	衣服	152.3		yònggōng	用功	231.3
yījià	衣架	152.5		yònglì	用力	231.4
yīliào	衣料	152.4		yòngxīn	用心	231.5
yī	医	85.1		yǒu	友	22.1
yīkē	医科	85.5		yǒuhǎo	友好	22.4
yīshēng	医生	85.2		yǒuqíng	友情	22.2
yīwùsuǒ	医务所	85.3/247.5		yǒuyì	友谊	22.3
yīyuàn	医院	85.4/187.3		yǒu	有	45.1
yí	宜	169.1		yǒude	有的	20.4
yírén	宜人	169.3		yǒuhài	有害	45.5
yímā	姨妈	49.4		yǒumíng	有名	45.2
yǐ	以	240.1		yǒuqián	有钱	45.3/161.3
yǐbiàn	以便	240.2		yǒu shíhou	有时候	216.3
yǐhòu	以后	208.5/240.3		yǒu yìsi	有意思	45.4
yǐqián	以前	240.4		yòu	右	210.1
yǐwéi	以为	240.5		yòubian	右边	210.2
yì	意	181.1		yòucè	右侧	210.3
yìjiàn	意见	181.2		yòushǒu	右手	210.3
yìsi	意思	181.3		yǔ	雨	149.1

yǔjì	雨季	149.4
yǔsǎn	雨伞	149.5
yǔ	语	102.1
yǔfǎ	语法	102.3
yǔkuài	鱼块	163.2
yǔqì	语气	102.5
yǔyán	语言	102.4
yuán	元	162.1
Yuándàn	元旦	162.3
yuán	园	192.1
yuàn	院	187.1
yuànzi	院子	187.2
yuè	月	139.1
yuèliang	月亮	139.5/178.5

Z

zài	在	56.1
zài jiā	在家	56.2
zàinèi	在内	56.3
zàiwài	在外	56.4
zài	再	32.1
zàicì	再次	32.2
zàijiàn	再见	32.3/33.5
zàisān	再三	32.4
zàishuō	再说	32.5
zánmen	咱们	17.2
zǎo	早	221.1
zǎoché	早晨	221.4
zǎofàn	早饭	221.2
zǎorì	早日	221.5
zǎoshang	早上	221.3
zěn	怎	172.1
zěnme	怎么	25.3/172.2
zěnmeyàng	怎么样	172.4/173.2
zěnyàng	怎样	172.3
zhāng	张	238.1
zhāngkāi	张开	238.2
zhāngluó	张罗	238.4
zhāngyáng	张扬	238.5

zhàngjià	涨价	167.5
zhè	这	182.1
zhè ge	这个	182.2
zhè ge xīngqī	这个星期	140.3
zhè ge yuè	这个月	139.2
zhèlǐ	这里	59.3
zhème	这么	25.1
zhèr	这儿	182.3
zhèxiē	这些	182.4
zhèyàng	这样	182.5
zhěnsuǒ	诊所	247.4
zhènyǔ	阵雨	149.2
zhī	只	95.0
zhī	知	96.1
zhīdao	知道	96.2
zhījǐ	知己	96.4
zhīshi	知识	96.3
zhīyīn	知音	96.5
zhíjiǎo	直角	164.2
zhōng	中	62.1
Zhōngcān	中餐	62.5
Zhōngguó	中国	62.3
Zhōngguórén	中国人	35.3
zhōngjí	中级	62.2
Zhōngwén	中文	62.4
zhōngwǔ	中午	224.2
zhōng	钟	217.1
zhōngqíng	钟情	217.5
zhōngtóu	钟头	217.4
zhōu	周	225.1
zhōumò	周末	226.2
zhōunián	周年	225.3
zhōurì	周日	225.2
zhōushēn	周身	225.4
zhōuwéi	周围	225.5
zhuāng	装	157.0
zhuāngbèi	装备	157.2
zhuāngpèi	装配	157.6
zhuāngshì	装饰	157.5
zǐ	子	87.1

zǐnǚ	子女	87.3		zuówǎn	昨晚	145.4
zǐsūn	子孙	87.4		zuóyè	昨夜	145.5
zì	字	28.1		zuǒ	左	209.1
zìdiǎn	字典	28.2		zuǒbian	左边	209.2
zìmǔ	字母	28.3		zuǒpiězi	左撇子	209.4
zìmù	字幕	28.4		zuǒshǒu	左手	209.3
zìwǒ	自我	13.4		zuǒsī-yòuxiǎng	左思右想	210.5
zǒu	走	75.1		zuǒyòu	左右	209.5
zǒudòng	走动	75.5		zuò	作	81.1
zǒulù	走路	75.2		zuòjiā	作家	81.2
zǒu-qīn fǎng-yǒu	走亲访友	22.5		zuòwén	作文	81.3
zǒushī	走失	75.4		zuòyè	作业	81.4
zǒuyùn	走运	75.3		zuòyòng	作用	81.5
zǔfù	祖父	76.4		zuò	做	79.1
zuó	昨	145.0		zuòcài	做菜	79.2
zuórì	昨日	145.3		zuòmèng	做梦	79.5
zuótiān	昨天	145.1		zuò shēngyì	做生意	79.4
zuótiānde	昨天的	20.3/145.2		zuòshì	做事	79.3

Radical Index

The number on the right of each column refers to the character number.

[人] #18		
个	ge	37
会	huì	98
今	jīn	143
人	rén	35
以	yǐ	240
[亻] #19		
便	biàn/pián	168
但	dàn	242
候	hòu	216
价	jià	167
件	jiàn	159
们	men	17
你	nǐ	14
什	shén	24
他	tā	15
作	zuò	81
做	zuò	79
[儿] #21		
儿	ér	58
元	yuán	162
[几] #22		
几	jǐ	54
[厶] #23		
么	me	25
能	néng	232
去	qù	184
[又] #24		
对	duì	69
欢	huān	67
双	shuāng	160
友	yǒu	24
[阝] (left) #27		
院	yuàn	187

[阝] (right) #28		
都	dōu/dū	202
那	nà	183
[刀] #30		
分	fēn	166
[力] #31		
男	nán	89

3 strokes

[氵] #32		
汉	hàn	101
没	méi	46
漂	piāo/piǎo/piào	177
[忄] #33		
快	kuài	138
慢	màn	74
[宀] #34		
宾	bīn	197
家	jiā	34
客	kè	72
它	tā	94
宜	yí	169
字	zì	28
[广] #36		
店	diàn	189
[门] #37		
问	wèn	20
[辶] #38		
边	biān	214
道	dào	97
还	hái/huán	246
迎	yíng	38

这	zhè	182
[工] #39		
工	gōng	80
左	zuǒ	209
[土] #40		
城	chéng	195
地	dì	193
块	kuài	163
去	qù	184
在	zài	56
[士] #41		
喜	xǐ	106
[艹] #42		
茶	chá	235
花	huā	190
英	yīng	64
[大] #43		
大	dà	175
美	měi	63
太	tài	171
天	tiān	133
[寸] #46		
对	duì	69
[扌] #49		
报	bào	237
打	dà	115
[小(⺌)] #49		
少	shǎo/shào	40
小	xiǎo	176
[口] #50		
吧	ba	248

吃	chī	108
哥	gē	50
喝	hē	234
和	hé	44
后	hòu	208
叫	jiào	23
可	kě	239
口	kǒu	36
吗	ma	26
名	míng	27
哪	nǎ	57
呢	ne	249
史	shǐ	126
听	tīng	233
喜	xǐ	106
右	yòu	210
只	zhī	95
知	zhī	96

[囗] #51

国	guó	61
四	sì	4
园	yuán	192

[巾] #52

| 师 | shī | 70 |

[山] #53

| 岁 | suì | 55 |

[彳] #54

| 很 | hěn | 30 |
| 行 | xǐng/háng | 200 |

[彡] #55

| 影 | yǐng | 114 |

[夕] #56

| 多 | duō | 39 |

| 名 | míng | 27 |
| 岁 | suì | 55 |

[夂] #57

| 冬 | dōng | 132 |
| 夏 | xià | 130 |

[犭] #58

| 狗 | gǒu | 90 |
| 猫 | māo | 91 |

[饣] #59

| 饭 | fàn | 109 |
| 馆 | guǎn | 198 |

[弓] #63

| 张 | zhāng | 238 |

[女] #65

好	hǎo	31
姐	jiě	51
妈	mā	49
妹	mèi	53
女	nǚ	88
她	tā	16
姓	xìng	29
要	yào	107

[子] #67

孩	hái	86
学	xué	83
子	zǐ	87

[纟] #68

| 练 | liàn | 117 |

[马] #69

| 马 | mǎ | 93 |

4 strokes

[灬] #71

| 点 | diǎn | 218 |
| 热 | rè | 134 |

[文] #73

| 文 | wén | 103 |

[方] #74

| 方 | fāng | 194 |
| 旁 | páng | 213 |

[火] #75

| 火 | huǒ | 247 |

[心] #76

您	nín	66
想	xiǎng	174
意	yì	181
怎	zěn	172

[户] #77

| 所 | suǒ | 247 |

[衤] #78

| 视 | shì | 113 |

[王] #79

| 球 | qiú | 116 |
| 现 | xiàn | 227 |

[木] #81

校	jiào/xiào	186
末	mò	226
样	yàng	173

[戈] #85

| 我 | wǒ | 13 |

[比] #86		
比 bǐ	241	

[日] #90		
春 chūn	129	
明 míng	144	
暖 nuǎn	135	
日 rì	142	
时 shí	215	
是 shì	19	
晚 wǎn	222	
星 xīng	140	
早 zǎo	221	
昨 zuó	145	

[日] #91		
者 zhě	246	

[贝] #92		
贵 guì	170	

[见] #93		
见 jiàn	190	

[父] #94		
爸 bà	48	
父 fù	76	

[毛] #97		
毛 máo	165	

[气] #98		
气 qì	73	

[攵] #99		
数 shù	73	

[斤] #101		
所 suǒ	247	

[月] #103		
服 fú	153	
脑 nǎo	151	
朋 péng	21	
期 qī	141	
有 yǒu	45	
月 yuè	139	

[欠] #104		
欢 huān	67	

[风] #105		
风 fēng	148	

[母] #108		
每 měi	201	
母 mǔ	77	

5 strokes

[穴] #110		
穿 chuān	15	

[立] #111		
亲 qīn	151	

[衤] #113		
衬 chèn	156	
裤 kù	154	
裙 qún	155	

[目] #118		
看 kàn	110	

[田] #119		
男 nán	89	

[钅] #122		
错 cuò	179	
钱 qián	161	

银 yín	199	
钟 zhōng	217	

[矢] #123		
知 zhī	96	

[禾] #124		
和 hé	44	
科 kē	124	
秋 qiū	131	

[白] #125		
百 bǎi	12	
的 de	20	

[鸟] #128		
鸟 niǎo	92	

[用] #128		
用 yòng	231	

6 strokes

[衣] #132		
衣 yī	152	
装 zhuāng	157	

[羊] #133		
美 měi	63	

[老] #136		
考 kǎo	121	
老 lǎo	60	

[西] #139		
西 xī	206	
要 yào	107	

[页] #140		
题 tí	43	

Answer Key to Activities

Lesson 1: Review Activities

A. Pronunciation and *Pinyin* Practice

1	(一)	yī/yí/yì	2	(二)	èr	3	(三)	sān
4	(四)	sì	5	(五)	wǔ	6	(六)	liù
7	(七)	qī	8	(八)	bā	9	(九)	jiǔ
10	(十)	shí						

11	(十一)	shíyī	12	(十二)	shíèr	13	(十三)	shísān
14	(十四)	shísì	15	(十五)	shíwǔ	16	(十六)	shíliù
17	(十七)	shíqī	18	(十八)	shíbā	19	(十九)	shíjiǔ
20	(二十)	èrshí						

10	(十)	shí	20	(二十)	èrshí	30	(三十)	sānshí
40	(四十)	sìshí	50	(五十)	wǔshí	60	(六十)	liùshí
70	(七十)	qīshí	80	(八十)	bāshí	90	(九十)	jiǔshí
100	(一百)	yībǎi						

B. Number Identification

(I)

五	5	十七	17	二十三	23
四十一	41	八十六	86	九十九	99
一百	100	五百五十	550	七百二十五	725
九百零一	901				

(II)

16	十六	38	三十八	400	四百
205	两百零五	370	三百七十		

(III) (Open answer)

C. Chinese Language Sudoku

六	一	四	七	二	三	九	八	五
八	二	五	一	九	六	七	四	三
七	九	三	五	四	八	一	二	六
五	六	七	三	八	四	二	一	九
一	四	二	九	六	五	八	三	七
九	三	八	二	七	一	五	六	四
四	五	六	八	一	七	三	九	二
二	七	一	六	三	九	四	五	八
三	八	九	四	五	二	六	七	一

Lesson 2: Review Activities

A. Identification and Pronunciation

1. 我是 — wǒshì
2. 你是 — nǐshì
3. 她是 — tāshì
4. 我们不是 — wǒmen búshì
5. 你们是 — nǐmen shì
6. 他们不是 — tāmen búshì
7. 我的朋友 — wǒ de péngyou
8. 你的朋友 — nǐ de péngyou
9. 她们的朋友 — tāmen de péngyou
10. 他的女朋友 — tā de nǚ péngyou

B. Answer the Questions

1. 她是我的朋友。/ 她不是我的朋友。
2. 你是我的朋友。/ 你不是我的朋友。
3. 我是他的朋友。/ 我不是他的朋友。
4. 他们是我们的朋友。/ 他们不是我们的朋友。
5. 她们是我们的朋友。/ 她们不是我们的朋友。

C. Diagram

(Open answer; here is one posible response.)

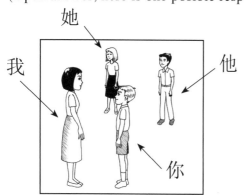

Lesson 3: Review Activities

A. Character Identification

	Pinyin	Stroke Order										
什	shén	丿	亻	仁	什							
么	me	丿	厶	么								
好	hǎo	乚	夂	女	奵	奷	好					
吗	ma	丨	冂	口	叩	吗	吗					
再	zài	一	厂	冂	冃	禹	再					
见	jiàn	丨	冂	贝	见							
叫	jiào	丨	冂	口	叫	叫						
名	míng	丿	夕	夕	夕	名	名					

B. Reading Comprehension

1. Her name is Li Chunhua.

2. Her family name is Li.

3. Her personal name is Chunhua.

4. She is 22 years old.

5. They were elementary school classmates.

C. Creating a Conversation

(Open answer)

Lesson 4: Review Activities

A. Pronunciation and *Pinyin* Practice

一个人	yíge rén	两个人	liǎngge rén	三个人	sānge rén
四个人	sìge rén	五个人	wǔge rén	六个人	liùge rén
七个人	qīge rén	八个人	bāge rén	九个人	jiǔge rén
十个人	shíge rén				

十个问题	shíge wèntí	二十个问题	èrshíge wèntí	三十个问题	sānshíge wèntí
四十个问题	sìshíge wèntí	五十个问题	wǔshíge wèntí	六十个问题	liùshíge wèntí
七十个问题	qīshíge wèntí	八十个问题	bāshíge wèntí	九十个问题	jiǔshíge wèntí
一百个问题	yìbǎige wèntí				

十一口人	shíyī kǒurén	十二口人	shíèr kǒurén	十三口人	shísān kǒurén
十四口人	shísì kǒurén	十五口人	shíwǔ kǒurén	十六口人	shíliù kǒurén
十七口人	shíqī kǒurén	十八口人	shíbā kǒurén	十九口人	shíjiǔ kǒurén
二十口人	èrshí kǒurén				

B. How Many?

人	家人	问题	朋友
四个人（四口人）	五个家人	七个问题	两个朋友

C. Sentence Completion

(Open answer)

Lesson 5: Review Activities

A. Pronunciation and *Pinyin* Practice

1. Nǐ yǒu wǔ ge jiā rén ma?
2. Nǐ shì bú shì wǒ de hǎo péngyou?
3. Nǐ yǒu méiyǒu jiějie?
4. Nǐ yǒu duōshaoge wèntí?
5. Nǐ de bàba jǐ suì?
6. Nǐ jiào shénme míngzi?

B. Family Members

(Open answer)

C. Paragraph Describing a Family

(Open answer; here is one possible response.)

我的朋友有四个家人。他的家有五个人。他有父亲和母亲。他有哥哥,也有妹妹。他的妹妹八岁。他的哥哥二十岁。他十五岁。他没有姐姐。他也没有弟弟。他是他哥哥的弟弟,也是他妹妹的小哥。

Section 1 Review (Lessons 1–5)

A. Numbers and Sentence Construction

2	二	7	七	14	十四	25	二十五
63	六十三	89	八十九	105	一百零五	250	两百五十
580	五百八十	999	九百九十九				

B. Grammatical Particles and Translation

1. 对不起, 你姓王 吗 ?
   Excuse me, is your family name Wang?

2. 你的妹妹 几 岁?
   How old is your younger sister?

3. 我的好朋友 没 有两个弟弟。
   My good friend does not have two younger brothers.

4. 她的问题也 很 好。
   Her question is also very good.

5. 请问：你 的 家有多少人?
   May I ask: how many people are there in your family?

C. Family Description
(Open answer)

D. Reflective Questions
(Open answer)

Lesson 6: Review Activities

A. Pronunciation and *Pinyin* Practice

1. Nǐ zài shénme guójiā?
2. Nǐ de hǎo péngyou zài shénme guójiā?
3. Nǐ de lǎojiā zài shénme guójiā?
4. Shénme rén zài Měiguó?
5. Shénme rén zài Zhōngguó?
6. Shénme rén zài Yīngguó?

B. Hometown Description

(Open answer; here are some possible responses.)

1. 我朋友的老家在美国。   4. 我的老家也在美国。
2. 我的朋友跟家人在她的老家。   5. 我老家的国家人口很多。
3. 我也在她的老家。

C. Different Countries

(Open answer)

Lesson 7: Review Activities

A. Response and *Pinyin*

你好   (你好) nǐ hǎo   谢谢   (不客气) bù kě qì
欢迎   (谢谢) xiè xiè   慢走   (再见) zài jiàn
你好吗   (你好 / 我很好) nǐ hǎo/wǒ hěn hǎo

B. Politeness Crossword

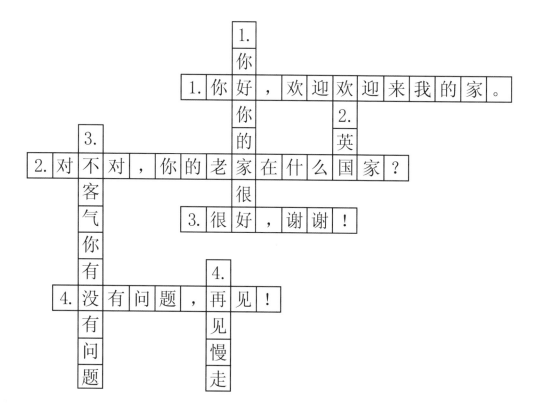

C. New Friend

(Open answer; here are some possible responses)

1. 你叫什么名字?
2. 你有什么家人?
3. 你的老家在哪儿?

4. 你做什么工作?
5. 你会说汉语吗?

Lesson 8: Review Activities

A. Sentence Creation

(Open answer; here are some possible responses)

我 学生　　　我的父亲 老师　　　我的母亲 医生

1. 我是学生。　　　　2. 我的父亲是老师。　　　3. 我的母亲是医生。

B. Reading Comprehension

1. My friend is a doctor.
2. She enjoys her work.
3. Her mother is a teacher of doctors.
4. Yes it is interesting.
5. The mother teaches doctors, the daughter is a doctor.

C. Short Description

(Open answer)

Lesson 9: Review Activities

A. Vocabulary Classification

The sentence portion is open answer; some possible responses are shown below.

有工作	没有工作
女朋友　　男朋友 我　　我的父母	狗　猫　马 孩子
1. 我的父母有工作。 2. 她的男朋友有工作。	3. 孩子没有工作。 4. 猫没有工作。

B. Answering Questions

(Open answer)

C. Expressing Opinion

(Open answer)

Lesson 10: Review Activities

A. Character Recognition

	Pinyin	*2-Character Word*		*Pinyin*	*2-Character Word*
汉	hàn	汉语	知	zhī	知道
中	zhōng	中文	生	shēng	学生
英	yīng	英国	国	guó	国家
字	zǐ	名字	文	wén	文学
人	rén	家人	语	yǔ	语言

B. Sentence Completion and Translation

(Open answer)

1. 我的朋友不认识我的哥哥。

   My friend does not know my older brother.

2. 我也有两只猫。

   I also have two cats.

3. 你的同学会说汉语吗?

   Does your classmate know how to speak Chinese?

4. 他喜欢写汉字, 他也喜欢说汉语。

   He enjoys writing Chinese characters and he also enjoys speaking Chinese.

5. 我不能回答你的问题, 我不知道。

   I cannot answer your question, I do not know.

C. Expressing Opinion

(Open answer)

Section 2 Review (Lessons 6–10)

A. Word Completion

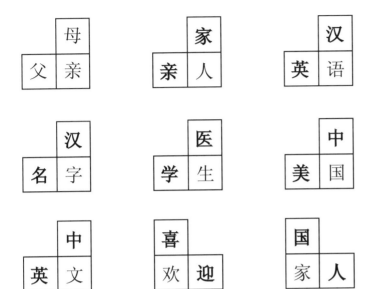

B. Occupation Description

(Open answer)

C. Describing a Place

(Open answer)

D. Reflective Questions

(Open answer)

Lesson 11: Review Activities

A. Pronunciation and *Pinyin* Practice

1. (*Pinyin*) <u>Nǐ shì bú shì xuésheng?</u> <u>我是学生。</u>

2. (*Pinyin*) <u>Nǐ yàobúyào kàn diànshì?</u> <u>我不要看电视。</u>

3. (*Pinyin*) <u>Nǐ yào zuò shénme?</u> <u>我要吃饭。</u>

4. (*Pinyin*) <u>Nǐ xǐbùxǐhuan kàn shū?</u> <u>我喜欢看书。</u>

5. (*Pinyin*) <u>Nǐ de jiārén zuò shénme?</u> <u>我的家人喜欢看电影。</u>

B. Verb Object Matching

(Open answer)

吃 <u>饭</u>　　打 <u>球</u>　　看 <u>书</u>　　喜欢 <u>看电视</u>　　是 <u>老师</u>

1. <u>我的好朋友很喜欢看电视。</u>
2. <u>我的哥哥不是学生, 他是老师。他也喜欢上课。</u>
3. <u>有时候小孩子看书、有时候听父母念书。</u>
4. <u>每天三次人应该吃饭。</u>
5. <u>有一些朋友天天打球。</u>

C. Comparative Discussion

(Open answer)

Lesson 12: Review Activities

A. Word Completion

B. Sentence Completion and Translation

1. 我的妹妹喜欢<u>上</u>数学课。

   <u>My younger sister likes to go to math class.</u>

2. 我们一起<u>练习</u>说中文。

   <u>We practice speaking Chinese together.</u>

3. 你的母亲是<u>老师</u>, 她也上课。

   <u>My mother is a teacher and also goes to class.</u>

4. 科学课的<u>考试</u>很难吗?

   <u>Are tests in science class very difficult?</u>

5. 你跟谁<u>复习</u>汉语生词?

   <u>Whom do you review Chinese vocabulary with?</u>

C. Short Description of Examples

(Open answer)

Lesson 13: Review Activities

A. Vocabulary Matching

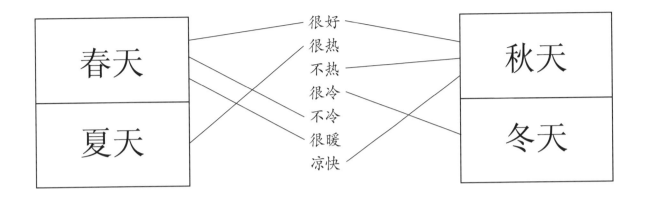

B. Reading Comprehension

1. The speaker's friends are: 王光仁, 郑慧, 吴东梅, and 周正义。
2. 郑慧 enjoys hot weather.
3. She enjoys going to parks.
4. 王光仁 enjoys cold weather.
5. 吴东梅 and 周正义 enjoy the weather in the spring and fall.
6. 吴东梅 enjoys flowers and 周正义 enjoys going to school.

C. Short Description of Examples

(Open answer)

Lesson 14: Review Activities

A. Pronunciation and *Pinyin* Practice

下雨

xià yǔ

很热

hěn rè

刮风

guā fēng

下雪

xià xuě

B. Reading Comprehension

星期三	星期四	星期五（今天）	星期六	星期天

C. Questions and Responses

(Open answer)

Section 3 Review (Lessons 11–14)

A. Verb Object Matching

(Open answer)

1. 上　课
5. 学习　数学

2. 下　雨
6. 练习　汉语课

3. 看　电影
7. 要　吃饭

4. 吃　饭
8. 喜欢　下雪

1. 有空时，我跟朋友去看电影。
2. 在学校学生喜欢下雪。
3. 每个人有学习数学的经历。
4. 你喜欢吃自己做的饭还是从饭店买来的饭？
5. 现在你上什么课？
6. 在你的老家天气常常下雨吗？
7. 什么时候你要跟我一起练习说汉语？
8. 我有一点儿饿，现在我想吃饭，想吃小吃？

B. Describing an Image

(Open answer)

C. Describing a Day

(Open answer)

D. Reflective Questions

(Open answer)

Lesson 15: Review Activities

A. Pronunciation and *Pinyin* Practice

裤子	裙子	两件衬衫	一双鞋子	衣服
kùzi	qúnzi	liǎng jiàn chénshān	yì shuāng xiézi	yīfu

B. Sentence Completion and Translation

1. 今天你穿很好看的衣服。
   <u>Today you are wearing nice-looking clothing.</u>

2. 我喜欢你的鞋子; 请问你什么时候买的?
   <u>I like your shoes; can I ask when you got that pair?</u>

3. 他们的衬衫都一样, 请看! 很有意思!
   <u>Their shirts are all the same, take a look, it is really interesting!</u>

4. 明天, 你要穿裙子还是裤子?
   <u>Tomorrow, do you want to wear a skirt or pants?</u>

5. 什么时候女人要穿洋装?
   <u>When do women want to wear dresses?</u>

C. Illustrative Discussion

(Open answer)

Lesson 16: Review Activities

A. Character and Pronunciation Practice

Amount	Characters	*Pinyin*
$2.50	两块五毛钱	liǎng kuài wǔ máo <u>qián</u>
$1.99	一块九毛九分钱	yí kuài jiǔ máo jiǔ fēn <u>qián</u>
$10.10	十元一角钱	shí yuán yī jiǎo <u>qián</u>
$45.05	四十五块零毛五分钱	sì shí wǔ kuài líng máo wǔ fēn <u>qián</u>
$100.00	一百块钱	yī bǎi kuài <u>qián</u>
$450.75	四百五十块七角五分钱	sì bǎi wǔ shí yuán qī jiǎo wǔ fēn <u>qián</u>
$205.21	两百零五块两毛一分钱	liǎng bǎi líng wǔ kuài liǎng máo yī fēn <u>qián</u>

67¢	六毛七分钱	liù máo qī fēn qián
25¢	两毛五分钱	liǎng máo wǔ fēn qián
$51.50	五十一块五毛钱	wǔ shí yī kuài wǔ máo qián

B. Price Descriptions

(Open answer)

C. Money Comparison

(Open answer)

Lesson 17: Review Activities

A. Pronunciation and *Pinyin* Practice

1. Chūn tiān de huā hěn piǎoliang ma?

2. Zhè jiàn máoyī hěn hǎokàn, nǐ tóngbùtóng yì?

3. Nǐ de gōngzuò zěnmeyàng?

B. Descriptive Sentences

1. 这些衣服很好看。我要买这些衣服。
2. 今天的天气不好的, 大风刮了。
3. 我的朋友很好!

C. Short Description

(Open answer)

Lesson 18: Review Activities

A. Vocabulary Identification and *Pinyin*

1. D huā yuán
2. C shāng diàn
3. F gōng yuán
4. A xuéxiào
5. B dàxué
6. E yīyuàn

B. Descriptive Sentences

(Open answer; here is a possible response.)

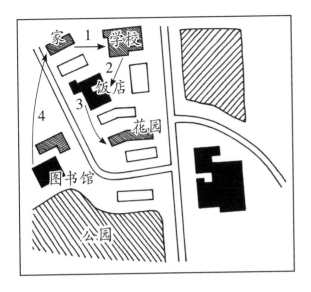

1. 天一早, 我从家去学校。

2. 十二点钟下课。我从学校走到饭店,
   我要吃午饭。

3. 吃午饭以后我要休息。我从饭店走路到花园。

4. 吃晚饭以前我在城市的图书馆练习写字。
   练完以后我从图书馆回家。

C. Comparative Discussion

(Open answer)

Lesson 19: Review Activities

A. Pronunciation and *Pinyin* Practice

纽约

伦敦

洛杉矶

Zhè ge chéngshì shì Měiguó
zuì dà de chéngshì.

Zhè ge chéngshì shì
Yīngguó de shǒudū.

Hěn duō yǒumíng rén
zhùzài zhè ge chéngshì.

B. Completion and Translation

1. 每个<u>学生</u>都喜欢练习汉语。
   <u>Each and every student enjoys Chinese writing / characters.</u>

2. 我朋友的每件<u>衣服</u>都非常好看。
   <u>Each and every piece of my friend's clothing is good looking.</u>

3. 每个<u>城市</u>都有邮局。
   <u>Every city has a post office.</u>

4. 每个<u>书店</u>都卖有意思的书。
   <u>Every bookstore sells interesting books.</u>

C. Descriptive Sentences

(Open answer)

Section 4 Review (Lessons 15–19)

A. Items and Prices

东西：	衣服	毛衣	饭店	宾馆
多少钱：	二十五块钱	四十五块钱	三块钱	两百五十块钱

B. Reading Comprehension

1. <u>The speaker is talking about her hometown.</u>

2. <u>A city needs a school, police station, post office, etc.</u>

3. <u>Yes, this small city does have all of those.</u>

4. <u>She feels a large city should have a nice park.</u>

5. <u>Yes it does have one and it is near the city center.</u>

6. <u>It is a small city; though not one that has many visitors.</u>

C. Location Comparison

(Open answer)

D. Reflective Questions

(Open answer)

Lesson 20: Review Activities

A. Vocabulary and *Pinyin* Practice

	pinyin		*pinyin*		*pinyin*		*pinyin*		*pinyin*
北	běi	东	dōng	前	qián	左	zuǒ	内	nèi
南	nán	西	xī	后	hòu	右	yòu	外	wài

B. Location Description

1. (左边) <u>饭店在宾馆的左边。</u>
2. (右边) <u>在我的右边是我的朋友。</u>
3. (旁边) <u>在公园的旁边是商店。</u>
4. (东边) <u>学校在公园的东边。</u>
5. (后边) <u>宾馆在我的后边。</u>

C. Short Description

(Open answer)

Lesson 21: Review Activities

A. Character and Pronunciation Practice

Time	Character	*Pinyin*
10:00	十点(钟)	shí diǎn (zhōng)
5:30	五点半	wǔ diǎn bàn
2:05	两点五分(钟)	liǎng diǎn wǔ fēn (zhōng)
7:15	七点一刻 (钟)	qī diǎn yí kè (zhōng)
8:45 P.M.	晚上八点四十五分(钟)	wǎn shàng bā diǎn sì shí wǔ fēn (zhōng)
9:10 A.M.	早上九点十分(钟)	zǎo shàng jiǔ diǎn shí fēn (zhōng)
3:50 P.M.	下午四点差十分	xià wǔ sì diǎn chà shí fēn
11:00 A.M.	早上十一点(钟)	zǎo shàng shí yì diǎn (zhōng)

B. Descriptive Sentences

1.（看电视）我看电视的时候，我也喜欢打电话。
2.（跟家人吃饭）我跟我的家人吃饭的时候，我们谈话。
3.（想我的老家）我想我的老家的时候，我做我最喜欢吃的饭。
4.（写汉字）我写汉字的时候，我也练习说汉语。
5.（跟朋友们一起玩儿）我跟朋友们一起玩儿的时候，我们非常非常高兴！

C. Short Description

(Open answer)

Lesson 22: Review Activities

A. Pronunciation and *Pinyin* Practice

师	shī	十	shí	谢	xiè	写	xiě
电	diàn	店	diàn	数	shù	书	shū
市	shì	识	shì	学	xué	雪	xuě
买	mǎi	卖	mài	是	shì	史	shǐ
友	yǒu	有	yǒu	左	zuǒ	做	zuò
工	gōng	公	gōng	南	nán	男	nán

B. Sentence Completion and Translation

1. 你的意见很好，真的有道理。
   Your opinion is really good, it honestly has merit.

2. 我的母亲说这个冰箱很好，冰箱很有用。
   My mother said this refrigerator is very good, refrigerators are very useful.

3. 老师说："这个文章明白吗？学生们，你们有没有问题？
   The teacher said: "Is this essay clear? Students, do you have any questions?"

4. 如果很多人都知道你的名字，我们就可能说你很有名。
   If people all recognize your name, we can then say you are famous.

5. 学生常常觉得学习汉语很有意思。
   Students often feel that studying Chinese is very interesting.

C. Comparative Description

(Open answer)

Lesson 23: Review Activities

A. Pronunciation and *Pinyin* Practice

1. Nǐ de tóngxué yào xuéxí Yīngwén dànshì nǐ yào xuéxí Zhōngwén ma?

2. Jīntiān de tiānqì hěn měilì, wǒmen dōu qù huāyuán ba!

3. Nǐ zhùzài guójiā de běibù háishì nánbù?

B. Sentence Completion and Translation

1. 在饭店你可以吃饭, 可是你不可以做饭！
   At a restaurant you can eat food but you cannot cook food.

2. 美国的英语比英国的英语好听, 你同意吗？
   American English is nicer to hear than British English, do you agree?

3. 我们可以在什么地方踢足球？
   Where would we be allowed to play soccer?

4. 我们两个人一起上课, 好吧！
   The two of us go to class together, great!

5. 对不起, 我不会开车所以现在我不可能开车。
   Excuse me, I do not know how to drive a car so I cannot drive right now.

C. Describing Consequence

(Open answer; here are some possible responses.)

1. (所以) 所以你问老师可以不可以借公用的词典。
2. (于是) 于是你的老师让你用公用的词典。
3. (而且) 公用词典很大而且非常好。所以你考得很好。
4. (以后) 考试以后, 你要买一本新的一样的词典。
5. (可是) 可是书店都没有。你找不到一样的词典！

Section 5 Review (Lessons 20–23)

A. Vocabulary and *Pinyin* Review

	Pinyin	English		*Pinyin*	English
但是	dàn shì	but	还是	hái shì	or
可是	kě shì	but, expresses some surprise	以前	yǐ qián	or beforehand

而且	ér qiě	and, but, yet		以后	yǐ hòu	afterwards
就是	jiù shì	then, thus		然后	rán hòu	after, then
所以	suǒ yǐ	therefore, so		而已	ér yǐ	that is all

B. Short Description

(Open answer; here are some possible responses.)

1.（这里）这里是一个很美丽的花园。

2.（前边）在这个人的前边是一个小湖。

3.（后边）在这个人的后边是一棵很大很老的树。

4.（现在）现在天气很好，很舒服。这个人看一看觉得这是很漂亮的地方。

5.（以前）一天以前天气不太好。那天下了雨。

6.（以后）休息以后她走路。

C. Relationship Description

(Open answer)

D. Reflective Questions

(Open answer)